To Karin
a friend to remember JB 10/27/80

CONQUEST OF THE TROPICS

READY FOR A THREE-THOUSAND-MILE JOURNEY

Romance of Big Business. Vol. I.

CONQUEST OF THE TROPICS

The story of the Creative Enterprises conducted by the United Fruit Company

By FREDERICK UPHAM ADAMS

Author of "John Burt," "The Kidnapped Millionaires," "The Bottom of the Well," etc.

ILLUSTRATED

GARDEN CITY, NEW YORK
DOUBLEDAY, PAGE & COMPANY
1914

PUBLISHERS' NOTE

This book is the first of a series planned to describe certain big businesses whose histories and operations concern and should interest the public. The publishers do not wish any one to be deceived into believing that this series is any different from what it pretends to be as now announced. It is planned as an open and above-board presentation frankly putting forth the interesting points of large business enterprises. In the chapters which follow, a large portion of the information as to facts has been obtained through courtesy of officials of the United Fruit Company. The deductions of the author stand on his reputation as a student and an analyst of issues of public concern. This method will be pursued in the preparation of the books of this series, which later will be announced. It is the belief of the publishers that a series of books thus planned will possess an interest and have a real value not only to those who are investors in these great enterprises, but also to a public which is demanding that far-reaching corporations shall give an account of their stewardship.

CONTENTS

ILLUSTRATIONS

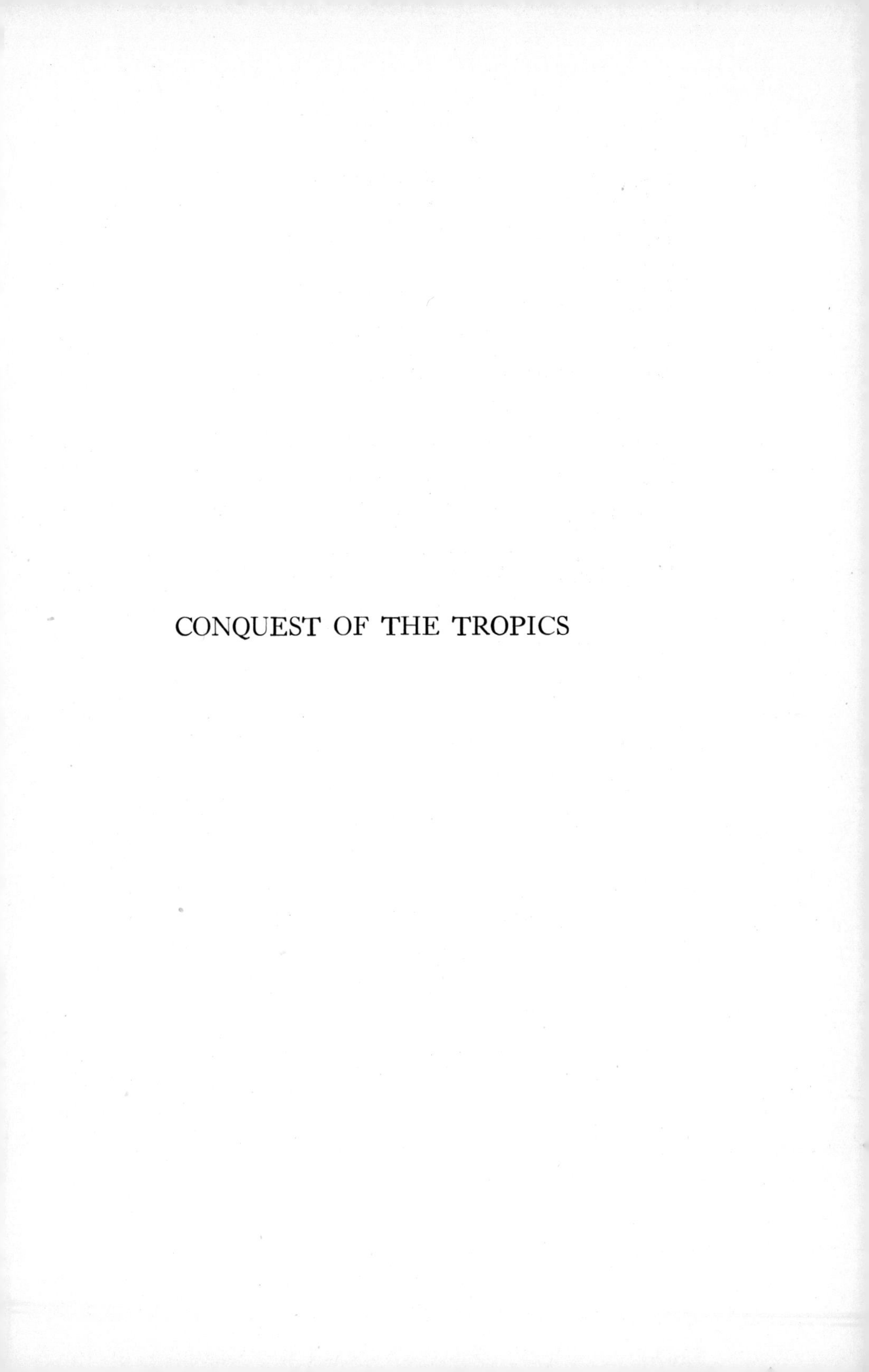

CONQUEST OF THE TROPICS

"I am not jealous of the size of any business. I am not jealous of any progress or growth no matter how huge the result, provided the result was indeed obtained by the processes of wholesome development, which are the processes of efficiency, of economy, of intelligence, and of invention."

— President Woodrow Wilson.

CHAPTER I

Our Neglected Tropical Neighbors

IT is a peculiar and mysterious trait of a considerable portion of the people of the United States that they know little and seem to care little about their national neighbors to the tropical south. This is a regrettable, expensive, and inexcusable fault. Our insular indifference concerning the sentiments, problems, and aspirations of the southern peoples on this continent is construed by them to imply contempt. This has engendered in most of Latin America a feeling of resentment, suspicion, and unfriendliness toward the United States. It certainly is not an asset to acquire and retain the ill-will of those who should be allied with us in ties of friendly intercourse.

The plain truth of the matter is that we have over-cultivated and over-expressed an attitude of self-sufficiency. We are so sure that the United States is the greatest country in the world that we are inclined at times to act as if it were the only country in the world. Some of us are so narrow that we find it impossible to understand why a citizen of the United States cares to live or dares to invest a dollar outside of the confines of his native country. The broad spirit of initiative and enterprise recognizes no national lines.

The great nations of history are those which encouraged their citizens to go out into the world and develop it commercially and industrially. Carthage was great because of citizens who dared to be the pioneers in the developments which created its stupendous commerce. Spain became great because of merchants who followed fast on the heels of her military adventurers, and because of colonies which sprung up in all parts of the world. Great Britain is great because her sons have been trained for centuries to know and act on the truth that there are no geographical boundaries and no national limitations to the enterprise of a British subject.

The coast near Port Antonio

All the world pours its wealth into London. Why? Because Englishmen, Irishmen, and Scotchmen have had the bold spirit of enterprise which has impelled them to undertake the development of natural resources in every part of the habitable globe. And the protection of the British flag and the unanimous defensive spirit of the British people follow its adventurous sons wherever they may go. There is not a nation on earth, no matter how crude and insecure its form of government, whose executives do not know and respect the fact that the British Government stands ever ready to protect the lives and the properties of its subjects, no matter where they may be.

This is a splendid racial trait, a just and righteous national spirit. No nation is sufficient unto itself. We of the United States of America have great resources, we possess wonderfully varied products of the soil, but despite the boastings of the uninformed we cannot create from them all of the necessities which belong to modern civilization and which are at the easy command of commerce.

A morning stroll in the tropics

We are of the temperate zone. Not even the most southerly points of Florida, Texas, or California contain districts which partake of the true characteristics of the tropics. It is doubtful if there be a square foot of tillable soil in the United States which has not been stricken with frost within the present generation. It therefore follows that we are dependent on the real tropics for the numerous indispensable foods and fruits foreign to our own soil. Even Cuba is not a tropical island. It is true that there is no record of frost on its plains and fertile valleys, but Cuba is only subtropical, and does not possess those climatic qualifications which render practical the extensive and permanent cultivation of coffee, cocoanuts, chocolate, bananas, and other delicacies which long ago ceased to be luxuries and became necessities.

A part of the low coast lands of southern Mexico and sections of its interior are truly tropical, but Central America and the north coast of South America constitute the real tropical domain from which the United States naturally should draw its supplies of indigenous products.

The New World has a very small and sparsely inhabited tropical area, and one wofully disproportionate to that of Europe, Asia, and Africa. If we include in the tropics of the New World the countries of Central America, and the West Indies, Mexico, Colombia, Venezuela, Ecuador, Peru, Brazil, Bolivia, and the British, Dutch, and French Guianas, we have an area of approximately 6,361,000 square miles, and with a total population of about 57,000,000 people, most of whom are Indians and negroes.

The tropics of the Old World cover an area of not less than 21,000,000 square miles, and they support more than half of the population of the earth, or not less than 800,000,000 people. To put it another way, only 7 per cent. of the tropical inhabitants of the earth live in the Western Hemisphere.

The disproportion in area is vastly greater in reality than is indicated even by these startling figures. I have included in the tropical area of the New World the vast undeveloped and unexplored wildernesses of South America, a large portion of which can never be reclaimed by cultivation. The problems raised by the Andes and by the swamps and jungles of the Amazon and its tributaries will not be solved in generations, if ever.

In a practical sense, and so far as the United States and its people are concerned, the tropical districts within commercial reach include southern Mexico, all of Central America, the coast lands of Colombia, Venezuela, and the British, Dutch, and French Guianas, together with Cuba, San Domingo, Porto Rico, Jamaica, and the remainder of the West Indies. This constitutes an area which roughly may be estimated at 600,000 square miles. Barren mountains and unwatered plains constitute a considerable portion of this area, and it is extremely doubtful if more than 300,000 square miles will ever be available for cultivation in what may be termed the American Tropics.

In other words, the tillable acreage of our tropics is about equal to that of Texas and Louisiana combined, or that included in the states of Illinois, Nebraska, Kansas, Iowa, and Kentucky. With the exception of Porto Rico and the few square miles of the Panama Canal Zone, not a foot of this 300,000 square miles of tropical possibility belongs to the territorial domain of the United States. True, we own Hawaii and exercise sovereignty over the Philippines, but geographical barriers shut these islands from easy contact and a large commerce.

Contrast this situation with that of Great Britain. Possessed of only nominal natural advantages, the wonderful inhabitants of that nation have extended their rule over 4,500,000 square miles of tropics in a broad belt which circles the world. The flag of Great Britain floats over 325,000,000 tropical natives, and the seas are dotted with British ships which furnish tropical products to the world, and bring untold annual profits to her merchants.

Germany has reached out into the tropics in recent years and has accomplished commercial miracles. Her merchants, farmers, miners, and engineers are in Africa, Asia, South America, Central America, Mexico, and are scattered over the tropical islands of the Pacific. Millions of the surplus population of the German Empire are participating in the development of neglected tropical opportunities, and are adding immeasurably to the total productivity of this small earth of ours.

France is engaged in this work on a smaller scale. Within the memory of men who deny that they are old, the miracle has been accomplished of linking commercially the temperate and the tropical zones. Only a few decades ago the mer-

Clearing a jungle for a banana plantation

chants who sent ships to the tropics with cargoes or for cargoes were classed as adventurers. It was not deemed legitimate trade, but a gamble. The man who made his residence in the tropics was regarded by his relatives and friends practically as one dead.

The commercial conquest by Europe of the tropics of Africa, Asia, and the islands of the Pacific will be recounted by future historians as the monumental achievement of this age. That development is still in progress. It consists in applying the methods of a high civilization and scientific industry to great tropical sections which have remained undeveloped.

There is one dominant reason why the American tropics have not participated in the stupendous progress of all other tropical sections, and that reason is this: Instability of their governmental conditions has estopped the capital and the enterprise of the world from undertaking the development of their wonderful tropical resources. For this state of affairs the United States is largely to blame. Our national sins are not those of commission, but of omission. We have paid no attention to the welfare of our tropical neighbors for the purely selfish and ignorant reason that we did not consider the matter worth our while.

It has not yet dawned on our political leaders that our tropics are a great but unused asset. We are so accustomed to the careless or wilful destruction of forests and other of our own natural resources that it is a matter of slight interest to us whether our tropical neighbors make a specialty of anarchy or of productive peace. We will one day learn, as financiers already have learned at their bitter cost, that each civilized nation shares in the prosperity or distress of all other nations. We of the United States pay our share of the losses in the periods of lawlessness which blight Mexico and other tropical republics. The revolution, equally with the hurricane which destroys crops in the adjacent tropics, adds to the cost of living of the dwellers in every city, village, and section in the United States. On the other hand, any enterprise or any statesmanship which increases the productivity of these tropical sections adds directly to the assets and welfare of all of the people of the United States.

The United States is and always will be the chief market for the agricultural products of these tropical nations. The United States should supply to them in return the innumerable much needed products of its factories and mills, but even the share of this trade which we now hold will be lost unless we meet this situation with intelligence and sympathy.

Our school-books and our histories dwell with pride on the records of the pioneers who braved the wildernesses and paved the way of our empire from the Atlantic to the Pacific. Our national prosperity is founded largely on the achievements of those who risked their lives in the conquest of nature. These men did not stop at a river because it marked the then existing territorial limits of the United States. France and Spain were the owners of the domains which now constitute the great Middle West when the men from New England and from the Atlantic Coast colonies cut their paths through the solitude and laid the foundations of that galaxy of States which now contain more than half of the population of the United States.

These hardy men had no thought of adding to the territory of the United States. Opportunity called them, and they heeded its invitation. We praise them in story and song, and teach our children that much of the glory of the Republic is due to their conquest of the then Unknown West.

The instinct which lured them to plant the flag of progress in new fields still exists. The untilled plains of the Canadian Northwest have drawn from the United States hundreds of thousands of American farmers who unhesitatingly act on the principle that opportunity and enterprise halt not at national boundary lines. These men love their native country, but they obey the instinct which makes of some men, and the best of men, pioneers.

Mexico, Central America, and the West Indies beckoned to others, and they responded. They dared to cast their lot amongst peoples who spake other tongues and followed customs strange to the Anglo-Saxon. It was inevitable that the American tropics should demand its quota of pioneers.

It would naturally be supposed that the Government of

A typical scene in Central America

the United States, the press, and the popular sentiment of the people would encourage all effort and applaud any movement looking to the development of the tropics. We have no tropics of our own.

Great Britain, Germany, France, and other progressive nations were eager to undertake this work, but they realized that the proximity of the United States gave its citizens an overwhelming commercial and financial advantage. The world accepted it as a certainty that the United States would be swift and alert to complete the commercial and industrial conquest of the American tropics. There was no thought and no necessity for the annexation of territory, but the world assumed that the Monroe Doctrine and the Panama Canal both implied that the United States was fully awake to the urgency of exerting every fair effort and using every legitimate influence to encourage its citizens to embrace this obvious and patriotic duty.

Every consideration, selfish and unselfish, political, commercial, social, economical, practical, and sentimental, demanded that the Government of the United States and its people should give loyal support and every possible encouragement to those of its citizens who were willing and able to undertake this task.

The reverse has happened. Successive administrations have treated the questions arising from our relations with our tropical neighbors in a manner calculated to convince them that we took slight interest either in their welfare or in that of the Americans who had cast their lot with them. No official in recent years has greatly distinguished himself in tropical affairs, and we are in sad need of men who will take sufficient interest in these questions to qualify as experts.

What has been the consequence of all this? There has been inculcated in the public mind an impression that the American who ventures into the tropics is either a fool or a knave. It has openly been affirmed by public men of influence that American citizens have no rights which tropical nations are bound to respect or our Government obligated to protect. If an individual attains in the tropics a measure of success after great risks and hardships, and despite absolute lack of sympathy or support from his home Government or his home people, he is likely to be rewarded with the insinuation that he has "exploited" the tropics and its natives.

It is high time that the sober, thoughtful, and just majority of the America people called a halt on this discrimination against the pioneers in the development of the tropics bisected by the Panama Canal. The day has arrived when we have the choice of accepting and profiting by a legitimate opportunity, or of neglecting it and reaping thereby a harvest of misfortune and a loss of national prestige.

Every American citizen should in this connection know, consider, and profit by the history of the inception and development of the United Fruit Company. It is a story of the peaceful and honorable conquest of a portion of the American tropics, and one of which every citizen should be proud. It is a record of a monumental constructive work performed amid surroundings so difficult that the plain narrative seems more like a romance than the account of deeds actually performed.

It is an accepted truism that within the borders of the United States and in the last quarter century, private initiative has mounted to heights of achievement not reached in any nation at any time in history.

When the shock and stress of the Civil War were over, there was witnessed the birth of an era of invention. War was declared on useless labor, and the peaceful genius of the nation set itself to the problem of perfecting the Machine.

The future historian will recognize the fact that the thirty years from 1870 to 1900 constitute a distinct and wonderful period worthy to be designated as "The Age of Invention." In these short thirty years invention gave to the world most of the basic mechanical and electrical discoveries whose services we now enjoy. The telephone, the typewriter, the linotype, the phonograph, the wireless telegraph, the automobile, the electric light, the trolley car, the third-rail, the innumerable forms of electrical power and communication, the air-brake, the turbine, elevated and underground railroads, the steel-constructed building—practically all of the mechanical marvels which now are familiar were unknown and undreamed of by the dwellers in the United States prior to 1870.

This Age of Invention came to a close, as a distinct era, in or about 1900. Since that time there have been no great inventions comparable with those announced to the world in the marvelous period of 1870–1900. The reason is plain. The Machine was perfected, or practically so. It still was possible to add a detail or eliminate a slight defect, but the model of 1900 still retains its approximate proportions, and posterity will credit its perfections to the inventive genius of the thirty years ending in 1900.

The Age of Invention was also an "Age of Panics," and the basic cause was the rapid development and approximate perfection of what may be expressed as "The Machine." By the "Machine" I mean the aggregate result of the work of the thousands of inventors and experimenters who had striven to attain mechanical efficiency, and who had wonderfully succeeded. It was the Machine which precipitated a series of devastating industrial and financial panics, but the fault lay with the system, or, rather, the lack of an adequate system for handling and distributing the enormously increased products of the Machine. It was like placing the turbine engines of a *Mauretania* in the warped and weakened hull of an antique Coney Island excursion boat. The obsolete and planless institution of "cut-throat competition" shuddered and intermittently broke down under the impulse of the new machinery of production bequeathed to the world by its brilliant corps of inventors.

The Machine thundered the doom of the type of competition which prevailed in the years devoted to its perfection. The Machine was the relentless incarnation of efficiency. It had no useless parts. It made no useless motions. It made no mistakes. The quantity and quality of its output was a known factor. It had been created to perform a mission. The outworn institution of petty, planless, and wasteful Competition stood in the way, and the Machine crushed in its massive cogs the type which prevailed prior to 1900.

Another type of competition has succeeded it, and still other types may follow, but the Competition which was crushed in the maw of the Machine is as extinct as the fabled dodo, and will continue so despite all the laws and all the court decisions which may be invoked for its resurrection.

The Machine was a big thing. It was immeasurably the greatest achievement of Man. Only those who can remember back of 1870 can realize its colossal proportions. Within the last fifty years this world of ours has made a material advancement greater far than was accomplished in the preceding twenty centuries, and the sole cause for this phenomenon was the perfection of the Machine in the thirty and

Brewing a tropical storm

odd years prior to 1900. Washington, Jefferson, Franklin, and all of the revered figures in our early national history lived and died years before our present form of material civilization was born.

At the risk of an abrupt descent let us consider the humble banana in this connection. The banana, as an article of import and consumption in the United States, is purely a product of what I designate as the Machine. Jefferson and Franklin never had a chance to eat a banana. There did not then exist the machinery of production and distribution by which it was possible to raise bananas in commercial quantities in the tropics and transport them to Philadelphia, New York, and Boston and deliver them to our ancestors in an edible condition. Bananas might as well have been solely a product of Mars so far as the people of the temperate zones were concerned.

The masses of the people who lived in the United States in 1870 were as unfamiliar with bananas as they were with electric lights and automobiles. It was known to them that bananas grew in the tropics, but the Machine had not yet been constructed which commercially merged New York, Chicago, and San Francisco with the fertile valleys of Costa Rica and Colombia. If a famine had occurred in the United States in the years prior to the birth of the Age of Invention, it would have been practically impossible to have levied on the fruits of the tropics.

But there is another and equally important reason why the banana could not have been transported from its native tropics and offered at retail prices which would have placed it at the command of the consuming public. There were no industrial enterprises with a capital and a scope fitted to undertake the huge task of producing and importing bananas. Industrial production was still on a small scale, practically local. The revolution which made industry national and international in its scope had not yet occurred.

The reorganization and amalgamation of productive energy which marked the period of 1898–1901 was not the result of a conspiracy on the part of unscrupulous business men. The small industrial units of the United States and of other countries did not merge into corporations national in their scope because of a desire to despoil the public. The so-called "trusts" which were incorporated in and around 1900 were not forts; they were shelters to which productivity had fled for protection against a welter of warring and wasteful effort.

This reorganization of corporate industry was, whether its participants knew it or not, an evolutionary movement calculated to build for the Machine a foundation fitted to its stupendous energy and possible productivity. The creation of monopolies did not enter into this evolutionary movement. Evolutions are natural; monopolies are artificial.

The new order of things decreed that production should

be on the largest practical scale, and that distribution should be on a national or international scale. This presupposed a large amount of capital, ample credit, the speedy adoption of improved processes, the elimination of waste effort; in a word, the highest possible efficiency in all of the details of financing, production, and marketing. None of these attributes precluded competition, but the new order of productive energy made it imperative that the new competition should be based on carefully planned efficiency and not, as in former years, on the test of a blind and savage struggle in the dark.

The great enterprises conducted by the United Fruit Company are worthy of a careful study in this connection. A better example could not be found to indicate the vast gulf which exists between the industrial and commercial methods which now prevail as contrasted with those in operation prior to 1899, the year of the corporate organization of this company.

The United Fruit Company is not an industrial "trust" in the economic or legal sense of the word. It does not operate as a monopoly, it having many capable and alert competitors, but it is by far the largest factor in its particular field and ranks as one of the conspicuous industrial corporations of the time. Its productive operations are entirely confined to the tropics, none of them being within the limits of the legal jurisdiction of the United States. The latter is, however, the chief consumer of its products, but most of the civilized world is now served by the commerce originated by its American founders and owners.

It is a mere coincidence that the birth of this great corporation occurred in the period of the national reconstruction of industry. The prime causes which impelled the hundred or more leading industries of the United States to abandon old competitive methods and adopt new ones were absent and without effect in the incorporation of the United Fruit Company.

The vast and complicated manufacturing interests of the nation were constantly menaced with over-production. The Socialist declares that the fault lay with "under-consumption," and asserts that this was due to the fact that the worker was unable to purchase with his wages his share of the product of the machine he operated. Be this as it may,

Washday in Jamaica

there was no method then known by which prices could be adjusted to secure a fair profit and a steady market for manufactured goods, and over-production and panics ensued.

The problem which confronted the banana industry in

1899 was an entirely different one. The producers and importers of bananas were constantly confronted with the problems of *under-production.* They were constantly menaced with the fact that they were unable to obtain bananas with which to hold the trade already won, to say nothing of meeting the constantly increasing demands of new consumers attracted by the quality and cheapness of a tropical fruit to which they had been strangers.

The contrast was vital and interesting.

The manufacturing interests of the nation merged in defense against creative possibilities so great that they were destructive of profits. Certain of the banana producers and importers united for the purpose of insuring the production and speedy distribution of an increased output of that tropical fruit. "Too many manufactured shoes and no protection against lessened demand," was a typical industrial problem in the United States. "Not enough bananas, and no protection against the destruction of what we have got by floods and hurricanes," was the vital problem in the tropics.

I have had an exceptional opportunity to study the work and the results obtained by the great tropical enterprise known as the United Fruit Company. Students of social and political economy and all who are sincerely desirous of aiding in the solution of the problems involved in the phenomenon of the increased cost of living should find much of interest in the chapters that follow. The statistics quoted have been obtained from authoritative sources and can easily be verified, and I am under obligations to many officials of the Government and heads of the competing banana corporations for aid extended in preparing this history.

CHAPTER II

The Modest but Mighty Banana

I RETAIN a fairly vivid recollection of eating my first banana. It was in 1876, and I, then a youngster, was visiting the Centennial Exposition in Philadelphia with my father as guide and treasurer. When a young man, my father had spent some time in the tropical sections of Central America and the West Indies, and I had often heard him talk of revelling in bananas and other fruits of those then fever-stricken districts.

On the afternoon of the day when I encountered my first imported banana we had visited the horticultural department of the great exposition, and there was then pointed out to me one of the leading attractions of that exhibit, a scrubby banana tree from beneath whose fronds actually grew a diminutive bunch of bananas. My recollection is that this was a part of the government exhibit. In any event it was surrounded by a crowd of spectators, most of whom would have been delighted to have plucked a banana, a strip of bark, or even a bit of the earth which surrounded its roots in the huge box which served that purpose. The craze for the collection of "souvenirs," regardless of property rights or possible damage, was then already in vogue, though it had not sunk its victims to such deplorable depths of peculation as at present.

An attendant restrained the bolder of those who longed to touch or dissect this banana tree which was doing its feeble best under artificial conditions far removed from its native habitat. To my young and impressionable mind this was the most romantic of all the innumerable things I had seen in any of the vast buildings. It was the tangible, living, and expressive symbol of the far-distant and mysterious tropics. I had seen pictures of banana trees in text and Sunday-school books, and I had derived from them the pleasing but — as I have since learned — inaccurate information that the fortunate natives of the tropics have nothing to do but roam the flowery glades and live on bananas. I had no difficulty in picturing such natives lounging beneath the small banana tree now before me, and I conjured from my imagination a boa constrictor emerging from the surrounding jungle and making away with a swarthy savage who was about to pluck his evening meal from the ripened bunch of bananas.

I presume my father was the only one there who had ever seen bananas growing in the tropics. He explained to me the difference between this hot-house product and that of the warm and humid coast lands near the equator, and as he talked the throng gathered about him and asked questions.

The "long arm of coincidence," as literary experts term it, was extended to me that day. On the same evening we took a walk along one of the business streets of Philadelphia. My father was fond of fruits, and he paused at a store and we looked over the tempting array. He was about to buy some peaches, when his attention was diverted to a basket containing small, cylindrical objects wrapped in tin foil.

"What are those?" he asked of the clerk, taking one from the basket and looking at it curiously.

"Bananas," proudly replied the salesman. "Bananas just imported from South America. They are a great luxury, sir, and this is the only place in Philadelphia which handles them."

"Bananas in tin foil!" exclaimed my father. "I presume most of your customers think they grow that way?"

"They are a novelty, sir, and only our best customers call for them. May I wrap up some for you?"

"How much are they?"

United Fruit Company Hospital at Bocas del Toro

"Ten cents apiece, or six for half a dollar."

"That is more money than the native who raised them could earn in a month," laughed my father. "I will take half a dollar's worth."

Back in the room in our hotel I stripped the tin foil from one of them and revealed a substance which looked like the bananas I had seen that afternoon, save that this one was nearly black and the growing ones were green. I was about to bite into the skin when my father interfered and removed the peel, looked at the interior critically and rather doubtfully, tasted it, and gave it to me.

"It is not very good, but it is a banana," he said, peeling one for himself. "How do you like it?"

I assured him that it was delicious, but I presume that the novelty of the thing gave my taste a zest and the fruit a flavor not justified by its condition. Two of the six bananas were in such an advanced stage of decay that they were rejected, but we shared the others. They were small bananas, and it would have taken three of them to make the bulk of one of the delicious yellow bananas now at the cheap command of practically every consumer in the United States.

Thus in 1876 we paid about twenty times the present retail price of bananas, considering the bulk alone. The bananas which we bought and ate as a curiosity would now be condemned by the first food inspector who took a glance at them, but I suffered no harm and fell into pleasant dreams of tropics through which I roamed and ate lavishly of bananas which drooped from graceful trees and asked me to pick them.

We lived in Illinois and it was a number of years before I ever had a chance to see or eat another banana. It is my recollection that on various occasions I boasted to my schoolmates and others of having eaten my full of bananas in Philadelphia during the wonderful Centennial, and it is also my recollection that this recital of mine was greeted with mingled doubt and envy. I brought the banana peels back with me, but they did not survive in a shape to verify conclusively the tale of my gastronomic distinction.

In the thirty years which followed this experience I read

and heard considerable about bananas. It was not until the middle eighties that we of the Middle West became fairly familiar with the banana as a fruit. The price still made it a luxury, and it occupied the relative position now held by the grapefruit and other tropical or subtropical products which have established their places in our ever-increasing national

Photo by A. Duperly & Son, Kingston, Jamaica

Under the shade of banana fronds

menu. With my youthful start as a banana expert I took more than the average interest in bananas, and managed to accumulate by reading and listening a mass of impressions, most of which I ascertained to be false on my first visit to the tropics.

One of my most cherished delusions was that the banana which comes to us is a vastly inferior article to that which is enjoyed in the tropics. You doubtless have heard many times the same assertion made with calm superiority by some person who pretended to familiarity with the tropics. The subject of bananas arises. You express your like or dislike of the banana. With this as a cue the presumed globe-trotter, who claims that he knows the tropics as you know the arrangement of your bedroom, turns on you and asks: "What do you know about bananas? These things which are sold here in the United States neither look nor taste like the banana known to the tropics. The banana which you eat was picked green from the trees and was ripened artificially. Nature did not have a chance to perfect her work. It is true that some of the bananas offered for sale here in the United States are fair — just fair, mind you — but you should eat a banana picked from its native stem, its glossy, smooth coat a golden yellow, and its tender pulp a food fit for the gods. I plucked some bananas in Costa Rica which ——"

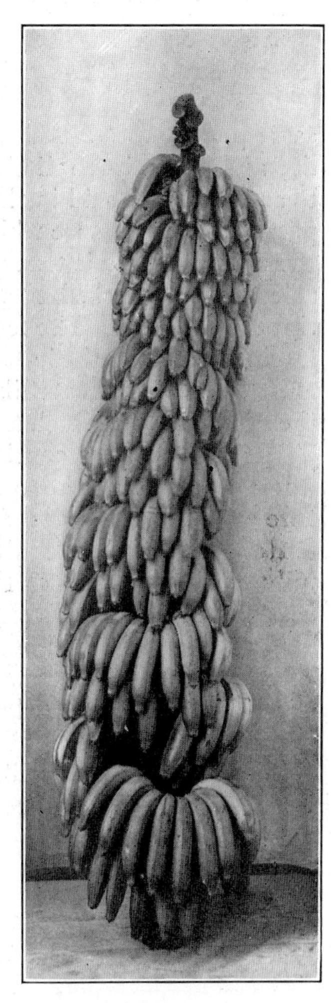

Record bunch of bananas, with 22 "hands" and 300 pieces of fruit

But enough of this recital. You have heard or read something like it many times. The next time you listen to such a narrative or read such a statement you will be safe in assuming that the author never saw a growing banana and knows nothing about the tropics.

The natives of the tropics do not permit a banana to ripen on its stem for the good and sufficient reason that such a banana is hardly fit to eat. A chemical process sets in which partially disintegrates the pulp, destroys the fine flavor, and renders it insipid and almost tasteless. More than that, the rind cracks when the banana starts to ripen on the plant, and insects burrow in the pulp and thus mar or spoil the fruit. The natives pluck the bunches from the stem at about the same period of their development that the leading importers do, and there is so little difference between an exported banana and one sold in the native markets that even an expert could not be sure which is which.

The same thing is true of most other tropical fruits. As a rule they are picked green by the natives and allowed to ripen artificially. The fecundity of the tropical soil and the forcing powers of the humidity and the sun are so great that most tropical fruits are likely to break their envelopes under the pressure of an accelerated ripening process.

Therefore do not continue to think you are getting the worst of it because the bananas which you eat at home come here green. The high grade bananas brought to the United States by the United Fruit Company and its competitors are fully equal to most of those offered for sale in the markets of Havana, Kingston, or Panama City. Nature knows how to grow bananas; man had to learn how to ripen them. Tropical nature left to herself creates foodless jungles and miasmic swamps. The banana of commerce is one of Man's proud triumphs over Nature.

Possibly the reader still entertains another of my former delusions; one to the effect that bananas grow wild and that the lucky native need only venture into the jungle to find this fruit awaiting him. This is another myth which I acquired in school-book days. The authors of my favorite works of fiction and of fact in those days educated me to believe that the wild banana was food, drink, raiment, and shelter to the fortunate and indolent natives of these sections.

It is possible that there are parts of the globe in which wild banana plants bear edible fruit, but none of the banana authorities knows of any such section, and I have never met any one who claims that he ever saw or heard of a wild banana plant which bore anything fit to eat. The jungles of

SCENE IN GUATEMALA

A small squad of the army of 60,000 which enables the United Fruit Company to help satisfy the hunger of the world

Central and South America are filled with wild banana plants, and there are districts covered so thickly with the tangle of their vegetation that they cannot be penetrated, but these indigenous plants bear no fruit and do not respond to attempts to develop them by cultivation.

Banana fruit is the product of cultivated banana plants, and the cultivated banana of commerce was introduced into certain sections of the American tropics several hundred years ago by their Spanish conquerors. The seeds or bulbs were brought from Asia or Africa. The native of our tropics who cares to feed on bananas must either raise them or obtain them from some one who has the enterprise and energy to do so. Despite a cherished popular delusion to the contrary, the jungle is not much of an asset or convenience even to the native. Its only free gifts are choice assortments of pests and fevers.

The popular writers and text-book makers of a generation ago doubtless confused the banana with the plantain. The latter is also a cultivated product, but it is purely a vegetable and not a fruit. The banana is both, but until recently it has had little utility save as a fruit.

For centuries the plantain has been the leading food staple of hundreds of millions of people. It has performed for them the double function which bread and potatoes do for us of the temperate zone. The plantain has the appearance of a very large banana, but does not much resemble it in flavor, texture, or uses. It is cultivated more extensively than the banana and over a wider area, and ranks in the tropics as an indispensable food product. The time is not far distant when the plantain will take its place in our menu. It has already secured a foothold in the southern section of the United States, and there is no reason why it should not play an important part in checking the rise in the cost of living. Humboldt must have confused the plantain with the banana when he ascribed to the latter a productivity to the acre forty times that of potatoes. Even under most favorable conditions this is not so with the banana, but it is possible that Humboldt established this comparison with the plantain.

The early missionaries doubtless fell into the same error. Many of them probably never saw a banana either at home or in the tropics, and confused it with the plantain. The banana never was extensively cultivated in the American tropics until the founders of the United Fruit Company and its competitors established for it a market in the United States. Grim necessity had ever forced the natives to cultivate the plantain, but the banana was considered more of a luxury, and tropical negroes and Indian tribes spend little time or effort in the quest for things not absolutely needed. It is probably not an exaggeration to assert that the people of the United States eat ten times more bananas than are consumed in the Latin-American countries which produce them.

The "American Encyclopædia," published in 1873, in its article descriptive of the banana, makes no mention or hint that this fruit was known outside of the tropics. There was then no thought that the banana would create a commerce amounting to tens of millions of dollars annually. The misinformation contained in most of the encyclopædias of that period now seems amusing, but there was not enough popular interest in the subject to warrant investigation by the compilers of these presumably authoritative volumes.

Botanical history still gropes in the dark in the search for accurate knowledge concerning the origin and development of the banana. Where it came from, what it was called in olden times, who was responsible for its transplanting from one country to another, the part it played in various stages of the world's history? — all these are mysteries yet hid from those who seek to learn the truth. Some botanist gave the banana the title of *Musa sapientium*, and we are informed that it is intended to convey an allusion to a statement by Theophrastus concerning a fruit which served as food for the wise men of India, and which, from his description, is supposed to have been the plantain or banana. Certain authorities try to prove that the banana originated in India, but there is little to show that this section of the globe has any just claim which sets aside those of equally favored tropical localities.

Some primordial Burbank back in the buried centuries undertook the cultivation of the wild banana plant, was greeted with the jibes of his cave-dwelling neighbors, but attained a measure of success which warranted others in following him. This first banana expert may have been a native of India, but there is nothing to prove that he did not conduct his experiments in Central or South America. There is good historical authority to prove that banana cultivation flourished in parts of South America long before Vespucius, Pinzon, Magalhaes, Balboa, Cabot, Cortes, Pizarro, and other Spanish explorers, adventurers, and soldiers first laid foot on the southern half of the New World. It is true that later Spanish colonists brought and planted Asiatic and African types of bananas, but it is a certainty that the wild banana plant is indigenous to the New World tropics, and it is probable that the highly advanced people ruled by the Incas had added the banana to their natural resources.

Fifty centuries or fifty thousand centuries may have passed since man plucked the first edible banana from its drooping stem. Science will never master this riddle. The wonderful thing is that in all these centuries there is no record that any traveller from the tropics ever was able to convey a banana from its place of growth to the temperate zone. Rome extended its rule over the world and its soldiers and merchants levied tribute on the tropics. The luxurious

The food "trust" of Jamaica

emperors and nobles of Rome ransacked the world for food delicacies, but not even the power of the Cæsars was sufficient to place the banana on their banquet tables. It was necessary to annihilate time and space to transport this perishable fruit from its parent stock to distant clime, and civilization was compelled to await the mastery of transportation before the banana became a world food product.

Since the origin of the banana is lost in the shadows of antiquity there is no reason why we should not entertain the theory that it was the banana and not the apple which played so important a part in the Garden of Eden. Certain it is that the early botanists had this thought in mind when they gave the fruit its names, *Musa paradisiaca* "Fruit of Paradise," and *Musa sapientium* "Fruit of Knowledge."

It is generally accepted by authorities on this subject that the banana was not a native of the West Indies. Sloane says: "The banana was brought to Hispaniola (Hayti and San Domingo) from the Canary Islands by one Thomas di Berlanga, a friar, in the year 1516, from whence they were sent to the other islands in the Spanish Main, and they, being very useful and taking extremely, were planted everywhere, but in all probability this plant came first from Guinea to the Canaries."

The Canary Island banana (*Musa Cavendishii*) is better known to the American trade as the "dwarf Chinese banana," and has been quite extensively raised in sections of Central and South America in sections where other types of bananas have been destroyed by a soil disease peculiar to this fruit — the Chinese banana being immune to the parasite responsible for this disease. But the fruit lovers of the United States are familiar with and partial to the "Gros Michel," which roughly may be translated as "Big Mike,"

Tunnel formed by arching banana fronds

the large, smooth and yellow product of Jamaica and Central America, and it has been found difficult to introduce the smaller but equally well flavored Canary or Chinese banana.

The "Claret" or red banana is grown in various parts of the world, including the American tropics, and seems to be popular with the public, but this fruit is difficult to ship because of the fact that the individual bananas do not cling firmly to the stem. This is a fatal defect, shippers having established the rule that the bunches must be delivered in perfect condition.

Not more than twenty-five years have passed since the banana became generally known to the consumers of the United States. Less than half that short span of years has elapsed since the banana became an article of import in Great Britain and the nations of Europe. Fate had decreed that it should be the lot of a small group of American citizens, most of whom are now living and active in this mission, to give to the peoples of the temperate zones a fruit and food product denied to their ancestors through all the ages. This is a real achievement. It is a part of the contribution of our age to the sum total of human progress.

CHAPTER III

Attacking the Wilderness

JUST when or how the first banana was brought into the United States is a matter of conjecture. Bananas were introduced in Cuba several centuries ago by the Spanish conquerors of that island, and some ship may have brought a few over-ripe specimens of this fruit to a port of one of the colonies prior to the War of the Revolution, and its owner might have done this without knowing that he had the distinction of indicating the possibilities of a new commerce.

It is asserted that in 1804 the schooner *Reynard*, on a voyage from Cuba, brought thirty bunches of bananas to New York. If this be true, the feat was rendered possible by favorable temperatures and kindly winds. There are records that at long and irregular intervals small consignments of red bananas arrived at Atlantic coast ports from Cuba, but in all of the years prior to the advent of steam navigation the banana necessarily remained a curiosity and not an extensive article of commerce.

The actual inception of the banana trade dates back to 1866, immediately following the close of the Civil War. In that year Carl B. Franc entered into an arrangement with a steamship company and began on a small scale the importation of bananas from Colombia, South America, to New York City. He shipped from Colon, and his plantations were in or near the present Panama Canal Zone.

For a number of years Mr. Franc and his associates had

New York, Philadelphia, and other eastern markets to themselves. Being the sole producers and importers of bananas, they had a monopoly, and this was the only time a monopoly ever existed in the banana trade. It was not, however, a grasping and merciless monopoly. The banana was then recognized as a luxury of a rare type, and it was not dreamed that a day ever would come when this delicacy would be at the command of every consumer in the United States, and that it would be offered for retail sale at prices a fraction of those charged for native fruits. No one thought of accusing Mr. Franc and his associates of "exploiting the tropics." It was then deemed an admirable thing for Americans to venture their lives and their fortunes in the development of natural resources within commercial reach of the United States. This is still deemed an admirable thing by all of our citizens who are capable of broad and enlightened thought and who have no political or legal axes to grind.

This proved a profitable venture for these pioneers in the banana industry, but fully six years passed before they were confronted with anything resembling competition. And they were shipping bananas to New York from South America! Here is something for the reader to ponder. Bananas are now raised on most of the islands of the West Indies, and along all of the Gulf and Caribbean coasts from Vera Cruz to the mouths of the Amazon. Why did not rival importers rush into competition with Mr. Franc? Why did such rivals not embrace this glittering chance to "exploit the tropics" and cheat the natives of the fruits of their flourishing banana groves and plantations?

There was a very simple reason why this was not done. The natives of the American tropics raised no bananas in commercial quantities. They had no extensive banana groves and plantations, flourishing or otherwise. There was no native agriculture in the American tropics to "exploit," and it may astound the reader to know that there never has been and that none exists to-day. These tropics are productive just about in proportion as American initiative, American capital, and American enterprise make them productive.

The sooner the people of the United States come to know

this fundamental fact, the sooner will they be able to meet the problems which the tropics present.

Cuba, with its unrivalled natural resources of soil and climate, offered no chance to those who would compete with Carl B. Franc in the New York banana market. Cuba was

Cocoanut tree

raising what General Sherman fittingly characterized as "hell," and a people cannot raise that and sugar, tobacco, and bananas at the same time. Cuba raised nothing but revolutions, anarchy, and chaos until the United States was compelled, against its will, to interfere for the purpose of eradicating an international nuisance. Hayti and San

Domingo were confining their activities almost exclusively to pillage and bloodshed. Central America was not yet on the commercial map. Jamaica was in the happy position of not enjoying self-government — being under the domination of Great Britain and denied the pastime of "revolutions" — but her people were devoting their lands and energy to the cultivation of sugar-cane, pending the time when enforced peace would permit Cuba to take her proper place as the great sugar-producing section of the globe. Mexico — well, Mexico was in its normal condition. Porfirio Diaz had not yet clubbed its semi-savage factions into a coma of temporary peace and prosperity.

These are some of the reasons why Mr. Franc and his associates were able to control the banana market. They had preëmpted the only known spot in the American tropics where it seemed safe to raise and export bananas. The great stream of the world's commerce beat up against Colon. The Panama railroad was in operation, and the demands of international trade automatically decreed that peace and order should prevail in the territory adjacent to that natural pathway of commerce.

Thus it was that Mr. Franc became the commercial pioneer in the banana industry, and thus it was that a number of years passed before any rivals entered the field he had chosen. It is likely that the bananas wrapped in tin foil which I encountered in Philadelphia in 1876 were imported by his company, and he acquired a modest competence with an equipment and prices which would seem grotesque to-day.

But Mr. Franc was not the founder of the banana industry as we know it. He formulated no plan and took no effective steps to bring about a production of bananas adequate to meet the demands of a people ready to accept this fruit as a commodity and not as a high-priced luxury. He treated the banana as a specialty, and the business which he reared was lost sight of when others took the logical steps to enlarge and systematize this industry.

In 1870 Captain Lorenzo D. Baker, owner of a Cape Cod schooner, took a contract to convey a party of gold miners and their machinery and supplies 300 miles up the Orinoco

River in Venezuela. Captain Baker was a native of New England, born on Boundbrook Island, Wellfleet, Massachusetts, in 1840, of a mother who bore the old-fashioned Yankee name of Thankful Rich.

On his return from South America, Captain Baker stopped at Kingston, Jamaica, and looked about for a cargo fit for Boston consumption. Trade was dull and freights scarce. Whether or not he knew that Carl B. Franc was making occasional banana shipments to New York is uncertain, but the fact that he took a chance on carrying bananas by schooner from Kingston to Boston indicates conclusively either that he knew little about the perishable nature of bananas or that he was willing to take a decided speculative risk.

At any event, Captain Baker purchased a few bunches of bananas from a local dealer, loaded them on the deck of his schooner, and set sail for Boston. He made a quick voyage and docked in Boston with the bananas ripened and in eatable and salable condition. It is claimed that these were the first commercial bananas ever imported to Boston.

The important effect of this small shipment was to call the attention of shrewd fruit merchants to the possibilities of Jamaica as a banana competitor to Colombia.

Andrew W. Preston — who later became president of the United Fruit Company — and other New England investors made investigations which warranted them in stimulating and participating in the cultivation of bananas in Jamaica, and thus laid the secure foundations of an industry which bequeaths to that island most of its present prosperity, and which has saved its people from the bankruptcy that threatened to follow the supremacy of Cuba in the sugar trade. The tremendous importance of the enterprise thus started may dimly be realized when it is stated that, in the year when this is written, Jamaica will export probably 18,000,000 bunches of bananas, most of which will be sold at cheap prices to the consumers of average means in the United States. Bear in mind that Jamaica took slight part in the initiation of this vast industry. The credit for the decided benefits which mutually have accrued

How the jungle has been conquered

to her people and ours belongs to New England merchants who dared venture into uncharted commercial seas.

Andrew W. Preston comes from hardy New England stock of English origin, and he inherited from his ancestors an iron constitution which has stood him in good stead in upbuilding and directing the vast and far-reaching enterprises which now constitute the United Fruit Company. He was born in Beverly Farms, Massachusetts, on June 29, 1846, the son of Benjamin and Sarah Poland Preston. He received his education in the public schools of his native village, but as a youth determined that the local horizon was too contracted. Boston was not far away, and its greater and broader activities laid their spell on him even when he was poring over his books in the district school.

As a mere boy he left home ties and village associations and took his chance in the New England metropolis, obtaining a job in a Boston produce commission house which handled fruits among other things. Ships from all parts of the world came to Boston loaded with strange foods and fruits, with coffee and spices fragrant with the odors and charms of the tropics. But practical common-sense told him that the tropics could not be won by dreaming and that Boston was the place first to conquer. The time came when the young man went into business for himself on a modest scale, but he was quick to realize that the American tropics offered rewards to those American merchants who would develop their neglected valleys and offer their food and fruit products for sale in the northern markets.

An incident which illustrates the capacity of Mr. Preston to adapt himself to new duties and responsibilities occurred while he was managing the affairs of the Boston Fruit Company. The latter was a depositor in the Hancock National Bank of Boston, and Mr. Preston was a director and one of the vice-presidents of this bank. He was not, however, one of the more active officials in the bank, neither did he pretend to intimate familiarity with its affairs or expert knowledge of the banking business in general.

A United States bank examiner, after a rigid examination

of the affairs of the Bank, expressed dissatisfaction with the manner in which its business had been conducted. The matter was referred to the Comptroller of the Currency who, after a careful study of the conditions, stipulated that the bank should be permitted to continue business on the condition that Andrew W. Preston would assume active management of it. Despite the fact that the affairs of the Boston Fruit Company demanded his thought and time, Mr. Preston deemed it his duty to assume the additional burden suggested, and without hesitation agreed to do his best to reorganize the Hancock National Bank. For months he worked day and night, and was finally able to bring the matter to a succesful conclusion. This incident is still recalled by Boston business men who have not been surprised at the success of the United Fruit Company under the executive management of a man who has a genius for doing big things in a big and honorable way.

From 1870, when Captain Baker made his first famous shipment of a few bunches of Jamaican bananas to Boston, until 1885 there was no systematic attempt made to develop the production and transportation of this fruit from the tropical sections nearer the Atlantic coast line. Intermittent shipments were made by sailing ships from Cuba or Jamaica, but not in quantities sufficient to create a steady demand or a fixed market price for this tropical luxury. Mr. Franc, as has been explained, had a contract with a steamship company which gave him exclusive rights of shipment to New York, and his success in that line proved that there was a chance for a well managed competition.

In 1884 Andrew W. Preston was a fruit merchant in Boston. He purchased and sold bananas whenever he had a chance, and regretted the fact that the supply was incapable of giving this fruit the value of a staple commodity. A careful personal study and investigation of this subject convinced Mr. Preston that there was a promising business opportunity for a concern which would undertake the stimulation of the production and transportation of bananas from Jamaica, San Domingo, and Cuba, the three tropical islands within easier reach of the Atlantic seaboard.

But Mr. Preston was not financially able to undertake any such enterprise. There was a large amount of idle money in Boston. There were many New England capitalists who were able to advance the money which would have insured the speedy success of the plans which Mr. Preston was eager to put into effect. A half a million of dollars would have put the enterprise on a secure foundation in 1884, but Mr. Preston might as well have pleaded for that amount of money to construct a bridge to Mars.

After many efforts Mr. Preston finally induced nine men to join him in an association to promote the banana business with Boston as the port of entry. This association was formed in 1885. Mr. Preston and each of his nine associates advanced $2,000, giving this enterprise an original capital of $20,000. With the exception of Mr. Preston, all of the gentlemen contributing to this fund were engaged in lines of business which had no connection whatever with the fruit trade. This would seem to indicate that the "experts" in the fruit business shared with the men of large available capital the opinion that the American tropics was the last place in the world in which to invest money.

It is also evident that Mr. Preston had slight expectation of adding to the list of the nine men who had risked $2,000 each on this desperate speculation. It was at his suggestion that all of them should agree to waive dividends for a period of five years, and to reinvest all possible profits in the business. Such was the basis of organization of the association of the ten men who had a hope that it would be possible to raise bananas in the tropics and bring them to Boston. The amount of money then risked by these Boston merchants would not defray the expenses of a round trip of one of the steamships which constitute the Great White Fleet of the United Fruit Company. Mr. Preston is the sole living survivor of the ten who endowed the New England branch of the banana industry with $20,000.

The venture was a success from the start. Under the active management of Mr. Preston every honorable business expedient was employed to bring about an increased production of bananas in Jamaica and other sections, also to secure an increased consumption in Boston and other parts of New England. From the very beginning the policy of this partnership (it was not then a corporation) was to maintain the lowest possible retail prices consistent with fair profits. The problem was to create a demand for this tropical fruit, and no large demand was possible with fancy prices. Here is the key to the mystery of the success of the banana industry — small profits on enormous sales — and

Glimpse of the jungle

back in 1885 Mr. Preston and his nine associates initiated this policy and did not deviate from it.

The most beautiful business structure in the world, the wonderful Woolworth Building, was reared to the clouds by a man who derived a fortune by conducting a chain of "Five and Ten Cent Stores," in which millions of people buy thousands of things which are sold at a fraction of a cent profit on each article.

The United Fruit Company stands as the greatest agricultural enterprise in the world because it so handles its products that they reach the consumer with a unit of profit per banana so small that it cannot readily be comprehended.

When the banana growers of Jamaica, Cuba, and elsewhere learned that there was an increasing demand for their fruit they increased their acreage and adopted better systems of cultivation. But Mr. Preston did not intend to rely solely on the native growers. Investigation had convinced him that it would be more profitable to buy tracts of suitable lands and raise bananas than to buy them from others. A portion of the profits was set aside for this experiment. It was successful. By this time all of the gentlemen who had contributed to the $20,000 pool were convinced that they were on the right track and that there was business warrant to invest more in the project. Instead of depending entirely on the profits for reinvestment they added the further sum of $100,000 before the five years specified in their agreement of 1885 had elapsed. With this fund new plantations were developed in San Domingo, Jamaica, and Cuba, and new expedients were installed to facilitate production and distribution. Encouragement was given to the native growers. The secrets of refrigeration were studied and better methods installed to bring the fruit to market in prime condition.

When the five years had passed a careful appraisal showed that the association was the owner of properties conservatively estimated at a value of $531,000. This was the flattering result of the judicious management of an investment of $120,000 and the reinvestment of profits as they accrued. Good luck had played its share in attaining this success. Floods and high winds had not greatly damaged the new plantations, and the men who founded this enterprise had yet to learn the lessons of such disasters.

These men had called their association or partnership the "Boston Fruit Company," and when it was decided to incorporate the enterprise it was given the same name. This was in 1890, and the Boston Fruit Company was duly organized under the laws of Massachusetts with a capital stock of $500,000, and a surplus of $31,000.

The managing director of the newly incorporated Boston Fruit Company was Andrew W. Preston. He was peculiarly

HEART OF A BANANA PLANTATION

This gives an excellent idea of a flourishing banana district. Some of these plants are fully 40 feet high

fitted for the responsibilities of his position. For five years he had met and mastered the many problems which had arisen in the development of a new industry; an industry complicated by the fact that the sources of production and supply were far removed from the home sections of distribution and consumption.

The Boston Fruit Company did not depart from the policy of converting earnings into betterments, and the United Fruit Company has since followed in its footsteps. The steadily increasing consumption of bananas in the United States called for added sources of production in the tropics, and dividend rates were kept low, and the surplus devoted to the conquest of the tropics. Mr. Preston has ever adhered to this policy of devoting a large share of the earnings of the company to new banana plantings which would keep pace with the rapidly increasing consumption of this fruit and food product.

During all of the years from 1885, when the Boston Fruit Company was informally started, up to 1899, when the United Fruit Company purchased its corporate holdings, there were active competitors in the banana trade. There was competition to secure the fruit of the native raisers of bananas; there was competition in the planting of new fields of supply; there was competition in transportation and in marketing and in all of the branches of the industry. The field was one in which monopoly was impossible. There was practically an unlimited amount of virgin land fitted for the cultivation of bananas. Thousands of new independent growers were offering their fruit to those importers who would grant the best prices. There was an unlimited number of steamships eager to accept banana freight from any one able to pay for it, and the field was an open one to any individual or interest that cared to invade it.

But none of the competitors of the Boston Fruit Company imitated the far-seeing policy of Mr. Preston in building for the future. Most of those who took part in this competition seemed to regard it more as a speculation than as an enterprise requiring broad but conservative management. It soon became known that luck was a vital factor with the small planter or the small importer. A given district would be favored with bountiful banana harvests for a year or a period of years, then disaster would come from flood, drought, or hurricane. The average importer would pin his faith to the luck of a certain district. He would gamble that there would be no weather calamities in a certain year or period of years. If he won, his profits would be large, and he would put these winnings in his pockets or disburse them in dividends to his associates. If he lost, he usually went into bankruptcy.

Mr. Preston fully realized the nature of all of these risks, but bent every effort to reduce their effects to a minimum. The initial disasters which befell the Boston Fruit Company in the tropics and in the New England markets told him clearly that safety lay in securing the widest possible source of supply and the widest possible market outlet. In most lines of business the concern which scatters its energies and resources over a wide territory invites disaster. Mr. Preston made the discovery that the banana business was a startling exception to this time-honored rule. Concentration in any producing field or in any consuming market constituted a deadly risk. Minor C. Keith learned the same lesson in banana districts far remote from those which served the Boston Fruit Company, and every individual who engaged in the banana trade had this palpable truth shoved in his face sooner or later, but it is a remarkable fact that Mr. Preston and Mr. Keith were the only executive heads of banana enterprises who took the obvious precautionary measures to insure their interests against inevitable climatic disasters.

When Mr. Franc and Captain Baker discovered that it was possible to transport bananas from South America and Jamaica, there were few citizens of the United States who could boast that they had ever penetrated Central America. The word "penetrate" exactly describes the process then necessary to reach the cities and settlements of Guatemala, Salvador, Honduras, Nicaragua, and Costa Rica. Though all of these countries had extensive coastlines, their natives actually shunned them. The peoples of Central America were highlanders in the true sense of the word. Nothing but absolute necessity could induce them to venture into the disease-stricken wildernesses which bounded them on the Pacific Ocean and the Caribbean Sea. These desolate regions had for them an absolute terror, and that dread of the lowlands still exists in all classes.

Why the tropical death-rate once was high

In all of the centuries from the discovery of America down to a comparatively few years ago, the hundreds of miles of coast from Colon to Belize and from Panama City to Salina Cruz have remained practically uninhabited. There are unmistakable signs that thousands of years ago other races thrived and reared great cities and splendid palaces in the fertile valleys along both coasts, but it is certain that their conquerors were unable to master the problems of sanitation and were compelled to take refuge on the high plateaus where now stand the capitals and cities of their descendants.

No words can describe the horrors and dangers of the few squalid villages which once lay on the water edge of these jungles. Nature had infested these wastes with most of the enemies of mankind, but the ignorance and indifference of those who clustered there added new and more deadly menaces. The normal death-rate of a typical Central American seaport, in the years prior to the advent of the banana industry, was not less than 150 annually out of a population of 1,000! This is fully ten times what it is now. It was almost sure death for an unacclimated foreigner to remain a week in these unsanitary surroundings. The wealthy citizen of Costa Rica or Guatemala who wished to go to London, Paris, or New York on business or pleasure approached the Pacific port from which he was to sail in fear and trembling, and thousands who longed to make such trips could not be induced to take the risk.

In 1871 there was not a mile of railroad in all of Central America, with the exception of a short line having its terminal at Puerto Cortez, Honduras. There were no dependable foot or wagon roads from its capitals to either coast. In 1871 there was no steamship service from the United States or from any part of the world to any port in Central America. There probably was no inhabited spot on earth more isolated. These republics were cut off not only by the sea, but also by barriers of pestilential lands, which the natives dreaded to cross and which the outside world could not enter.

To-day these former wildernesses constitute one of the most productive agricultural sections of the globe. To-day the ships from all the world enter the beautiful harbors of Central America and land their passengers in ports which are as sanitary as those of Massachusetts. To-day most republics in Central America are served with well-managed and modernly equipped railway lines. The day is near at hand when one will be able to travel by rail from New York or San Francisco to Panama City in safety and luxury.

Who performed these miracles?

They were wrought by American citizens who had the imagination, the courage, and the ability to attack and conquer the countless dangers and problems of the tropical wildernesses, and who did this through the organization of enterprises which helped lay the foundations of the United Fruit Company.

The people of the United States have been slow to give just credit to those who have made this splendid contribution to the world's advancement. It is one of the things which cannot be dismissed with the sneer that it was undertaken in expectation of money profits. We give acclaim to the achievements of Morse, Field, McCormick, Edison, and honor the men whose constructive genius projected railways into the once trackless West and who set the pace for the most wonderful material progress the world has ever known. All of these men were inspired by hope and confident expectation of money gains, but something bigger and better led them on.

They devoted their lives to adding some new and great things to the world's assets. The world owes nothing to the man who attains money success by devoting his time and talents to a business or an avocation the mysteries and problems of which were already solved. It is not an important thing that an individual is able so to conduct a dry goods business that he amasses twenty or fifty millions of dollars. He can do this fairly and honestly, and die without having added anything of value to the era in which he mounted to rare heights of money success.

But the man who acquires riches by discovering and proving that some new method of production will vastly curtail human labor and increase human comfort stands on an entirely different plane. He has given the world a *quid pro quo* for the wealth which he has gained. The men who toiled and struggled and finally won in the campaign to prove that the Canadian Northwest was fitted to become one of the world's great harvest fields should be granted every honor

On the edge of a tropical jungle

in the gift of the British Empire, but current fame hardly knows their names. The men who turned the unused jungles of Cuba into sugar-cane plantations are well entitled to recompense and distinction for having placed an absolute necessity within the reach of all.

By the same token, the men who believed that it was possible to convert the miasmic swamps and jungles of Central America into vast plantations of nodding banana plants, and who had the courage and fortitude to act on that belief, need not fear that honest and intelligent men will fail to give them credit when the facts are known. It was not solely a desire for profits which caused these men to combat the seen and invisible dangers of the tropical fastnesses. They did it in response to that instinctive spirit which ever has urged the American to face and conquer the frontier.

CHAPTER IV

Laying the Foundations

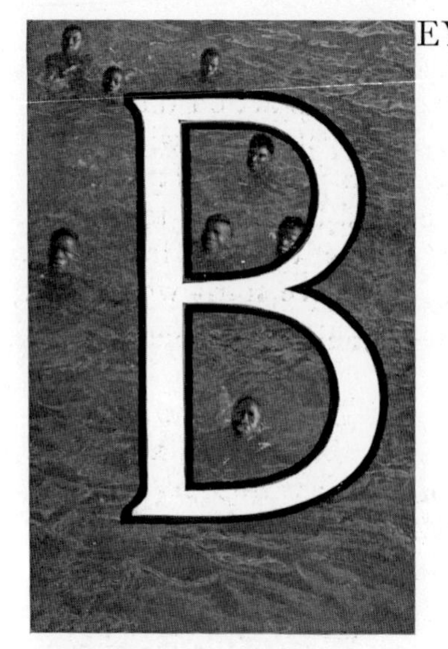

EYOND question the best known man in Central America is not a native of any one of her five republics, but a plain American business man, a resident of New York City — Minor C. Keith. There is not a Central American of any consequence from the Mexican border line to Colombia who is not aware that Mr. Keith is the particular *Americano* who made the commercial discovery of that section of the world, and there is not a fair-minded Central American who does not cheerfully admit that a large share of the prosperity of the five republics is due to the vast enterprises initiated by him.

Minor C. Keith was born in Brooklyn on January 19, 1848, and is the active head of most of the great enterprises with which his name is identified. He is vice-president of the United Fruit Company, and shares with its president, Andrew W. Preston, the distinction of having brought about the conditions which made that wonderful business organization possible. Mr. Keith is better known to the informed public as the head of what is popularly called the "Pan-American Railway," the tracks of which will soon connect the United States with the Panama Canal, and which, in the not distant future, will link New York with Rio Janeiro and Buenos Aires.

The two leading officials of the United Fruit Company started in life with none of the advantages which wealth and position are supposed to give. They had the inheritance of health, physique, energy, and that persistence which lends success to ambition. Both Mr. Preston and Mr. Keith took their first steps in business before they were of legal age, and both determined in their youth to seek opportunity for advancement in new and undeveloped fields. They were of the hardy American type which listens and responds eagerly to the call of the wild.

Before he was entitled to vote, we find young Keith in Texas, struggling to win and hold a place in the cattle business. He secured a foothold in 1869. The only railroad then in Texas was a short line, less than forty miles in all, connecting Galveston and Houston. It was then that this young man became possessed of an ambition to build a chain of railroads which would open up new and strange territories, but he stuck to the cattle trade as the most promising chance of making his dream possible. The time speedily came when the young cattleman owned 4,000 head of stock, also a cash surplus which lured him to begin the attempt to construct railroads through virgin lands.

In 1871 Mr. Keith went to Costa Rica to join his brother, Henry M. Keith, in the construction of a railway from Puerto Limon on the Atlantic coast to San José, the capital, on the Pacific slope. Henry Meiggs, of Peru, had contracts with the Costa Rica government to construct the railway, and transferred the contracts to Henry M. Keith, his nephew.

There was then not a mile of railroad in operation south of the Rio Grande to the Isthmus of Panama with the exception of the short line in Honduras. Two years were yet to pass before Mexico could boast of her first railway line, the product of British capital and enterprise, which connected Vera Cruz and Mexico City. It therefore stands to the credit of Minor C. Keith that he was the first citizen of the United States who had the courage and the enterprise to build a railroad in the American tropics, and it is a matter of history that he executed this work against handicaps and perils which cannot be imagined, much less described.

The Costa Rican railroad planned by Mr. Keith and his brother began in a jungle and for years ended in a jungle. It was necessary to traverse flood-swept valleys and deadly swamps, and then to climb a jutting barricade of lofty mountains to an altitude exceeding 5,000 feet in order to gain the plateau on which is located the city of San José. The reader should reflect that Minor C. Keith was then only twenty-three years old, an age at which many favored modern American lads are more interested in college athletic events than they are in tackling a great engineering problem in a tropical wilderness.

The appalling hardships and risks of this enterprise may faintly be understood when it is stated that the construction of the first twenty-five miles of this railroad cost the lives of more than 4,000 men. This was the tribute demanded by the fever-infested jungles, and it was obtained despite the fact that the average working force did not exceed 1,500 men. Almost three full corps of laborers gave up their lives in the fight to conquer the mere fringe of the wilderness. Only a very few of these were natives of Costa Rica or inhabitants of Central America, for nothing could induce the average native to enter the deadly zone of the *tierras calientes*, the dreaded hot lands of the Caribbean coastal region. The laborers therefore were drawn from Jamaica, and it is the Jamaican negro who does the bulk of the manual work in the banana districts of Central America to-day.

But it was not these humble Jamaican negroes who made up all of this death roll. Scores of young American engineers and others of skilled professions gave up their lives in this attempt to subdue the jungle. In the long list of those

A village plaza in Guatemala

who fell in this industrial battle were three of the brothers of Minor C. Keith, and only a splendid physique and a calm faith in his destiny preserved the latter in the long nineteen years while the railroad was climbing its tortuous way to San José on the Pacific slope of the plateau. Those American tourists and travellers who now journey in comfort over this railroad, and who are enchanted by scenic beauties not surpassed in any part of this beautiful world of ours, should pause and reflect that the trip which they make in a few happy hours was made possible by men who did not hesitate to risk and sacrifice their lives in a work which will ever stand as a monument to the constructive genius of American citizenship.

At one time the government of Costa Rica was unable to pay Mr. Keith a considerable sum of money which was due to him under the terms of the official agreement. Mr. Keith met the pay-roll of the 1,500 Jamaican negroes until most of his available funds were exhausted. He then called this small army together and explained to them the exact situation, and asked them if they would continue to work without pay until he could make financial arrangements which would permit a settlement, and pledged his word that not a man should lose thereby. Mr. Keith offered full pay and transportation to Jamaica to those who wished to quit.

Mr. Keith had every reason to believe that Costa Rica would quickly emerge from its financial difficulties, but event after event made it impossible for its officials to meet their obligations to Mr. Keith. It was a year of financial disaster and money scarcity all over the world. Month after month passed, and still the negro laborers worked on without pay. It was not the fault of Costa Rica; it was the fault of a panic which had chased the mobile money of the world into hiding.

Six months passed, and still no pay day for the 1,500 negroes. It was possible for Mr. Keith to feed and clothe them, but that was all. He called them together again, explained the situation, assured them of his belief that the financial skies soon would clear, and asked them if they still had confidence in his word. By an unanimous vote they again pledged their faith in the American who had attempted the seeming impossible. Many of them had wives and children back in Jamaica, but they stuck. Three more months passed before outside capital was ready or able to come to the aid of the young railroad builder, and then Mr. Keith paid his faithful army of men in full, and added a substantial bonus.

I doubt if a finer tribute ever was paid to a mere business man. For nine long months these Jamaican negroes performed their difficult and dangerous duties in the firm confidence that "Mistah Keith would make good." He was not of their race or of their country, but they had for him the faith and allegiance which inspired the soldiers of Napoleon to conquer Europe.

This incident had an interesting sequel. At the earliest opportunity the Republic of Costa Rica not only paid to Mr. Keith all that was due under his contract, but also reimbursed him for the losses sustained at the time he was denied the amounts due him. I will detail later how Costa Rica in after years proved in another most striking and substantial way that there are exceptions to the traditional rule that "Republics are ungrateful."

Passengers for Costa Rica now land at the beautiful and healthful city of Puerto Limon, and from there take a train for San José and other points between the Caribbean and the Pacific. Mr. Keith did not select Puerto Limon by reason of the fact that it was the principal eastern seaport of Costa Rica. That nation had no seaport, and little need of a seaport. Its few imports and exports were carried by rowboats to and from sailing ships which anchored at safe distances from shore.

The name of Limon was given on account of a lemon tree found in the jungle, and there was then nothing to distinguish the site from the dreary miles of uninhabited beach. At long intervals there may have been found the huts of a few Caribs and other Indians who existed by the primitive methods handed down by their ancestors. The real Republic of Costa Rica was far inland, as has been explained.

The manner in which Mr. Keith entered into the banana

Small growers bringing in bananas

business is peculiar and interesting. He had many ambitious plans, but the truth of the matter is that the banana did not originally enter into them. He went to Central America to build railroads, and from 1871 until the present day he has continued at that task, and will doubtless pursue his ambition until younger hands complete this great undertaking. It is very likely that Mr. Keith underestimated the difficulties which were ahead of him. There was no possible traffic from the outside for his new railroad until he came into touch with the populous interior of Costa Rica. It soon became apparent that for a number of years the railroad which started in a jungle would remain in the jungle, and the traffic possibilities of such a road are about equal to that of a "merry-go-round" with the North Pole as an axis.

Mr. Keith probably did not dream that nineteen years would pass before his road would reach San José, less than 100 miles away, but with every mile presenting some new and difficult problem. He soon realized, however, that he must secure some article of freight for his railroad and that this article must be found or developed in the jungle, and this is how Minor C. Keith became identified with the banana industry and stands as one of the pioneers of its systematic production on a large scale.

It was in 1872 that Mr. Keith planted the first marketable bananas which ever grew in Central American soil. Less than two years had passed since this youth quit Texas, and he never had seen a banana until he paid a visit to Panama. Therefore he was not an expert on bananas, but since there were no experts on this fruit he was not handicapped. Carl B. Franc was the sole importer probably in all the world, and it was from this pioneer that Mr. Keith obtained the bulb with which to make the experiment in the Costa Rican jungles.

Without waiting for these small plantations to develop, Mr. Keith decided to test New Orleans as a possible market for a fruit then absolutely unknown to its people. His brother owned the small steamship *Juan G. Meiggs*, and in 1872 Mr. Keith shipped on it 200 bunches of bananas purchased in Colon. These were sold in New Orleans at high prices and a large profit, and for some time he continued to make monthly shipments of from 250 to 400 bunches, which was all that the market consumed at the fancy prices then charged.

At this time the total shipment of bananas from all the tropics did not amount annually to more than 300,000 bunches, imported from the West Indies, Colon, and the Bay Islands off the coast of Honduras. To-day the importations amount to more than 50,000,000 bunches.

The experiment of planting bananas in Costa Rica was a success from the start. The partly completed railroad gave Mr. Keith a chance to initiate a system of rapid transportation from the fields to the ships, which system is the prime requisite in modern banana production. Thus was founded in the deadly jungles of Costa Rica an enterprise which was destined to make these waste lands not only highly productive but also sanitary. Instead of remaining an enemy the jungle became a friend — a friend who came bearing gifts of delicious fruit. It was not necessary for the railroad to await revenue until the peopled plateau was reached. Such waiting probably would have spelled disaster to Mr. Keith. This forcing the jungle to pay tribute was business genius of a high order. It helped to found a gigantic industry, and brought prosperity and an awakening to all of Central America.

Mr. Keith continued to extend his banana plantations in Costa Rica and to search for new districts where the soil and climate promised success. He discovered such a location in the beautiful region about Bocas del Toro, then a part of Colombia, but now a prosperous community in the Republic of Panama. He also decided to acquire banana interests in Santa Marta, Colombia, along the north coast of South America, the agricultural wonders of which will be described in a later chapter.

In 1878 Mr. Keith opened the first store in Bluefields, Nicaragua, and conducted a trade in rubber, sarsa and tortoise shell. No bananas had yet been planted in Nicaragua, but Mr. Keith induced friends to make the experiment, and in 1882 he shipped the first bananas from Bluefields to New Orleans by the steamship *Heredia*, owned by him. Mr. Keith subsequently turned his banana interests in Nicaragua

On the beach at Bocas del Toro

over to a business associate, and devoted his attention to other sections in Central and South America.

From 1872 until 1899, the latter being the date of the organization of the United Fruit Company, Mr. Keith devoted all of the time he could spare from his railroad enterprises to the development of the banana industry. As the years passed, and the demand for bananas stimulated by Mr. Keith and the New England pioneers increased, other Americans were attracted by the possibilities of this new industry, and competing concerns established footholds along various points of the coast of Central America. Some of these quickly failed from crop disasters, inexperience, lack of capital or credit, and from the causes which exist in all forms of business. Others succeeded and are in profitable operation to-day.

From the day that the Boston importers and Mr. Keith entered the field against Mr. Franc there has been active competition in the banana industry. In Central America Mr. Keith had certain natural advantages, but these were the ones which belong of right to the man who is first in a new field. The miner who has the daring, fortitude, and energy to prospect in a country which others ignore, and who has the good fortune to discover outcroppings of gold or silver which have escaped other eyes, acts within his legal and moral rights in locating claims which seem most promising to him. Others may come later and attain an even greater success because of taking advantage of the discovery made by this pioneer prospector in a virgin field, but fair-minded individuals and public opinion does not begrudge the discoverer of this wealth the share which is his because of his rights of priority.

The same just rule holds true everywhere. The hardy men who explored the Mississippi Valley would have been fools, and despised as such, had they not have claimed and pre-empted the choicer locations for farms and town sites. This is in accord with the unassailable rule, "First come, first served." Deny to the pioneer and the explorer these just rewards of risks and hardships and you put a brake and drag on material progress.

The men who first undertook the banana business in the American tropics had every right to acquire and hold the sections which seemed to give most promise for success in banana production and quick transportation. The field was so enormous and the then existing demand for bananas so small that the early advantages of the pioneers were about the same as those possessed by the original corn and wheat growers of Ohio, Indiana, and Illinois.

Minor C. Keith saw into the banana future and builded

A country road in Jamaica

for it. He foresaw that bananas would be carried from the tropics to the markets entirely by steamships. That meant that the fruit must be raised in districts adjacent to deep water harbors. There are only five natural harbors on all of the Caribbean coast of Central America. These are as follows: Trujillo, Honduras; Puerto Barrios, Guatemala; Puerto Cortez, Honduras; Puerto Limon, Costa Rica, and Bocas del Toro, Republic of Panama. Within close reach of all of these natural harbors are large tracts of land well adapted to the cultivation of bananas. All five of these harbors are the logical starting points of railroads built to reach into the populated highlands of their respective republics.

The opportunity was obvious. Every condition was in harmony. There were four locations possessed of deep water, banana lands, and river valleys through which railroads could reach the interior plateaus. None of these natural resources had been touched. There was a small settlement of negroes at Bocas del Toro, but only slight signs of villages where now are located the thriving cities of Limon, Barrios, and Cortez. The swamps and jungles were the property of anyone who cared to pay a small price for them. Mr. Keith was then the only man in the world who was willing to risk money in an attempt to make them of value. A somewhat similar situation existed in Santa Marta, the only seaport of consequence along the north coast of Colombia, South America. Mr. Keith purchased banana interests in and near Santa Marta.

Such was the manner in which Mr. Keith acquired whatever of natural advantage he possessed, and such was the manner in which a part of the foundation was laid for the great business structure which has been reared by the United Fruit Company. There are vast areas of banana lands remaining in all of these countries, areas which are as fertile as those selected for cultivation and sanitation by Mr. Keith, but they lack some of the advantages of the lands chosen by Mr. Preston and Mr. Keith in the years when the world thought them crazy for spending time and money in the swamps and jungles of an unknown section of the globe.

In 1898, after a continuous residence of twenty-seven years in Costa Rica, Minor C. Keith was the controlling factor in three banana enterprises. It is rather a significant fact that his associates in one of the corporations were English investors, and that the company was incorporated in London. It was, for reasons already stated and which should be deplored, almost impossible to interest the capital of the United States in the development of the sections over which was extended the uncertain sway of the

Photo by A. Duperly & Son, Kingston, Jamaica

Wives of Jamaica banana farmers

Monroe Doctrine. Our men of money shut their eyes to the facts and declined to listen to the arguments of Mr. Keith and others who attempted to enlist their wealthy countrymen in the development of the American tropics.

The Tropical Trading & Transport Company, Limited, was a Costa Rican corporation formed for the purpose of handling the properties which Mr. Keith had acquired in Costa Rica. The Colombian Land Company, Limited, was a British corporation formed for the purpose of developing the banana industry in and about Santa Marta, and Mr. Keith was the general manager and controlling factor in that company. The Snyder Banana Company, a New Jersey corporation, owned the plantations in Chiriqui Lagoon, of the Bocas del Toro district of Panama, and Mr. Keith owned a half interest and control of this company. Sir Alexander Henderson, Sir Thomas Kitson, Mr. Copperthwaite, Mr. James Lindsay, and other English investors were associated with Mr. Keith in the companies which were developing Santa Marta, and a group of London capitalists gave support to his operations in Costa Rica.

The regular ports of entry for the bananas produced by these companies were New Orleans, Mobile, and other Gulf and southern ports. The demand for bananas in the United States was limited because of the fact that there were no proper facilities for the transportation and distribution of this fruit to the interior markets. The three Keith companies made money in years when no disasters befell their growing crops, and lost money when floods droughts and high winds afflicted them.

CHAPTER V

Birth of the United Fruit Company

ONLY those who have lived in the tropics and are familiar with the hazards which confront the cultivation and marketing of its fruits can readily understand the motives which impelled a union of the interests of the Boston Fruit Company and those headed by Minor C. Keith. It was not a move calculated to control competition or to rear a monopoly; it was the business step imperatively required to secure the permanency of the banana industry.

In 1898, the year preceding the organization of the United Fruit Company, the total importation of bananas from the American tropics did not exceed 12,000,000 bunches, or about one-fourth of those imported in 1913. It is doubtful if any food product has shown a similar increase in any equal period in the world's history. The sole reason why more bananas were not imported in 1898 is that this was the total product available for importation. The sole reason why the year 1913 did not exceed the figure of 50,000,000 bunches of imported bananas is that no more were available for shipment to the consuming sections of the United States and Europe.

The problem in 1898 was to produce more bananas for a steadily mounting popular demand. That is the problem to-day. The field was open to all comers in 1898. It is open to all who care to enter it to-day. Under such conditions the presumption that a banana monopoly ever existed, now exists, or is possible cannot be entertained by those who understand the first rudiments of the laws of business and commerce.

At the time of the organization of the United Fruit Company the following firms, corporations, and persons were engaged in importing bananas into the United States:

Boston Fruit Company,
Tropical Trading and Transport Company, Ltd.,
Colombian Land Company, Ltd.,
Snyder Banana Company,
J. D. Hart Company,
J. M. Ceballos & Company,
Orr & Laubenheimer Company, Ltd.,
Camors, McConnell & Company,
New Orleans Belize Royal Mail & Central American Steamship Company,
W. W. & C. R. Noyes,
John E. Kerr & Company,
J. H. Seward Importing & Steamship Company,
Aspinwall Fruit Company,
West Indian Fruit Company,
Monumental Trading Company,
West India Trading Company,
Henry Bayer & Son,
Camors-Weinberger Banana Company, Ltd.,
J. B. Cefalu & Brother,
S. Oteri,
The Bluefields Steamship Company, Ltd.,
W. L. Rathbun & Company.

There were undoubtedly other firms and individuals engaged in a small scale in the banana business, but the above list includes all those of consequence in the trade. The first four were merged into the United Fruit Company. Some of the others have retired, others have been absorbed by the companies which now compete with the United Fruit Company, but not a firm, corporation, or individual engaged in the banana business at the time of the incorporation of the United Fruit Company has failed because of the operations of that company.

Photo by A. Duperly & Son, Kingston, Jamaica

Beyond the reach of frost and snow

Prior to 1899, the year of the formation of the United Fruit Company, there had been organized, according to the best available information, not less than 114 companies or firms which engaged in the importation of bananas to the United States. Of this large list — as has been stated — only twenty-two of any consequence were still in existence when the United Fruit Company was formed.

Most of these banana companies were inadequately financed, and most of them were under the management of men who had no practical knowledge of the banana industry. Few had been in business for as long a period as ten years, and most of them handled insignificant quantities of bananas. With monotonous regularity these mushroom banana companies would spring into being, struggle along for a short time, and then drop out of existence, leaving behind no assets for their stockholders.

Such experimental banana companies still are founded, most of them with capital stock ranging from $50,000 to $200,000. These amounts of money are sufficient to finance a banana plantation, but it is as idle to expect to become a producer, importer, and national distributor of bananas with such capital as it would be to expect to compete successfully with the Western Union and the Postal Telegraph with a new company thus financed.

When the banana industry was in its infancy there was a possibility of temporary success even with the most crude and wasteful of methods. The cargoes were small, and it was not difficult to dispose of the fruit over the ship's sides a few bunches at a time. The market was largely confined to the port in which the ship docked, the prices were high, and the consumption small.

The fruit was generally secured by purchase from the native tropical planters, sometimes by contract, but more often in the open market. Few companies, even in the late 90's, grew any bananas on their own plantations, and when they did, these formed merely the nuclei of their cargoes, the remainder being secured by purchase. Practically all of the importers of this early period looked to one source of supply and had only one port of entry in the United States. In some instances, the importer simply chartered space on steamers and stored it with bananas; the more ambitious importers chartered ships, but these were of low speed and had a capacity for a comparatively small number of stems of bananas.

Arriving in the United States, the fruit was unloaded by hand, and in the early days the prospective purchasers would assemble on the wharves to secure their supplies. Naturally, they chose their own fruit, buying as they did only a few bunches at a time. In later years, however, the importers adopted the custom of selling the fruit by "steamer run," viz: as it came out of the steamer, declining to permit the buyer to pick out the best bunches. Some importers had stores and ripening rooms where they could keep a portion of their fruit and sell it gradually. What was left, after every possible local demand had been satisfied, was then shipped to various interior points usually consigned to some broker. Sometimes the fruit was shipped a long distance, from New Orleans to Chicago, but it was not often necessary to assume such risks.

The importers knew little concerning the business as a whole; they were not familiar with the interior markets or how to reach them, and the industry in all of its departments was conducted in a wasteful and haphazard manner, the public paying their share of these blunders in high prices for bananas, and the importers paying their share in losses which generally ended in bankruptcy.

New Orleans took the first step for a business organization designed to secure a proper distribution of bananas in 1896, three years prior to the formation of the United Fruit Company. In this year, four of the New Orleans companies formed the New Orleans Importing Company, a selling organization intended to dispose of the fruit imported by its members. The New Orleans experiment was successful while it lasted, but jealousies and dissensions among the heads of the four companies requiring its services caused its dissolution after a few months.

Another effort in the same direction was made early in 1899 when similar problems resulted in the formation of the Southern Banana Exchange. Like its predecessor, it worked satisfactorily, but its usefulness was cut short in three or four months by the inability of its members to get along without friction.

The truth of the matter is, that the banana industry, prior to the formation of the United Fruit Company, had made sorry progress compared with other importing enterprises. The Boston Fruit Company and those concerns headed by Mr. Keith were the most progressive in their methods, but they were handicapped by conditions which will now be considered.

The Boston Fruit Company and the Keith interests were the leading factors in the banana industry. The Boston Fruit Company derived its product solely from the West Indies and confined its market to the Atlantic coast and to the northern sections of the interior of the United States. The Keith interests cultivated bananas in Central America and Colombia and shipped them mainly to New Orleans and other Gulf ports, but lacked the facilities for reaching far into the southern and western territory naturally tributary to these shipping and railroad termini. The conditions were such that there was nothing approaching competition between the Boston Fruit Company and the Keith interests, nor was there any prospect that their activities would conflict.

Neither of these interests had the capital with which to take advantage of obvious opportunities, but the time had arrived when moneyed men were willing to listen to the possibilities of the banana as an investment. They still declined to class it as a conservative investment, and, such is the proverbial timidity of capital, it is not so considered to-day, as stock quotations eloquently testify. Your cautious man of money seeks investments which he can look at and study personally from day to day, the securities of which he can convert into cash almost at a moment's notice, and the tropics —well, the tropics are far from New York and Boston.

Hence a tropical investment must prove and double-prove itself before the average man of money will consider it, and then the lure must be attractive, in dividend per cents. But in the years which had passed since Carl B. Franc, Captain Lorenzo D. Baker, Andrew W. Preston, Minor

C. Keith, and others faced the hardships and risks of the pioneer, certain things had been proved beyond possibility of doubt.

The most favorable thing proved by these pioneers was that the people of the United States liked bananas and would eat them in unlimited quantities if offered at prices which

Photo by A. Duperly & Son, Kingston, Jamaica

Family life in Jamaica

would compete with such home fruits as apples, peaches, pears, and oranges. The second favorable consideration proved was that bananas could be grown cheaply and in large quantities in certain tropical sections, provided weather conditions continued favorable.

The disturbing and discouraging element was found in the fact that a flood, drought, or high wind would destroy a crop in a given section and eliminate it as a source of production for a year or more. Capital pays more attention to one flaw in a new proposition than it does to ten of its glowing promises. Possibly this is the reason why we have such a thing as capital. In any event, capital in 1898 declined to enthuse over an enterprise which could not prove its ability to supply at all times the commodity in which a large investment was to be made.

There was ample justification for this attitude. The Boston Fruit Company had learned by grim and expensive experience that the tropics could frown as well as smile. Hurricanes levelled some of their best plantations in Jamaica. The replanted tracts would later be swept away by roaring floods. Droughts shrivelled the fronds of the banana plants in Cuba and San Domingo. Nor was nature the only one to strike blows. Warring factions waged revolutions and counter-revolutions in Cuba and San Domingo. There was no stability of governments, no assurance that the field workers of to-day would not follow some ambitious "general" on the morrow in the quest of "liberty" or loot. The Boston Fruit Company did not have a source of banana supply which it could insure against sweeping disaster without warning. Under the most favorable circumstances its total supply was insufficient to meet the rapidly increasing demand, and any curtailment meant not only money losses but damaged prestige as well.

The enterprises headed by Mr. Keith faced the same menaces. Terrific floods in Costa Rica and Panama swept away the railroad tracks and bridges and overwhelmed the loaded banana plants in large districts. In one year a protracted drought in the Santa Marta district of Colombia practically killed all of the plantations. Revolutions in some of the Central American republics played their part in determining whether crops would be harvested or not.

But luck, chance, or the law of average decreed that these disasters to the banana crops should be local, and that a large portion in the American tropics would survive in any year despite the rage of the elements and the fury of warring political factions. The obvious remedy of a banana import-

Street scene in San José, Costa Rica

ing concern was to provide for sources of supply in many districts scattered all over the American tropics. This expedient was so obvious and so imperative that it should have suggested itself and been adopted years prior to the formation of the United Fruit Company. It was the natural, reasonable, sensible, and logical thing to do.

The consolidation of the interests of the Boston Fruit Company and the companies controlled by Minor C. Keith was brought about, as a matter of fact, not as the result of a carefully considered plan, but through a financial disaster which seriously threatened Mr. Keith. In the latter part of 1898 the firm of Hoadley & Company failed. Mr. Keith had drawn bills against this company to the amount of more than $1,500,000. He was conducting extensive operations in many tropical sections, and this failure was a serious blow. For years Mr. Keith had consigned his bananas to Hoadley & Company, through the port of New Orleans. There was a consequent shattering of his plans for the marketing of bananas.

I told in a former chapter of the time when 1,500 Jamaica negroes worked nine months for Mr. Keith without wages owing to the inability of the Government of Costa Rica to pay money due for railroad construction. The failure of Hoadley & Company and the financial crippling of Mr. Keith gave Costa Rica a chance to prove that republics are not always ungrateful. This crisis found Mr. Keith obligated to Costa Rica, which held his drafts in large amounts, but this made no difference. The government officials of that republic promptly offered to lend Mr. Keith any reasonable amount of money to tide him over his difficulties, and he accepted their aid. The Costa Rican banks and others coöperated, and two weeks after the failure Mr. Keith arrived in New York City and made a settlement in full with his creditors.

Mr. Keith, on account of the failure of his agents, was compelled to make new arrangements for the sale of his fruit and entered into negotiations with Andrew W. Preston, president of the Boston Fruit Company. The latter organization had just formed the Fruit Dispatch Company for the purpose of expediting and extending the distribution and sale of bananas. An arrangement was made by which a portion of Mr. Keith's product would be handled by the Boston Fruit Company or its branches, and it was in this manner that Mr. Preston and Mr. Keith came in closer business contact.

It has been explained that Mr. Keith took up banana

Glimpse of the interior of the SS. *Sixaola*

cultivation and transportation as a means to supply freight for his tropical railroads, but in the years which had passed since 1872 his banana enterprises had progressed to a stage which demanded a large share of his time. Instead of being a secondary interest, as Mr. Keith had intended it to be, his banana enterprises threatened to divert his whole time from the railroad projects on which he had set his ambition.

Andrew W. Preston, president and directing spirit of the Boston Fruit Company and its branches, was anxious to secure new sources of banana supply, and was fully aware that some of these should come from Central and South America.

Under such conditions it was easy to initiate and conclude negotiations looking to the lawful consolidation of the properties of these two non-competitive groups of banana companies. Mr. Preston, Mr. Keith, and their associates were also influenced by a hope that such an amalgamation would create an enterprise sufficiently conservative and devoid of risks to attract the outside capital required to place the banana business on a more secure financial foundation.

It had been obvious for years that the banana industry was one which must be conducted on a large scale. It could be gambled in on a small scale, but there is a wide difference between rearing a conservative banana enterprise and taking a chance on the luck of a ship and a local banana plantation. Most agricultural products can be raised on a small scale. Wheat, corn, oats, barley, garden truck, apples, pears, grapes, and scores of other food and fruit products can be brought from the soil by individuals of limited means, who can compete successfully with those who cultivate much larger tracts. Cotton is in the same class, but sugar and bananas are in an entirely different class.

Sugar and bananas can be produced on a small scale, but their economical production positively demands vast acreage and vast expenditures for the complicated equipment of handling and transportation. It was a demonstrated fact in 1899 that no banana enterprise could hope for permanent success unless financially equipped to insure a widely scattered source of supply, adequate means of transportation, and, finally, methods of distribution which would place bananas within speedy reach of all of the consuming centres in the United States.

Investors had never been offered a chance in a banana enterprise of this character. Would it prove attractive? Mr. Keith, Mr. Preston, and their associates discussed the question of a consolidation of interests and gave careful

A temple in Costa Rica

consideration to the various details. It was found possible to enlist financial support for the organization of a properly equipped banana enterprise. The United Fruit Company was not, strictly speaking, a consolidation of the interests of the northern and southern groups headed respectively by Andrew W. Preston and Minor C. Keith. The United Fruit Company was incorporated on March 30, 1899, under the laws of New Jersey, as a single, individual corporation, with an authorized capital of $20,000,000. Shortly thereafter $1,650,000 capital was subscribed and paid for in cash at par, and during the first year $11,230,000 in stock was subscribed. It was authorized under its charter to acquire, by purchase or development, banana and other properties and to conduct them in the manner provided by law.

Under this charter the United Fruit Company, on April 1, 1899, offered to purchase all the property, business, and shares of the Boston Fruit Company and of its associated companies for $5,200,000 cash. This offer was later accepted and resulted in the acquisition by the United Fruit Company of the assets of the Boston Fruit Company, and its seven branch companies, viz: the American Fruit Company, Banes Fruit Company, Buckman Fruit Company, Dominican Fruit Company, Quaker City Fruit Company, and Sama Fruit Company, also the Fruit Dispatch Company.

These seven branches of the Boston Fruit Company were organized from time to time for business convenience, and were owned outright or largely controlled by the parent company. This system of branch companies was the conventional expedient of the time and was not a subject of comment or criticism.

The Banes Fruit Company, Dominican Fruit Company, and Sama Fruit Company were companies organized and owned by the Boston Fruit Company, and were operated solely for the purpose of owning plantations and growing bananas in Cuba and San Domingo. They were strictly agricultural propositions. The American Fruit Company, Buckman Fruit Company, and Quaker City Fruit Company were organized by the Boston Fruit Company to transport bananas from Cuba, San Domingo, and Jamaica to the United States, and to sell them in different points in the northern and northeastern sections of the country. The Boston Fruit Company imported bananas into the port of Boston; the American Fruit Company imported bananas to New York City, the Quaker City Fruit Company to Philadelphia, and the Buckman Fruit Company to Baltimore. The Boston Fruit Company furnished to the American, Quaker City, and Buckman companies all of the

Photo by A. Duperly & Son, Kingston, Jamaica

A tropical fern bank

bananas imported and sold by them. In other words, all of these companies were merely branches of the Boston Fruit Company.

The Fruit Dispatch Company was organized and wholly owned by the Boston Fruit Company, and was a selling corporation only. It still maintains a separate corporate existence, but is owned outright by the United Fruit Company.

To all intents and purposes the Boston Fruit Company and the branches organized and owned by it were one corporation in 1899. The branches were organized and maintained for purposes of convenience and for conventional business reasons, mainly local. It was within the power and the right

Constructing the hull of a modern banana ship

of the Boston Fruit Company to absorb its branches at any time, or to make such other disposition of them as it saw fit. Despite this obvious fact, it has been alleged that the United Fruit Company acquired these branch companies because they were competitive with the Boston Fruit Company — an absurd and utterly unfounded statement. The source of banana supply did not extend south of Jamaica and there was no port of entry south of Baltimore. So much for the northern or Boston group.

On April 5, 1899, the United Fruit Company purchased from Minor C. Keith and his associates all of the properties owned by the Tropical Trading and Transport Company, Ltd., the Colombian Land Company, Ltd., and the Snyder Banana Company, all three of which had been under the management and control of Mr. Keith. These three properties were acquired for about $4,000,000. The Colombian Land Company, Ltd., and the Tropical Trading and Transport Company, Ltd., were corporations whose operations were restricted solely to the cultivation of banana plantations in Colombia and Costa Rica respectively. The Snyder Banana Company owned plantations in Panama and chartered a few steamers which carried its fruit and other freight from Bocas del Toro to New Orleans and Mobile. The width of the Caribbean separated this group from the one to which it had been united, and the ports of entry and distribution were no nearer than Baltimore and Mobile.

Such is the plain history of the organization of the United Fruit Company. Its legal incorporation meant more than the birth of a corporation. It was the actual birth of the banana industry. It had taken thirty-four years of blunders, experiments, disasters, partial successes, and the assumption of the innumerable risks and hardships incident to a struggle with the virgin tropics to create an enterprise fit to take advantage of the experience which had so dearly been bought. The great experiment of whether bananas could be produced and handled on a vastly larger scale had yet to be made, and there were many who did not hesitate to predict that the ambitious plans of the heads of the newly organized United Fruit Company would end in overwhelming failure.

CHAPTER VI

Growth of a Great Enterprise

EVERY reader of the preceding chapter must be aware that the United Fruit Company started its career without any of the advantages which conduce to monopoly. It was the owner of no patents. It had the benefit of no tariff favors. Its land holdings in the tropics were insignificant compared with the total of banana tracts available for cultivation. It held no exclusive concessions from any of the governments of the tropical countries in which it operated. It had no contracts — and never has entered into contracts — with steamship or railway lines giving it any advantages over its competitors. The Gulf of Mexico and the Caribbean Sea were open waters to all of the ships of the world which cared to engage in the banana trade. The ports of the tropics and of the United States were open to such ships.

There was nothing to prevent other groups of investors from entering the field against the newly organized United Fruit Company. Such interests might have purchased the properties of the companies which were already in competition with the United Fruit Company, or they could have acquired most of the lands on which now are located the banana plantations which give to the United Fruit Company the bulk of its supply.

The United Fruit Company was formed in the year when the American public was possessed of a mania for risking its money in new and vast undertakings. Any plan of reorganization or consolidation of industry which could be so presented as to offer a reasonable chance of success had its securities snapped up by thousands of investors who besieged the offices of the underwriters and deluged them with letters containing remittances. It was a period when billions of dollars were turned into the coffers of the "New Industry." It goes without saying that the newly formed United Fruit Company had no prestige, advantage or financial backing which would deter promoters from organizing an even more powerful company along the same lines and for the purpose of entering the same broad field of enterprise.

No, it was not fear of the competition of the newly launched United Fruit Company which prevented the great captains of finance and industry from bidding for popular support for a corporation which would rival and possibly supplant the one then in the field. They made no move because they lacked faith both in the success of such an undertaking and in the support of the investing public.

The modern fruit ship

There was another reason. It was impossible to draft a prospectus which would convince an intelligent investor that one banana producing concern would have any marked natural advantage over another. The investing public was in a frenzy to escape the effects of a system of cut-throat competition which had brought ruin to producer and consumer alike. The most popular of the new stock and bond securities were those which gave assurance that their holders would be immune from profit-destroying competition. No industry based on agriculture offered that inducement. What had bananas to offer? The public had been educated to believe that bananas flourish in most parts of the tropics, and careful investors knew that the price of bananas would ever be fixed by competition. Competition was very unpopular in

1899, and the average investor and underwriter looked with suspicion on any security based on the alleged possibilities of the banana industry.

The blunt truth of the matter is that the United Fruit Company was forced into its present leadership in the banana industry because of the ignorance and indifference of the investing public of the United States concerning the tropics at their southern gates.

The United Fruit Company to-day has certain assured advantages, and these advantages must be taken into account by any new rival which bids for its trade and business. How did the United Fruit Company obtain these advantages? By what right does it exercise these advantages?

The great wholesale dry goods firm of Marshall Field & Company has certain decided advantages over all of its competitors in the United States. How did this corporation obtain these advantages and by what right does it exercise them? Here is the answer: Marshall Field & Company created these advantages by the exercise of constructive business genius in a field open to the investment capital of all the world. Marshall Field & Company holds these advantages by the right of honorable business conquest.

The same thing is true of hundreds of other corporations, concerns, and individuals who have reared great business enterprises in fields where monopoly is impossible, and who now possess the legitimate advantages which come from good will and prestige honestly won and fairly exercised.

The annual reports of the company during the thirteen years of its corporate existence form an interesting study. President Preston has condensed in these reports a frank and lucid history of a progress which has been halted at times by climatic disasters, sweeping calamities which would have spelled ruin to a concern not fortified by a wide distribution of its sources of supply.

The reading public has always associated the United Fruit Company solely with the banana industry, and there prevails a popular belief that its success has been due en-

SCENE ALONG THE SEA WALL IN PUERTO LIMON, COSTA RICA
This was a wilderness before the founders of the United Fruit Company developed the coast lands and harbors of Central America

tirely to a mastery of the production and distribution of that tropical fruit. This is not so. From the very beginning the company was engaged in other forms of activities. It was a carrier of freight and passengers. It was a raiser of cattle

AFTER A TROPICAL FLOOD
Repairing a bridge on a banana railroad

and other live stock; it was an owner and builder of railroads; it was preparing to engage in the extensive production of sugar in Cuba, and it was cultivating many tropical products besides bananas.

On August 31, 1900, we learn from the first annual report

of the United Fruit Company that it owned 212,394 acres of land in Costa Rica, Cuba, Honduras, Jamaica, San Domingo, and Colombia. It had leased lands in Costa Rica and Jamaica to the extent of 23,807 acres, making its total holdings 236,201 acres. Of this area 66,294 were under cultivation of some sort, and 169,907 acres were unimproved. Much of this unimproved land was unfitted for cultivation, and belonged to tracts which had to be purchased intact in order to secure an acreage suitable for bananas or other purposes. All save a small portion of the lands then owned by the United Fruit Company had been acquired by purchase from the Boston Fruit Company and from the interests headed by Minor C. Keith.

The company had 38,463 acres planted to bananas, as is shown in the following table which is of interest as showing the agricultural resources of the enterprise in its initial year of operation:

STATEMENT SHOWING THE LOCATION AND THE ACREAGE OF THE UNITED FRUIT COMPANY'S FRUIT, SUGAR CANE, AND MISCELLANEOUS CULTIVATIONS, AUGUST 31, 1900

LOCATION AND ACREAGE

Description	Costa Rica	Cuba	Honduras	Jamaica	San Domingo	Colombia	Total
Fruit:							
Bananas	10,626	5,841	400	5,749	3,300	12,547	38,463
Oranges	......	......	...	315	......	......	315
Pineapples	......	......	...	17	......	......	17
Sugar Cane	......	7,803	....	......	......	......	7,803
Miscellaneous:							
Cocoanuts	......	......	...	1,830	......	12	1,842
Coffee	46	......	...	10	......	2	58
Cocoa	......	......	...	115	......	140	255
Rubber	65	......	...	79	......	163	307
Para Grass	2380	......	...	......	......	78	2,458
Guinea Grass	3,417	......	...	......	......	......	3,417
Vegetables	......	......	...	......	......	12	12
Other lands	3,276	3,539	100	4,151	200	81	11,347
Total Acreage	19,810	17,183	500	12,266	3,500	13,035	66,294

On these plantations were 13,932 head of live stock, apportioned to the various countries as follows:

STATEMENT OF LIVE STOCK OWNED BY THE UNITED FRUIT COMPANY ON AUGUST 31, 1900

LOCATION

Description	Costa Rica	Cuba	Honduras	Jamaica	San Domingo	Colombia	Total
Cattle:							
Cows	2,907	12	....	611	.....	132	3,662
Bulls	43	1	2	26	.....	5	77
Oxen	46	783	24	1,290	13	.....	2,156
Steers	3,416	5	6	482	.....	37	3,946
Calves	1,357	.....	....	281	.....	24	1,662
Heifers	.....	....	....	442	.....	....	442
Total	7,769	801	32	3,132	13	198	11,945
Horses and Mules:							
Stallions	8	2	..	......	....	5	15
Mares	166	1	2	66	....	3	238
Geldings	120	51	2	51	....	38	262
Colts	109	...	..	29	12	7	157
Mules	271	104	1	774	96	36	1,282
Asses	......	...	..	19	....	4	23
Total	674	158	5	939	108	93	1,977

The cattle were used for three purposes: Stock cattle were raised in Costa Rica and Cuba, and were killed for consumption on the plantations or for shipment to the markets of these and other countries. Dairy cattle furnished the milk, cream, butter and cheese supplied to the employees from the commissary stores which the company maintained and conducted at prices strictly regulated to meet the mere cost of maintenance. The oxen, steers, horses, and mules were employed mainly in the transportation of the fruit and other products from the fields to the railroads or to the wharves.

The newly formed company came into possession of several small railways which served as the foundation for the comprehensive systems now in operation in all of the countries of its activities. Speedy and adequate railway trans-

Washday in Costa Rica

portation of bananas from the great plantations to the docks, and rapid steamship transportation from the tropics to the markets of the United States and Europe is the expensive but imperative prerequisite of a modern banana enterprise. The banana is the most perishable of all tropical products, and one of the vital problems is to provide sure and swift transportation from all parts of the plantations to the awaiting ships. How scantily equipped was the United Fruit Company at the end of its first corporate year may be judged by a glance at the following table:

RAILROADS OWNED BY THE UNITED FRUIT COMPANY ON AUGUST 31, 1900

Location	Miles of Road	Equipment	
		Number of locomotives	Number of freight cars
Costa Rica	33.18	3	49
Cuba	28.50	4	104
Jamaica	8.12	2	32
Colombia	37.73	6	76
San Domingo	4.50	2	28
Total	112.03	17	289

The utter inadequacy of these diminutive railroad lines to penetrate the tropical jungles and convert them into productive banana plantations is apparent when it is stated that the United Fruit Company now owns and operates more than 1,000 miles of well-constructed and finely equipped railroads and tramways, and that banana transportation from the fields to the wharves requires the service of more than 100 locomotives and 2,500 freight cars!

This is a giant step forward from the year of 1900 when 112 miles of poorly laid track and less than a score of light locomotives were forced to serve as best they could. At that time the patient ox and the impatient mule did much of the work now done by steam and electricity.

But the tropical assets of the United Fruit Company in 1900, crude and small as they were compared with those of the present day, were much superior to those of any other fruit company in the American tropics or in the world. The greatest single asset of the company was its plan of self-insurance against the effects of the devastation of a plantation or all of the plantations of a district.

During all of the years of the corporate existence of the Boston Fruit Company no destructive hurricane had swept Jamaica, its chief source of banana supply. More than average good luck had attended its operations in San Domingo and Cuba, but Mr. Preston was alive to the fact that climatic disasters would break sooner or later. It is rather a remarkable coincidence that all of the districts of banana production of the old Boston Fruit Company were smitten in the very year following its purchase by the United Fruit Company. The season opened with the first hurricane in twelve years in Jamaica, the blasts of which levelled a large percentage of the growing banana plants on that island and

Stateroom of modern fruit boat

seriously crippled its supply. A few months later San Domingo was swept by a hurricane which did great damage to the plantations formerly owned by the Boston Fruit Company. To make the coincidence complete, a deadly and very unusual drought simultaneously afflicted Cuba.

Not a district formerly depended on by the Boston Fruit Company was exempt from these afflictions. It is possible that the company would have survived these blows of misfortune, but its losses in money, trade, and prestige would have been enormous. Banana importers from Central and South America would have invaded its field and derived large temporary profits by taking advantage of the plight of consumers.

But how fared it with the newly organized United Fruit Company and the public it served? The company lost the

A nook on the United Fruit Company's SS. *Calamares*

bananas destroyed by the hurricanes and the drought and was compelled to meet the expense of bringing new plantations into bearing, but the bananas raised by the company in Colombia and Central America were still at its command and there was no delay in shipping them to Boston, New York, Philadelphia, Baltimore, and other ports formerly dependent almost entirely on the islands of the West Indies. Prices to the jobbers or retailers continued low and reasonable, and the public was not called on to pay an excessive price for bananas on account of these climatic disasters.

It will hardly be denied that this was a desirable outcome for the public. There was a time when each section of the United States was compelled to depend on the wheat and corn raised within easy reach of the individual consumer. It naturally followed that a disaster to local crops meant famine or abnormally high prices. The development of transportation and methods of storing grain products insured consumers against the worst of the effects of local crop disasters. This progress put an end to the activities of those who are eager to derive unfair profits from calamities.

The sensible and logical plan initiated by the United Fruit Company performed for the banana exactly the same service that improved methods of transportation and handling wrought for wheat, corn, and other grain products. It removed the banana from the list of speculative products and elevated it to the grade of a fruit and food staple.

CHAPTER VII

Twelve Years of Creative Work

LET us review briefly the manner in which the United Fruit Company attempted the industrial conquest of the tropics.

Reference to its first annual report shows that in 1900 it had tropical investments conservatively estimated at a value of $16,949,753. Nearly ten millions of this amount had been expended in the purchase of plantations, their cultivation, and the erection of suitable buildings. Approximately $400,000 was represented by live stock, $1,253,428 by railways, $74,000 by telephones, $95,673 by towboats, launches, and lighters, $233,560 by wharves, and $365,000 had already been expended in the construction of a sugar mill in Cuba. The United Fruit Company owned $1,244,096 in the stock of other companies. This included all of the stock of the Belize Royal Mail and Central American Steamship Company, which owned and operated ten ships of tonnage from 1,000 to 1,600. It also included all of the stock of the Fruit Dispatch Company, which has always been maintained and operated as a distinct corporation.

In addition to the ten ships owned by the company it was necessary to charter or lease many others. This number ranged from thirty to fifty steamships, and varied according to the season and to the productivity of the plantations. The fruit boats of 1900 were a sorry lot compared with the large, speedy, and luxurious ships which now compose the famous Great White Fleet, and which are fitted with every convenience and safety which modern inventive genius can suggest and money provide.

The company had determined to make a comprehensive experiment in sugar cultivation, and the location selected was the beautiful Nipe Bay district of eastern Cuba. A sugar mill was under construction, and 7,800 acres had been planted to cane. In this same district the company owned 5,841 acres of banana plantations, and planned greatly to increase its banana acreage. It was later to learn that banana cultivation in Cuba was impracticable.

The officials of the company were fully alive to the fact that the duty was imposed on them of making sanitary all of the tropical ports from which their ships took freight. This duty, by custom and by right, devolves on the governments in which such ports are located, but, with the exception of Jamaica, none of the governments of Central and South America and of Cuba and San Domingo were capable of initiating the complicated and expensive work of scientific sanitation. I shall consider in detail in a later chapter the effective work which was planned and executed along health lines by the United Fruit Company, and will also give an account of other public duties which it has performed.

Those who risk their lives and their fortunes in tropical investments have a right to expect that success will yield handsome returns. There is always the chance that weather disasters or political revolutions will blot the ordinary tropical enterprise out of existence. This fact is recognized and acted on by bankers and private money lenders. The banks of Cuba, Mexico, and of Central and South America demand from 10 to 20 per cent interest on high class tropical loans. The sugar planter, tobacco grower, small banana raiser, or other participant in tropical agriculture is satisfied to pay 12 per cent for money borrowed to conduct his operations. He has an expectation of making from 20 to as high as 100 per cent under favorable conditions, and money is not forthcoming when an enterprise cannot prove that it has a reasonable chance of realizing from 20 to 30 per cent net profit.

The student of tropical industry should understand and

Street scene in Guatemala

keep in mind this basic fact. It is sometimes alleged that the profits of the United Fruit Company are excessive. The contrary is true. The risks assumed justify prices which would yield annual profits of 25 per cent, and even that figure might not tempt the conservative capital of New York, London, Paris, or Berlin to enter the field against the successful operators.

On this basis and with an actual investment of about $17,000,000, the United Fruit Company could not have been criticised had it realized net profits of $4,250,000 in its initial year of operation. It was compelled, however, to be content with $1,831,815, which justified a dividend payment of 10 per cent, and the application of an appropriate amount for improvements and betterments.

In 1901 the capital stock was increased from $11,230,000 to $12,369,500, and the money derived from stock sales was applied to new plantations and other productive assets. Despite this fact the net earnings showed a decided decrease, dropping to $1,098,557, and aggregate dividends of 9 per cent were paid.

The policy of the company toward the public and with its stockholders is well illustrated by the opening paragraph in President Preston's second annual report, in which he said:

"In presenting herewith the second annual report of your company the management has endeavored to inform you even more fully than previously as to the character, location, extent, and value of the company's several properties, as well as to show in detail receipts, expenditures, and other financial and business matters. The management desires to give all such statements, figures, and general information respecting your company's property and business to the stockholders as will enable them to share the confidence of the management in the stability and success of the company's business, a confidence which has been inspired by many years' experience in the businesses which your company has acquired, and which has been greatly increased by the success with which the risks and disadvantages under which such businesses were formerly carried on have been obviated by the formation and operations of your company. With this object in view the statements and figures given in our previous report have been subdivided and amplified."

It is doubtful if any great corporation has been equally frank in annually presenting to its stockholders, and through them to the public, all of the important details concerning its operations.

The destroyed banana plantations of Jamaica, San Domingo, and Cuba greatly curtailed the productivity of these sections in 1901, but despite this fact the company distributed in the United States and Canada approximately 14,000,000 bunches of bananas, nearly all of which were consumed in the United States. This was an increase of nearly three million over the first year. The sixty steamships owned or chartered by the company also brought up from the tropics 13,500,000 cocoanuts and 200,000 boxes of oranges.

The sugar mill at Banes, Cuba, was put into operation and yielded a profit of about $110,000 for the year. The price of bananas dropped in the United States to a point so low that fair business profits on them were impossible.

In 1901 the company increased its improved land holdings from 66,294 to 75,055 acres, and its total holdings, owned and leased, from 236,201 to 262,425 acres. The bulk of this increase was in Central and South America. Experience was proving that banana production was safer and more profitable in Central America and Colombia, but it was deemed best to give Cuba and San Domingo a further chance. During this year 3,500 acres in Costa Rica were set out to new banana cultivation, and 3,000 acres in Colombia made ready for such planting. The sum of $460,000 was expended on the Banes sugar mill.

The climatic disasters which had afflicted the company and diminished its profits did not swerve the management from its belief that it would be possible to rear a great business structure in the tropics, but the world of finance and investment looked with increased doubt on this venture, and there was limited public demand for its securities. If it

Banana-unloading machines in New Orleans

had been apparent to investors that there was a likelihood that the United Fruit Company would rear a monopoly in the banana industry there would have been a rush to acquire an interest in this investment, but well-informed capital knew then, and knows now, that the control of the banana industry by a single corporation is beyond possibility.

The company made a much better showing in 1902. Its plantations had recovered from the effects of hurricanes, droughts, and floods, and there was a better market and higher prices for bananas in the United States and Canada. No effort had yet been made to ship bananas to Great Britain and the Continent, and the consuming public abroad had yet to learn that it was possible to offer that tropical luxury at prices which would compete with their own native fruits.

The importations of bananas for that year reached about 16,000,000 bunches, most of which were consumed in the United States. The new sugar mill in Banes produced more than 40,000,000 pounds of sugar, but the market prices were so low that it was operated at a loss approximating $100,000.

The attempt to arouse the public against the alleged aggressions of a combination among the growers of sugar cane has always amused me, and it will interest and amuse any one who has personal knowledge of the facts. In the first place, sugar is the cheapest of all food products, with the sole exception of bananas, and it happens that a very large portion of the revenue of the United Fruit Company is derived from the production and sale of these two remarkably inexpensive food staples. It goes without saying that the United Fruit Company would not willingly produce and export sugar and bananas for any length of time at a loss, yet this is exactly what it has been compelled to do in many protracted periods during its corporate existence.

If the American sugar growers of Cuba had the power to fix prices you may rest assured that there would be no year which failed to show a reasonable profit. If the American banana cultivators in the tropics had the power to fix prices you may rest assured that not a bunch of this fruit would ever be sold at a loss. Yet we see this capably handled corporation losing $100,000 in a year when its cane fields were wonderfully prolific. In the winter season of 1911–12 the

Old method of loading bananas

United Fruit Company lost more than $800,000 on its banana shipments, and in the two weeks ending February 26, 1913, the losses incurred in its banana business exceeded $290,000!

Monopolies or near-monopolies are not compelled to submit, and do not submit, to such losses. The plain truth of the matter is that the market prices of sugar and of bananas are fixed by vast competitive factors absolutely beyond the control of any corporation or possible combination of corporations or individuals. Those who assert to the contrary insult the intelligence of a people who long have enjoyed the boon of cheap sugar and cheap bananas, and who know instinctively that such prices are not the logical outcome of monopoly.

The wisdom of the United Fruit Company in diversifying its tropical products was strikingly shown in this year of 1902. Competition frowned on sugar, but smiled on bananas and cocoanuts, which were in demand because of a scarcity of apples and other fruits and foods raised on home soil. After devoting $453,356 to betterments and allowing for depreciation and all other charges, there remained a net income of $2,185,000 available for dividend purposes, and the stockholders were paid total dividends of 8½ per cent for the year.

Several large new ships were added to the fleet, and the cost of transporting bananas from the tropical ports to the distributing domestic ports was reduced 3 per cent over the preceding year. The Fruit Dispatch Company greatly extended its operations and was busy with its function of placing tropical fruits at the command of new markets in the United States and Canada.

In the latter part of the fiscal year of 1903 the United Fruit Company made an important step. It began the exportation of bananas from the American tropics to Great Britain. A shipping arrangement was entered into with the English steamship line of Elders & Fyffes, which became an associate or subsidiary of the United Fruit Company.

It thus came about that, through the energy and foresight of an American corporation, the banana was introduced for the first time to lower the cost and raise the standard of living in the populous centres of the United Kingdom. This venture was a success from the start, and the banana was speedily introduced by the United Fruit Company and its American competitors into the markets of France, Germany, and other Continental nations to which it had been a comparative stranger. It is the strict truth to state, however, that the sole credit for this really important commercial step belongs to the United Fruit Company, and the reading public of the United States dimly realizes the extent of the benefits which have flowed to the consumers of average means from the introduction abroad of this cheap and wholesome fruit and food product.

It was another year of vast production but actual sugar losses for the company in Cuba. The fine new mill ground out 44,000,000 pounds of sugar, but the production of foreign beet sugar was so great that the market prices compelled the United Fruit Company to stand a loss of $70,800. Another hurricane swept and desolated Jamaica, and the losses from this disaster mounted to $168,000.

This year of 1903 was marked by extensive land purchases and improvements, entailing an expenditure of approximately $1,350,000. It was now a demonstrated fact that the bananas of Central America and Colombia were superior in quality and also in the quantity raised per acre of cultivation over those of Cuba and other parts of the West Indies. The wonderful Changuinola District of Panama was acquired by the company, the purchase including a canal twelve miles long and plantations already partially developed. Work was vigorously started on the railroads and equipment required to place all parts of this new district in quick communication with the port of Bocas del Toro. These and other land purchases increased the improved land holdings of the company to 97,609 acres, and its total possessions, owned and leased, to 288,177 acres.

The net income of the year available for dividends was $1,848,153, and the stockholders received 7 per cent on their money invested. They had a substantial equity, however, in the large sums which had been invested in new lands and improvements.

The year 1904 was marked by a decided increase in the fleet owned or controlled by the United Fruit Company. The Tropical Fruit Steamship Company, Ltd., was organized for the purpose of providing better freight and passenger facilities, more especially between the United States and the American tropics. This company made a modest start with three banana steamers, the *San José*, *Limon*, and *Esparta*. This was the modest beginning of the Great White Fleet, which has done so much for the commerce and prestige of the United States in the American tropics, and it is a matter deeply to be regretted that unwise laws operate to keep our flag from floating at their mastheads.

One of the luxuries of the Great White Fleet

Despite continued low prices for sugar the Cuban mill owned by the company showed, for a change, a fair profit for the year, and added $345,000 to the net income, which totalled $1,940,000 for 1904 from which divided payments aggregating 7 per cent were made. The total of bananas imported amounted to about 15,000,000 bunches, a decrease of 2,500,000 over the preceding year. This was occasioned by a decrease of 6,000,000 bunches from Jamaica, owing to the hurricane of August, 1903. This calamity would have crippled if not destroyed the former Boston Fruit Company, but the new plantations in Central and South America made up a large share of the deficit, and the consumers of bananas suffered nothing. The company expended more than a million of dollars in new plantations, new railroads, and new equipment in Central America during this year, a part of which sum was raised by the issuance and sale of new stock, the total capital stock of the company now standing at $15,782,000, which was far less than its assets.

The ensuing year, 1905, was one of low prices for bananas and comparatively high prices for sugar. As a result of this condition the profits from sugar were more than half of those derived from bananas and other tropical fruits, the figures being respectively, $1,044,703 for the latter, and $573,017 for sugar. This made it possible to declare dividends of 7 per cent.

The vicissitudes and uncertainties of the banana business are clearly shown by a comparison of certain items found in the annual reports of 1904 and 1905. In 1904 the company imported approximately 15,000,000 bunches of bananas, and realized on them a net profit of approximately $1,245,000. This was at the rate of 8.3 cents a bunch, or a profit of one cent on each eighteen bananas; surely not an extravagant return for a corporation with $20,000,000 invested in that enterprise.

In 1905 the importations made a startling increase from 15,000,000 to nearly 20,000,000 bunches, but the net profits tumbled from $1,245,000 to about $680,000. The latter figure shows that the United Fruit Company realized a net profit that year of only 3.4 cents a bunch, or a profit of one cent on each forty-two bananas sold!

Such facts are well known to the fruit trade, but now and then some sensationalist rushes into print with a fairy tale about the stupendous profits made by banana growers and importers. I have before me a page article from a Denver newspaper which would be humorous if intended as fiction, but it purports to state facts, and one of these alleged facts is that the United Fruit Company "pays 7 cents a bunch for bananas that sell in the United States for $1.50 to $2.50." This would lead the average reader to assume that the profits accruing to the company would range from $1.43 to $2.43 on each bunch of bananas brought to the United States. This particular falsehood multiples the truth by from 30 to 50, a freak of mendacity which ignores the fact that it costs about 95 cents to raise and transport a bunch of bananas from the tropics to the ports of the United States, and that $1.00 would be an acceptable selling price by the average importing company.

It may be taken for granted that the United Fruit Company did not willingly import bananas for a profit of less than 3½ cents a bunch. Sensible people who are compelled to pay extortionate prices for most that they eat, wear and use, would not indulge in riots even if it were proved to them that banana importers absorbed a profit of 10 cents for a

Building abridge for a banana railroad

bunch of from 100 to 150 luscious bananas. Nothing in the world is imported at any minimum profit rate approaching this, but the United Fruit Company seems to deem itself fortunate if it can derive a slight net profit on each bunch of bananas, and there are times when it brings in many shiploads at an actual loss.

It was in 1905 that the United Fruit Company decided

to abandon the cultivation of bananas in Cuba. Experience had demonstrated that the rainfall and general climatic conditions did not favor bananas as compared with available tracts in Central and South America. A fortune had been expended on these Cuban banana plantations, but it was finally decided to plant these tracts to sugar cane and this was done. It was a radical step, but it proved to be a wise one.

The year of 1906 was an important and successful one for the company. It marked the adding of Guatemala as a source of banana supply. This was not done until investigation had indicated that bananas could be raised profitably in a section with Barrios as its port.

The net earnings of the year, after deducting $638,867 for betterments, were $3,647,985 for bananas and other tropical fruits, and $72,416 for sugar, including deductions of $78,000 for betterments. This permitted dividend payments of 7 per cent, and left a handsome surplus in the treasury.

It was a year of extensive investments for the United Fruit Company. Approximately $1,100,000 was devoted to increasing the capacity of the sugar plant in Cuba, in order to attain a capacity of grinding 3,500 tons of cane per day. Eight thousand acres of new cane were planted, miles of new railroad constructed to bring the cane from the fields to the mill, and other construction work accomplished.

Panama had proved itself as a banana country, and $400,000 was expended in this year on new banana planting, farm buildings, hospitals, railways and trams. Costa Rica absorbed $565,000 of new capital, more than half of it being for railways, tramways and rolling stock. Guatemala made a modest start with $51,000 expended for banana planting and buildings. The total of capital expenditure and betterments in this progressive year reached the impressive figure of $2,386,690, which was far in excess of any year since the foundation of the company.

The demand for bananas was increasing enormously not only in the United States and Canada, but in Great Britain and the Continent. Other importers were competing for this trade, but the United Fruit Company was the only concern which had faith that this demand would continue to increase by leaps and bounds. Its earnings were ample to warrant the payment of dividends in excess of the 7 per cent distributed among the stockholders, but the officers of the company did not deviate from the original plan initiated by President Preston in the years of the Boston Fruit Company. This policy consisted of reinvesting a large part of the earnings in new plantations and new equipment, thus enabling the company to meet the demands of new consumers at prices which would make the banana a staple and a necessity, and not a luxury fluctuating widely in price and at the whim of climatic conditions.

In Jamaica

To help meet the demand for large expenditures it was the policy of the company to issue and sell new stock in such amounts as would be readily purchased by stockholders or by the general investing public. The consistent aim of the management was to keep pace with increasing consumption, and the present high standing of the company is due to the faith and courage of those who believed that the public would respond to prices established by adequate banana production.

We now come to a banner year in the history of the United Fruit Company, 1907, a year fraught with panic and financial depression in the United States, but one in which this tropical enterprise proved its stability and rewarded those who backed its prospects.

Almost every factor and condition favored the company in 1907. No disasters of consequence befel its plantations. Importations exceeding 22,000,000 bunches were sold in the United States and Canada at the highest prices in years. These slightly advanced prices were doubtless due largely to the fact that there was a greatly increased demand for bananas owing to the hard times which forced the average consumer to spend his money to the best advantage, and it was only natural that the low prices and high nutritive value of the banana should appeal to all who felt the pinch of hard times. As a result, hundreds of thousands of people discovered that the banana had the double merit of being cheap and wholesome.

The panic of 1907 had a remarkable effect so far as the United Fruit Company was concerned. It demonstrated that an investment in its stock, instead of being precarious, as had been regarded by some, was an effective insurance against the effects of general business depression. Not only did the company's earnings increase in this year of panic and depression, but its stock became the steadiest on the Boston Stock Exchange, investors quickly realizing that the panic had the remarkable effect of increasing the demand for bananas, especially among the working classes.

The United Fruit Company does not sell to the consumer, its entire product going to the dealer. The latter temporarily paid a few extra cents a bunch for bananas, but this meant much to the importing companies. The enhanced wholesale rates for bananas probably meant an extra profit of $2,000,000 to the United Fruit Company in this exceptional year. Its net earnings available for dividend purposes were $6,189,927, of which $5,441,319 were from bananas and other tropical fruits, and $620,590 from sugar, and dividends amounting to 7½ per cent for the year were paid.

In this banner year the company expended $3,525,000 for improvements and betterments, of which $2,841,000 was derived from the sale of new stock and $683,000 charged to operation. This increased the company's tropical investments to $20,628,000, and its assets had mounted to exceeding $32,000,000. This latter figure was more than 50 per cent in excess of its capital stock, and there has never been a time when this condition was not approximated. Unlike many great corporations, there has never been a trace of water in the securities of the United Fruit Company.

Cuba called for $535,000 of new capital in 1907. The

The United Fruit Company's SS. *Pastores* in her New York dock

Bocas del Toro district of Panama expended $547,000 in new banana planting, railways, wharves, and other facilities for the cheaper production and handling of fruits. The development expense in Costa Rica reached the impressive figure of $1,788,000, a large part of which was used in the purchase of banana lands. Guatemala called for $186,000, and her new plantations produced their first marketable fruit.

The company made a large investment in the stock of the Nipe Bay Company, whose sugar properties are near those owned outright by the company at Banes. New steamships were purchased or contracted for by the Tropical Fruit Steamship Company and Elders & Fyffes, Ltd.

There was a decided falling off in net profits in 1908, the total available for dividend purposes being under four million dollars. Less bananas were shipped to the United States and lower prices prevailed. The general prosperity of the enterprise was such, however, that in addition to the regular dividends, amounting to 8 per cent, it was deemed conservative to distribute an extra dividend of 10 per cent, which was paid on August 1st of that year, and which amounted to between $13 and $14 per share, to the stockholders. On account of the market value of the stock the company gave them the right to purchase at par with their dividends, and for the first time in the history of this corporation or its predecessors there was paid to stockholders a percentage of annual profit proportionate to the risks of a tropical investment.

This bonus meant far more than a mere money return. It meant the realization of years of hard work, relentless energy, courage, and fortitude. It meant that the banana industry had "arrived," to quote a descriptive word. It was a token and a reward of the faith which had supported those who had struggled against the hardships and dangers of the tropics. It proved to the world that the industrial and commercial conquest of the American tropics was possible, and it should have proved to the United States that it was the bounden duty of its people, its press, and its government to encourage and foster the speedy development of the tropics. Not for the mere purpose of obtaining money rewards, but for the larger, broader, and statesmanlike object of obtaining from the tropics such of its other products as would add to the happiness and raise the standard of living of the people of the United States.

The sum of nearly $2,400,000 was expended in betterments in 1908. These resulted in 8,000 acres of new banana plantings, which meant a future production almost equal to all of the plantations owned or leased by the old Boston Fruit Company. In addition to this there were added 1,800 acres of sugar cane, 3,500 acres of pasture, and about 2,000 acres of newly cleared land to be planted in bananas and cane. There was also constructed 43 miles of new railway and 61 miles of farm tramways, and the railway equipment was increased with 12 locomotives and 400 freight cars. In the live stock department there was noted an increase of 1,500 head in the number of horses and cattle.

This is what I call "creative work." I am reciting these rather dull facts in order that those who care to learn the truth can obtain a perspective of just how this corporation went about building up a business which is colossal in its extent and international in its scope. The preceding paragraph is eloquent in its suggestion of how the company won its present standing. It created it, fairly and honorably and splendidly.

The year of 1909 was one of greatly diminished banana earnings. Prices were low both in the United States and abroad. The Central American districts were swept by floods which entailed great losses both to growing crops and to railroad and other property. The net receipts from bananas and other tropical fruits dropped to $2,702,000, a sorry contrast to the $5,441,000 obtained in 1907 from a much less acreage and less efficient equipment. The sugar plantations made a better relative showing, and again vindicated the wisdom of diversified investments by returning a net income of $1,168,000. Regular dividends aggregating 8 per cent were disbursed to the shareholders, followed on November 15, 1909, by a second extra dividend of 10 per cent, approximating $18 in value, in consideration of the rights to subscribe to new stock issued at par as compared to its value in the open market.

The company sold all of its properties in Santo Domingo and invested the proceeds in sugar development in Cuba. The expenditures for new properties and improvements during the year aggregated $1,934,000. The railway mileage was increased 67, and 37 miles of new tramways were constructed. Three new and fine steamships were added to the

A sea of bananas

fleet of the Tropical Fruit Steamship Company, and four more were contracted for. The foreign business of the company showed a steady increase, and new centres of population were offered a fruit until then unknown to them.

Then arrived the prosperous year of 1910. Once again market conditions permitted the banana importers to realize slightly higher prices for bananas, with the result that the profits of the company for bananas and other tropical fruits mounted from $2,702,000 to the more cheerful figure of $3,943,000. On top of this came favorable prices for sugar, due to a shortage in the foreign beet sugar crop, with the result that the company's sugar mill in Cuba set a record which still stands — net profits of $1,968,491 — and this did not include the sugar profits from the Nipe Bay Company. This permitted the payment of the regular dividends of 8 per cent. On November 4, 1910, a third extra dividend of 10 per cent was paid to stockholders, which they were given the right to apply to the payment of new shares at par, which, with subscription rights netted the stockholders a return of 18 per cent from the extra dividend.

The capital stock stood at $23,474,000, with assets conservatively estimated at exceeding $45,000,000. The authorized capital was increased to $35,000,000 in order to make possible stock sales to meet required large investments. Four new ships were added to the fleet and three more ordered. In this year the company acquired all of the remaining stock in Elders & Fyffes, Ltd., thus giving it full ownership of that British steamship line with its large and well equipped fleet of fruit boats. The fleet of the Tropical Fruit Steamship Company, Ltd., now numbered seventeen ships, and the public had learned to know that they were the finest craft which connected the ports of the United States with the tropics.

The cultivated acreage was increased by about 6,000 in 1910. Guatemala had justified the hopes reposed in her soil and climate, and her banana plantations were supplying crops which compared favorably in quality and in quantity raised per acre to the older plantations in Costa Rica and Panama. The profits of this year were materially lessened

Photo by A. Duperly & Son, Kingston, Jamaica

The beach near Port Antonio

by the heavy cost of the practical reconstruction of an entire section of the railway line in Costa Rica, due to the almost unprecedented floods of the preceding year.

The year of 1911 was a fairly prosperous one for bananas, the net profits reaching $3,733,204, but there was a decided reduction in sugar profits, due to a severe drought in Cuba which was responsible for a greatly diminished output. As a result of this condition the sugar profits of the company dropped from $1,968,491 in 1910, to $544,418 in 1911, another striking illustration of the variations of tropical investments in agricultural products.

Extensive development work was carried on this year in Guatemala, Panama, and Colombia, the total expenditures for new plantations and improved equipment in these countries exceeding $1,483,000. There were thus added more than 7,000 acres of banana plantations in sections which had proved their excellence for that purpose. Three new ships were added to the Great White Fleet, and three others of increased tonnage and splendid accommodations for passengers were ordered from the builders.

Regular dividends aggregating 8 per cent were paid in the fiscal year of 1911, and again the company disbursed on December 19, 1911, an extra dividend of 10 per cent, giving its shareholders the right to apply their dividends to the purchase of stock at par. The stock was then selling at about 180, which made the extra dividend return 18 per cent to the stockholders.

In the following year, 1912, the earnings from bananas and other tropical fruits were $2,565,428, and those from the sugar business $1,930,186. The miscellaneous income of the company brought its net earnings to $5,332,112. In addition to the four regular quarterly dividends of 2 per cent each, stockholders were given the privilege of subscribing to shares of the company's stock at $150 per share to the amount of 20 per cent of their holdings, which gave shareholders rights having a market value of from $6 to $7 each.

In his annual report for this year President Andrew W. Preston makes this interesting comment:

"The growth of the demand for the company's bananas

necessitates continued extensive development work, and large purchases of banana properties and lands available for banana planting have been made in the Republic of Colombia, Republic of Panama, Costa Rica, and other parts of

Photo by A. Duperly & Son, Kingston, Jamaica

Rolling River Falls, Jamaica

Central America. A large program of development work is being carried on in Costa Rica, Guatemala, and Panama, the company's policy being to grow a large proportion of its fruit in order to insure an adequate supply and maintain a standard quality."

As a result of this policy the company increased its acreage of banana cultivation by more than thirty thousand acres, the figure rising from 84,549 acres of bananas in 1911 to 115,460 in 1912. Eliminating the discarded banana plantations of Cuba and San Domingo, this increase of 30,911 acres of growing bananas exceeded by nearly 2,000 the total acreage owned by the United Fruit Company in its initial year of operation. Yet such is the growing banana hunger of the world that this company and its competitors have found a ready market for their vast and rapidly mounting output.

Another important sugar investment was made in this year, through which the company acquired a 75 per cent interest in the Saetia Sugar Company, which owns 35,566 acres of land adjoining the property of the Nipe Bay Company in Cuba. Of this, some 6,350 acres were planted in cane and 558 acres to citrus and other fruits. The cane is ground in the great mill at Preston, the property of the Nipe Bay Company.

The fleet which delivers bananas abroad was increased by several new ships, and three splendid new boats were added to the Great White Fleet. These ships were christened the *Pastores*, *Tenadores*, and the *Calamares*, and are the last word in tropical freight and passenger service. They are 8,000-ton ships, each provided with accommodations for 135 first-class passengers.

Such is an epitome of the first twelve years of the creative work of the United Fruit Company. In those twelve years tens of millions of dollars were courageously but intelligently expended in a stubborn struggle with the known and unknown dangers of the tropics. An empire of agriculture was carved from the jealous and resentful jungles. Hundreds of miles of railroads were constructed into wildernesses where even the natives had not penetrated. From out the waters of the Caribbean steamed scores of ships to the marts of the Old and the New World bearing the commerce which Yankee enterprise had created in a crusade to attain the peaceful Conquest of the Tropics.

CHAPTER VIII

In the Wake of Columbus

SUPPOSE we plan a trip through the tropical sections in which grow the 50,000,000 bunches of bananas which are consumed in the temperate zones of North America and Europe. The ships of the United Fruit Company sail from many ports, but in this imaginative tour we will leave from New York and make our first stop in Jamaica.

The time was when the "fruiter" was only what its name implies — a steamship designed to carry bananas, and with limited and indifferent accommodations for those who were compelled to journey to the tropics. In the books of travel written twelve or more years ago the reader is entertained with the adventures and hardships of authors who reluctantly used the ships which went south with empty holds and returned with loads of bananas. These writers complain of lack of good food, of bad service, of poor ventilation, and of ships which pitched and rolled in ordinary weather and which were positively wicked when gales swept the Caribbean or howled about Cape Hatteras.

The passenger who has derived his impressions of the "fruiter" from a perusal of these probably truthful descriptions of the banana boats of former years has a delightful surprise in store when he steps on board one of the modern "fruiters" forming a part of the Great White Fleet of the United Fruit Company. It is the simple truth to state that these steamships are not excelled in comfort, luxury, and safety. My profession as a writer has compelled me to cruise in all of the Seven Seas, and it has been my fortune to enjoy the best and to submit to the worst of the ships which churn the waters on both sides of the equator.

It is a strange thing that, until recently, shipbuilders have ignored the fact that vessels designed to serve the tropics should conform to the conditions of the tropics. It is a sad fact that most of the ships which cater to tropical passenger trade are better fitted for arctic and antarctic explorations. It is not that the American tropics are cursed by hot weather — the thermometer seldom approaches 88 — but for the enjoyment of the delights of the Caribbean one must have broad and unobstructed deck spaces, commodious and well ventilated staterooms, spacious dining rooms, lounging and smoking saloons — in a word, the passenger ship in southern seas should offer the least possible obstruction to the free ingress of light and air. One aims to live out-of-doors in the tropics, in apartments so constructed that the air constantly circulates through screens which prevent flies, mosquitoes and other dreaded insects from entering living or sleeping quarters.

The ship which sails tropical seas should meet these specifications, and I believe that the ones comprising the Great White Fleet come nearer to the required ideal than any which have yet been constructed. The broad and spotlessly clean decks are a delight. There are no such decks on the *Mauretania*, the *Olympic* and other famous ships which are presumed to be all that luxury can demand or money can supply. The ordinary first-class staterooms on the best trans-Atlantic steamships do not begin to compare with those of the *Abangarez*, *Sixaola*, and a score of ships of their type, to say nothing of the peerless new additions to the Great White Fleet, the *Pastores*, *Tenadores* and *Calamares*.

All of the compartments on these modern fruit boats are fitted with every electrical equipment and accessory for the comfort of the passenger. In the deep hold of such a ship is the refrigerating apparatus, which reduces the temperature to the 53 degrees required to preserve the bananas on their trip from the tropics to the northern ports. Ducts lead

One of the ships of the Great White Fleet

from these huge cooling chambers to all of the staterooms. If the passenger finds it too warm at any hour of the day or night, he pulls a slide overhead and lets in a sufficient amount of fresh cool air to lower the temperature to the degree required. What millionaire in New York, London, or Paris can boast of this inestimable luxury? What terror is there to tropical heat or humidity when a touch of the hand can "turn on the cold" as easily as a child can turn the valve of a steam radiator? That is what I call a real luxury.

These 8,000-ton ships care nothing for any storm which sweeps the Atlantic, the Gulf or the Caribbean. There is something about the way in which they breast a gale which eliminates all thought of danger. Human skill and care cannot entirely remove the risks assumed by those "who go down to the sea in ships," but the record which has been established by the United Fruit Company is one possible only to capable organization and foresight.

These are worthy ships, strong and splendid ships, and it is too bad that it is possible neither to build them in the United States nor fly the American flag at their mastheads.

Most of those who make their initial trip to the American tropics choose the winter months, knowing that this will give them a respite from the rigors of blizzards, sleet and arctic cold. Those who really know the American tropics do not hesitate to select a summer month when the lure of the palm calls them. There is no better place to escape the blighting effects of the summer climate of New York, Boston, and other scorched centres of population than by fleeing to the temperate tropics. I use the word temperate advisedly. There is no temperate section in the United States. The schoolboy who was asked to define the temperate zone had it about right when he replied: "The temperate zone is the place where it is cold as Iceland in winter and hotter than Hades in summer."

In the tropics close to us there are no extremes of heat or cold, and the natives who foolishly venture north in the summer season are often compelled to return in haste to avoid serious consequences. When the travelling public learns the truth, as it soon will, Bocas del Toro, Panama, will

Tropical splendors of Castleton Gardens, Kingston, Jamaica

become one of the favorite summer resorts, and Port Antonio, Jamaica, will vie with Newport as the mecca of jaded wealth and fashion. You cannot determine the climate of a country by looking at a map.

But on this trip of ours we will sail from New York in December. Twenty-four hours later we are in the Gulf Stream, and already there is in the air a breath which whispers of the tropics. Before noon of the second day the heavy overcoat is discarded. It seems impossible to realize that yesterday we took a last look of snow-covered New Jersey headlands, and took that look through windows traced with frost. It is only a sea step these wondrous days from frost to balmy breezes. It is only two days from heavy woollens to white duck and lazy linens.

We glide past the Bahamas, score of islands lifting themselves out of the blue waters of the Atlantic as our ship heads steadily south. Some are inhabited, others show no signs of human life, but all of them hold the charm and mystery of a sea through which many ships pass and few pause, a sea which the great Columbus sailed and explored in his search for a new route to Asia. Speaking of the immortal Columbus, why do we call him by that name? He never bore while living any such name. He was born of the Italian family of "Colombo." When he entered the Spanish service he changed his name to "Cristobal Colon." And we insist on calling him "Columbus."

In Spain, Mexico, Central America, and all Spanish speaking countries the natives never heard of the "United States." They translate it into "Estados Unidos," and they have as much right to call it that as we have to call Espana by the title of "Spain," or Roma by the title of "Rome." I hold that we should call countries and cities and celebrities by their true names, and not stick to the clumsy derivations which have lazily been substituted. There is no such city as "Vienna," unless it happens to be some village in the United States. The great Austrian capital is named "Wien," and only those who speak the English language call it anything else. There is no such city as "Brussels," but the beautiful capital of Belgium is really named "Bruxelles."

It is time that we called the great discoverer by the name under which he achieved immortal fame, Cristobal Colon. We would not like it if the Russians insisted that the Father of our Country was named "Washeskivich."

Resuming our journey, we swing past the east end of Cuba within a hundred miles of the great sugar plantations belonging to the United Fruit Company. Some day, when the company gets time and can spare money from new banana

Hope Gardens, Kingston, Jamaica

developments, it may build a hotel along the shores of beautiful Nipe Bay, and thus permit tropical travellers to visit one of the most healthful and interesting spots in Cuba. It may form a link in the chain of attractions served by the future Great White Fleet, but it is not easily reached by the pleasure seeker at present. We will find it, however, on our way back.

We pass Cape Maisi, the extreme east point of Cuba, and head through the Windward Passage for Jamaica, taking a southwesterly course for Port Antonio. We have now entered the enchanted domain of the Caribbean, its surface and its skies glorious in sunshine and storm, in golden-houred day and star-studded night.

Hundreds of writers have attempted to describe the beauties of Jamaica, but none of them have succeeded. The only way to comprehend Jamaica is to see it and spend the rest of your time in dreaming about it.

Port Antonio is far more beautiful than the better known Kingston. There are few places in the world which can

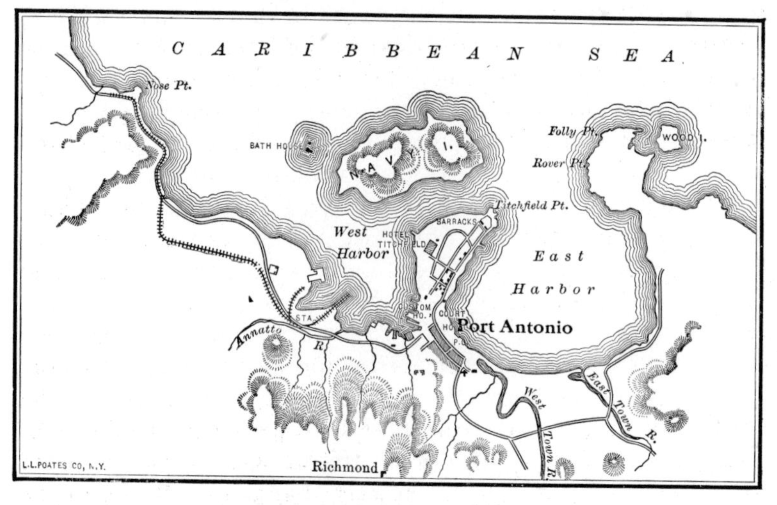

PORT ANTONIO, JAMAICA

match this harbor and its adjacent coasts and headlands in their combinations of tropical charms. In the background rise the cloud-wreathed heights of Blue Mountain Peak, carpeted to its very top with the innumerable forms of palm, fern, flowering tree, and entangled plants which constitute the jungle. Below these dizzy altitudes tumbles a sea of hills, a tumult of smaller mountains without plan or order, and twisting about them sprawls a bewildering labyrinth of valleys lacking seeming end or purpose, but all of this anarchy of nature is subdued and mellowed by the glittering fronds of palm and banana.

Through these valleys run 2,000 miles of roads which are the delight and awe of the automobile driver. Accidents are few and the enjoyment serene, but the man who drives an automobile a hundred miles through Jamaica derives a contempt for what the average car owner imagines to be curves and grades.

Not many years have passed since Jamaica made its living by raising sugar cane and grinding it into sugar. When the United States intervened and stopped anarchy in Cuba — against the tearful protest of all of our mollycoddles — that island leaped to prosperity through a peace which resulted in a vast development in the sugar industry, thus bringing wealth to Cuba and cheap sugar to the citizens of the United States. But this threatened disaster to Jamaica, whose law-abiding inhabitants had been raising the sugar the warring factions of Cuba could or would not produce. The reciprocity terms put Jamaica off the sugar map of the world.

The possibilities of banana cultivation saved the island. We have seen that the time came when the United Fruit Company cut down its banana groves in Cuba and planted the soil to sugar cane. The reverse happened in Jamaica. Her farmers abandoned their sugar fields and planted them to bananas. The United States has gained immeasurably from both operations. It is a perfect illustration of the wisdom of permitting natural laws to operate in the development of agricultural products. Cuba was naturally fitted for sugar; Jamaica could best raise bananas. Peace in the American tropics — enforced by the stern mandate of the United States or a combination of world powers, if necessary — will set in motion a stream of agricultural wealth which will bless the people of the tropics and the world which will bid for the released products of its waiting soils.

This is an obvious proposition to American citizens who think. The trouble with too many of us is that our mental horizon has a radius of about a mile.

The Island of Jamaica is still by far the greatest banana producing section on the globe. Its annual production at the present time approximates 17,000,000 bunches of this fruit, the sale of which brings to its people the larger propor-

Photo by A. Duperly & Son, Kingston, Jamaica

Cane River Falls, Jamaica

tion of their annual revenue. When our Congress threatened to impose a duty of approximately five cents a bunch on bananas, the people of Jamaica were dazed and terrified. Once again an artificial restraint of trade menaced them with destruction. A delegation of their leading officials and citizens went to Washington and joined their protest with that of the millions of American consumers who were indignant that this attempt should be made to impose a tariff duty on the one fruit-food product which had maintained low prices in an era remarkable for the steady and rapid rise in the cost of all other food products, sugar being the only other important exception. The press came nobly to the defence of the banana, and the foolish tax was finally stricken from the tariff bill.

Jamaica is and always will be an open market for any individual or concern that desires to import bananas. There are fully 11,000 producers of bananas on that island. The United Fruit Company and some of its competitors own and operate banana plantations, but the topography and land ownership of Jamaica are such that it is impossible to mass a large acreage into a single plantation and thus put into operation the economical system of cultivation and transportation employed in Panama, Costa Rica, and other places until recently undeveloped and uninhabited.

The United Fruit Company owns about 8,800 acres of growing bananas in Jamaica, which is less than 10 per cent of the total banana acreage of the island. On these tracts it raises about 2,000,000 bunches annually in seasons when the rainfall favors and no high winds sweep in from the Caribbean. This is about 12 per cent of the banana productivity of the greatest banana producing section in the world.

Banana producers, other than the United Fruit Company, raise annually in Jamaica about 15,000,000 bunches of this fruit, and there is no reason why this production should not be much increased. The United Fruit Company could not cultivate these thousands of small tracts with profit even if made a present of them. They will therefore ever remain as a source of banana supply open to any competitive interest which cares to bid for them.

What happens? The United Fruit Company and its various competitors bid for this enormous and constantly increasing output from the thousands of banana farms and plantations of Jamaica. Two methods are followed, viz.: The importer makes a contract with a banana producer for his crop for a year or a short term of years. Most of these contracts are renewed yearly. The grower naturally waits for the highest bid. He is under no obligations and stands in no fear of the United Fruit or any other company. Such contracts are made only with growers who own tracts of considerable extent, say from fifteen to twenty acres and upward. The second method is to purchase the product of the smaller farms in the open market.

Last year the United Fruit Company entered into about 700 contracts with independent growers, and under these contracts approximately 4,000,000 bunches of bananas were delivered and paid for. The price paid to growers varies, but its approximate range is from 35 to 45 cents a bunch. This yields the grower a revenue of from $40 to $75 an acre, which is double what our farmers can hope to realize on corn, wheat, or other staple products.

What does the importer make on the Jamaican bananas he buys by contract or in the open market? He will deem himself fortunate to realize profits ranging from 3 to 5 cents a bunch, and there will be times when he will lose heavily.

The point which I wish to impress is this: The banana consumption of the United States is approximately 42,000,000 bunches, of which the United Fruit Company supplies about 24,000,000. The Island of Jamaica alone offers to competition 15,000,000 bunches, to say nothing of the product of the thousands of other independent growers scattered over all of the islands and mainlands washed by the Caribbean. When it comes to buying these bananas the United Fruit Company has, of course, no advantage over any competitor.

The production of bananas in Jamaica in the fiscal year 1911–12 was 14,770,000 bunches. Of this amount the United Fruit Company raised 1,502,000 on its own plantations, and obtained by contracts with the native growers and

Photo by A. Duperly & Son, Kingston, Jamaica

The famous "Tom Cringle Tree"

in the open market 5,986,665 bunches, making its total of importations 7,488,665 bunches of bananas.

Competitors of the United Fruit Company imported 7,281,345 bunches. These official figures are more eloquent than any argument in disproof of the existence of a banana monopoly. So long as Jamaica remains above the Caribbean her fertile valleys and the thousands of tillers of her soil will insure the permanence of competitive conditions in the banana industry.

From the summits of twisting mountains which undulate from the main range one looks down on a rolling sea of bananas dotted with cocoanut palms. Some of the interlacing valleys are narrow, with precipitous slopes, but you will find bananas flourishing in places which would dishearten an ambitious goat. If you search you will find a bamboo hut somewhere in the valley, possibly a cluster of them, and here live the negroes who own or lease the semi-precipices on which grow the bananas.

Other valleys are wider, with brooks or small rivers running through them, and here we find plantations of more pretentious acreage. Sir John Pringle, who sells his banana to a competitor of the United Fruit Company, has more than 3,000 acres under cultivation. There are about 400 plantations in Jamaica which have 100 or more acres of bananas, and there are more than 10,000 growers who grade from this acreage down to the holdings of the lazy negro who is content and happy with a dozen plants scattered about his squalid hut.

As a rule the bananas are transported from the farms to the railroads by mules. On the uplands this is expensive work. The mule frequently is compelled to follow miles of winding roads and trails to cover what would be a very short distance in a straight line. There are many comparatively large tracts in the uplands which have been practically inaccessible for this reason.

The United Fruit Company has put into operation a system which solves this problem and which promises greatly to increase the banana productivity of Jamaica. In the place of mules or carts there is installed an "aerial banana conveyer," a strong cable properly supported and leading from the uplands in a fairly straight line to the valley below. This cable is an endless one revolving over drums, and is operated by gravity, the descending bananas bringing back to the top the devices which hold and carry them.

The average cost, at present, of carrying a bunch of bananas from plantations to railroads is estimated at about 8 cents a stem, and in many instances it greatly exceeds this. Experiments indicate that the "aerial banana con-

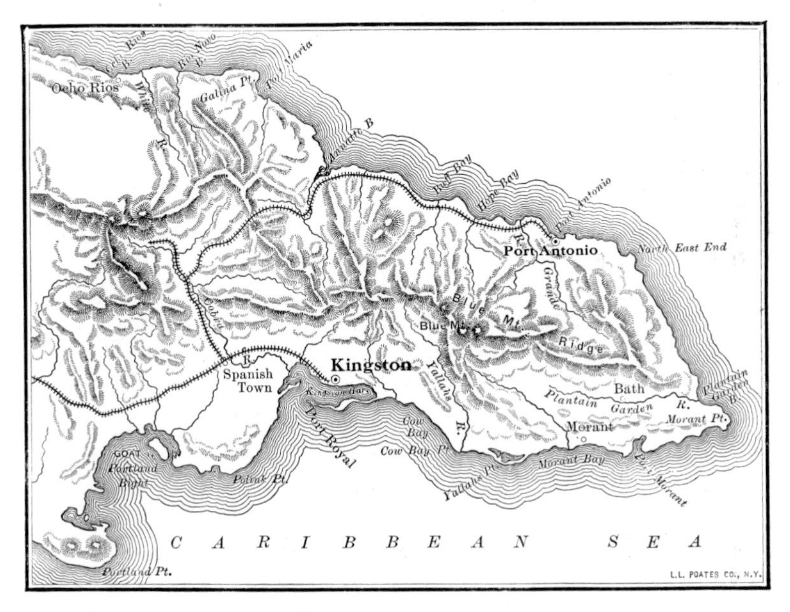

EAST PART OF JAMAICA

veyor" will reduce this cost by from 5 to 6, and even more, cents a bunch. Even more important is the certainty that this system will greatly increase the banana acreage of Jamaica. The company is also using auto trucks to good advantage in conveying bananas from plantations to the railroads.

The Jamaican banana is superior to the Cuban product, but much inferior in size to the magnificent fruit now being produced in the reclaimed swamps of Panama and Costa

Rica. A bunch of bananas consists of a stem, hands, and fingers. Each hand has from ten to fifteen fingers. A bunch of bananas is thus known to the trade as "a five-hand stem," "a six-hand stem," and from that up to the nine or ten-hand stems, which are the average commercial limit, though Costa Rica has produced stems containing as high as twenty-two hands — a veritable giant of tropical fecundity!

In Jamaica the bananas range from five to nine hands to the bunch, with an occasional one exceeding this grading, but the individual fingers are smaller than those which grow in the humid lowlands of the Central American coast. But they are good bananas, wholesome and marketable. The Jamaican negro is the workman who has made possible the wonders which the United Fruit Company has achieved in Central America, and Jamaica can lay just claim as the birthplace of the banana industry.

Bananas are shipped from Kingston and Port Antonio, but the great bulk of the fruit is loaded on ships which leave the latter harbor. Fully six hundred shiploads of bananas leave Jamaica annually to help satisfy the fruit hunger of the world, and most of these bananas come to the United States.

Port Antonio contains the best hotel in the American tropics, and, in my deliberate opinion, one of the best hotels in the world. Nothing can exceed the scenic possibilities of a headland jutting into a tropical sea with tropical mountains climbing ridge upon ridge until their heights are lost in the indescribable tropical clouds. Buttress this undulating coast with towering cliffs; spread at their bases jagged reefs over which the surge from the ocean beats forever in unappeased rage; fringe these cliffs with palms, drape their sides with ferns and clinging flowers; create as a foreground an island such as you pictured when you read of the criminal but glorious deeds of the buccaneers who sailed and plundered the Spanish Main; and amid such surroundings rear a beautiful hotel and conduct it as a hotel should be conducted — such is a faint impression of the Hotel Titchfield and its environment.

There are persons who go to Central Park to eat peanuts.

Photo by A. Duperly & Son, Kingston, Jamaica

Kingston Harbor

There are others who go to the tropics for the pleasures of shopping. Such will find the streets of Kingston more to their liking than the scenic marvels which are in and about Port Antonio, but I would rather spend one hour on the verandas of the Hotel Titchfield than to enjoy all of the pleasures Kingston has in store.

The United Fruit Company owns the Hotel Titchfield and should be proud of it. Its management is all that could be desired by the most exacting traveller. The pleasure-seeking public is discovering that the country in and about Port Antonio is the choicest bit of tropical paradise within easy reach of the coasts of the United States. Country clubs with golf links, tennis courts, and other out-of-door sports will logically follow, and the marvelous reaches of beach both sides of Port Antonio will be dotted with inns and palm-shaded hotels, and this part of Jamaica will outrival Florida as a winter resort.

The United Fruit Company owns an interest in the famous Myrtle Bank Hotel, of Kingston, the only one of consequence in the leading city and capital of the island. The service at the Myrtle Bank is excellent, and the hotel is an admirable base from which to explore the tropical beauties to be found in the uplands away from the dusty plain along this coast. Spanish Town, the peerless Bog Walk, Castleton Gardens, Hope Gardens, and other tropical attractions are within easy reach of Kingston, but none of these, in my opinion, can touch the natural charms of the district which lies on the other side of Blue Mountain, and of which Port Antonio is the centre.

CHAPTER IX

Where the Banana Is King

ROM Kingston we steam in a southwesterly course for Colon. Ones cherished geographical impressions are rudely shattered by travel. It was a shock to me to discover that the Panama Canal is almost due south of New York City, being about only 200 miles west of a north and south line. My mental map had located the Canal fully 1,000 miles to the west of New York, or about on the longitude of New Orleans and Chicago, instead of which it is due south of Buffalo, and far to the east of Havana. Most of us picture Havana as nearly south of New York, when in fact it is about south of Detroit. A study of a map of the New World discloses the disconcerting fact that all of the west coast of South America is east of Detroit, and that most of it is hundreds of miles east of New York City. The truth of the matter is that we should call that continent "Southeast America."

I also made the astounding discovery that a considerable portion of South America lies north of the southerly sections of North America. When we set sail from Colon for Santa Marta, Colombia, we do not head south or southeast, we point our prow northeast. This is almost as puzzling as the other fact to the effect that Colon, the Caribbean port (the supposed east port), is twenty odd miles *west* of Panama City, which is on the Pacific and presumably west end of the Canal. It is positively uncanny to look out of a window of the Tivoli Hotel in Panama City and watch the sun rise squarely out of the Pacific Ocean! Of course, an accurate map justifies the sun in selecting the Pacific for rising rather than setting purposes, but it never seemed right or proper to me. Oceans should stay where they belong, and the Pacific has no business to twist itself to the east of Panama.

We sail out of Kingston harbor and past what remains of Port Royal, and *over* the submerged ruins of the city which sunk into the sea in the great earthquake of 1692. This was then the Mecca of the pirates, adventurers and bad men of the world, and Port Royal made good its boast

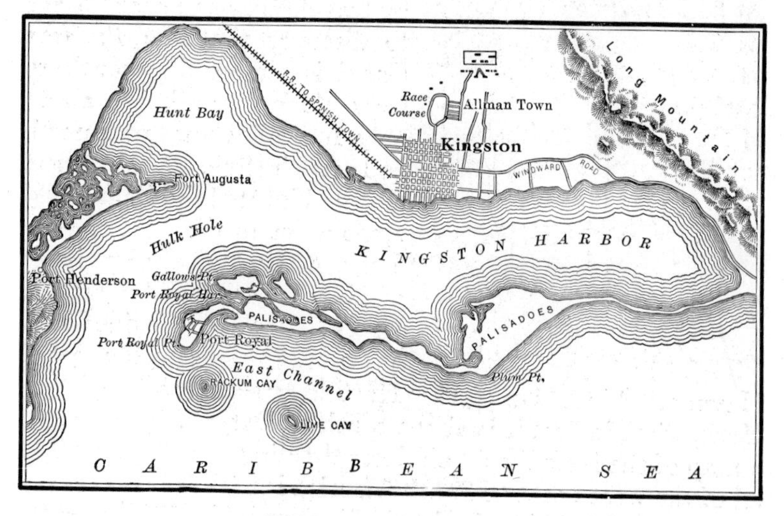

KINGSTON, JAMAICA

that it was "the wickedest spot in the world." History and romance invest the squalid segment which remains with a strange charm, but it looks best from the deck of a ship, and I would rather read about it than investigate it too closely.

It is claimed that when the water is calm one can make out the forms of the ruined buildings which slid into the sea that awful day when nature blotted from earth this nest of picturesque vice and storied crime. The fisher folk tell of nights when the ghosts of the buccaneers who perished three centuries ago hold high revel below and above the water, but

I have my doubts. I am inclined to the belief that their spirits are in a location far more tropical than Kingston harbor.

Two days of a cruise over the heart of the Caribbean brings us to Colon. In the winter months these are days of glorious sunshine, of wondrous skies, of sparkling waters, and of an air which one quaffs with delight as it comes on the perfumed breath of the trade winds. There is only one fault with this trip from Jamaica to Colon — it is too short.

Dining room of the SS. *Metapan*

The voyager treasures every minute of it, and rebels at the speed which limits this journey to a fleeting period of forty-eight hours.

It is not the province of this book to describe the wonders of the Panama Canal. The traveller will find at his command a wealth of books on this great project, some of which he can read with profit on the trip from Kingston to Colon.

Colon is the leading port of entry in the tropics for the United Fruit Company. From two to half a dozen and sometimes more of its ships can be found at the docks of

Colon. The company has under construction a system of extensive and modern docks and buildings in Cristobal, a contiguous part of Colon, but in the territory of the administration of the Canal Zone. The cities of Colon and Panama proper are under the jurisdiction of the Republic of Panama, with certain restrictions mutually agreed on and observed.

There is much which is attractive in Colon and Panama City and along the Canal Zone, and the visitor can spend many days with profit along the Isthmus now spanned by the great Canal. The city of Panama is distinct in type from any town in Central America or along the north coast of South America. Panama City is an architectural expression of the Spaniard in South America. The Republic of Panama is now a part of Central America, but it must be kept in mind that Colon and Panama City were founded and reared by men whose traditions and arts were those of South America. Spanish blood and Spanish temperament dominated in the construction of these cities, and Panama City in particular stands as an interesting and pleasing type of urban construction for which the architecture of Castile is responsible, and which is blended only faintly with the conceptions of the native Indian races. The Indian dominates in all other parts of Central America and Mexico, and in many sections of South America, but Panama City typifies the pleasing attempt of Spanish art to master the architectural requirements of the tropics.

The scenery along the Canal Zone will prove disappointing to those who have approached it either from Jamaica or from the ports of Central America. High mountains are almost indispensable in a proper arrangement of scenic charms, and the absence of high mountains was the consideration which led to the selection of this spot as the best place to bisect two continents. But that is not the only scenic handicap of the Canal Zone. Its soil is poor and its rainfall uneven and seasonal. As a result of these and other conditions there is a lack of that riotous luxuriance of tropical foliage which one demands of the jungle. It would be beautiful, perhaps, if one had not been educated to expect

A SUPERB ROW OF ROYAL PALMS

A view taken on one of the plantations of the United Fruit Company in Costa Rica

much from revelling in the tropical glories of more favored sections.

About 100 miles to the west of Colon, and along the Caribbean coast of the Republic of Panama, we arrive at one of the great productive centres of the United Fruit Company, the country contiguous to the port and city of Bocas del Toro, which translates as "The Mouths of the Bull," the bay or lagoon having some fancied resemblance to a bull, but with an extra mouth or two.

Let me confess in advance that I am violently prejudiced in favor of this Bocas del Toro country. It does not yet provide adequate hotel accommodations for the tourist, but these will come in time, and Bocas del Toro will become the Thousand Islands of the Tropics, with beauties and attractions far exceeding the wonder spot of the St. Lawrence.

I presume that the average person who never has visited the tropics goes there with a mental picture based on what he has read. This picture is a composite of impressions derived from a reading of "Robinson Crusoe," "Treasure Island," "The Swiss Family Robinson," and other classics of the tropical seas, but in all of these fond imageries there is a sheltered lagoon opening from an ocean which tosses its spume high up from jagged rocks and cruel coral reefs on which lie the bones of the ship from which the hero and heroine have been miraculously saved.

Prior to my first visit to the tropics I had the audacity to write a tropical novel, being encouraged by the fact that Robert Louis Stevenson created his best sea tale before he took his first long sea voyage. In this novel of mine, "The Kidnapped Millionaires," I created an ideal lagoon opening in from a tropical sea, and I embellished the shores of this sequestered spot with all the glories of plant and sea life for which the encyclopædias gave authority, and added a few of my own. It was a tropical paradise, this lagoon of mine to which the "kidnapped millionaires" were lured, and I doubt if nature will ever be able to create anything equal to it, but nature has its limitations and an author has none.

Bocas del Toro is in the western part of the Republic of Panama, this country running east and west, not north and south as many suppose. The banana plantations of the United Fruit Company cross the border line between Panama and Costa Rica. This boundary line is in dispute, and for years has been the subject of arbitration. Both Costa Rica and Panama impose an export duty of about one cent a bunch on bananas, and it thus happens that the United Fruit Company has been paying an export duty to

ALMIRANTE BAY AND CHIRIQUI LAGOON, PANAMA

both countries for all bananas raised in the sections over which both nations claim sovereignty.

Indented from the Caribbean is a huge lagoon about fifty miles long and from twelve to twenty miles wide. A cluster of islands protects this lagoon from the Caribbean, and another row of islands divides it into two parts. The town of Bocas del Toro is situated on an island which helps enclose what is known as Almirante Bay, and the Chiriqui Lagoon connects it to the south and west. The Chiriqui Lagoon is a mass of islands. The exact number is unknown, but there are several thousands of them — a perfect labyrinth of tropical islands in a setting which mocks description.

Some of these islands rise in cliffs hundreds of feet sheer above the crystal waters which lave their bases. The crests of these heights are fringed with palms and with other tropical trees laden with huge flowers of flaunting colors. Ferns and clinging vines soften the lines of the cliffs. In places the passage between these precipitous islands is so narrow that there is barely room to float a canoe. Only the Indian

Early morning on Almirante Bay

guides can safely find a way in and out of this tropical wonderland.

In the air are myriads of the feathered denizens of these interlocking islands. Monkeys and jabbering baboons swing from branches and jeer at those who dare penetrate their haunts. In the depths of the clear waters are swarms of fish of all colors and sizes. They dart amongst a wealth of sea plants, and in and out of tunnels formed by the rocks which have tumbled from the beetling cliffs. The thought comes that you are an atom floating in a vast aquarium. You call aloud, the rocks send the echoes flying; the parrots and monkeys return a chorus of insolent protest. If lucky you may venture on a pair of Central American tigers, an animal larger and more dangerous that our mountain lion, one with the general appearance of a small specimen of the African tiger. Alligators and crocodiles lurk about the mouths of the rivers which enter into Almirante Bay and Chiriqui Lagoon, but the tourist need have no fear of them.

Hundreds of miles of these passages between the islands can be explored in a motor boat. Here is a practically unknown paradise for the hunter, fisherman, and the devotee of the beautiful.

The traveller who lacks the time to explore the wonders of Chiriqui Lagoon can obtain an impression of them by visiting the present site of the hospitals of the United Fruit Company on Nances Cay — a large island about two miles to the southwest of Bocas del Toro.

In some respects the view from the verandas of these buildings is the finest I have ever seen in the tropics. Imagine yourself on the corner of a cliff forty feet or more above rocks through which the surf breaks lazily after having been checked by reefs which for ages have withstood its unceasing attack. Two miles to the north is the deep blue of the Caribbean seen through a fairway opening into the protected harbor of Almirante Bay. To the right is Flat Rock Point, a frowning promontory against which the sea beats and sends its storm spray a hundred feet in air. To the left is Columbus Island, comparatively low, with its crescent beach lined with palms and bamboo. No houses or native huts intrude on either side of this picturesque inlet through which the ships pass. It was on the dazzling white sands of such a beach that Robinson Crusoe saw the footprints of savages, and it was amid such surroundings that he and his man Friday lived their entrancing life.

On the inner edge of Bocas Island is the town of Bocas del Toro, its white buildings showing vivid against the foliage of its streets and parks. To the left are the smooth waters of Almirante Bay, shimmering twenty miles or more until the surface blends into the haze of an illusive shore line. Towering into the sky beyond the waters of the bay are terraced ranges of mountains which constitute the backbone of the continent, weakened at the Isthmus and now broken by the cutting of the Panama Canal 150 miles to the east. Within our range of vision are the Chiriqui, Pico Blanca, Talamanca and other lofty ranges, some of them in Panama and others in Costa Rica. Extinct volcanos — which may become active at any time — lift their conical crests into the Italian blue of cloud-flecked skies, great dreamy masses of uplifted verdure punctured with crags and capped with fleecy clouds.

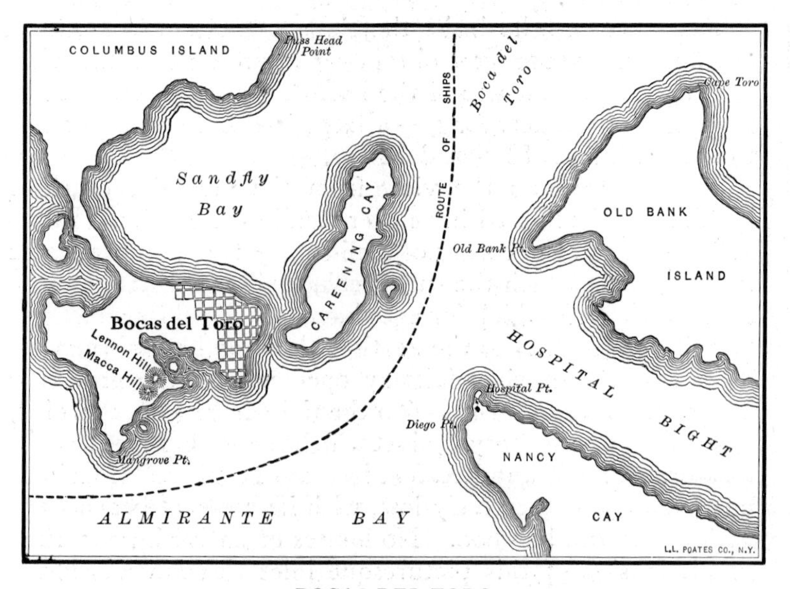

BOCAS DEL TORO

And all about us is a veritable exposition of tropical vegetation. Surrounding the hospital buildings are scores of forms of palms, some of them dwarfed and squat, others towering to the blue before the fronds burst into the gorgeous plume of the royal palm. High up in cieba and ebo trees cling festoons of orchids, absorbing from the air the beauties of its stars and the tints of its rainbows. But what's the use! When no man can paint, much less describe a single lily, what chance is there to compose in words

SITE OF ALMIRANTE

These native huts have disappeared and a massive sea wall insures the safety and health of the town created by the United Fruit Company

a single strain in the divine scenic harmony of this gem of the tropics?

It is only 150 miles from here to the Panama Canal Zone, but we are in another world so far as climate is concerned. The Bocas country is one of the rare districts in the tropics which is not handicapped with distinct dry and wet seasons. These seasons are the "intemperate" feature of the tropics. When it rains it rains too much, and when it quits it stops too long. The Panama Canal Zone and many other sections are afflicted with this sort of climate. In the winter months hardly a drop of rain falls, but in the spring and summer the flood-gates of the heavens are opened. On the Pacific side of the Canal Zone *a rainfall of nearly five inches in three minutes* has been recorded! A veritable deluge which tore the very earth in its violence!

It rains every month in Bocas del Toro. At times the rains are excessive and do great damage. Bananas grow best where nature has violent moods, and only those who are able financially to recover from the effects of these moods are justified in undertaking this enterprise. Bananas require an enormous amount of water, and Bocas del Toro is ideal in this respect.

Rarely does it happen that a week passes in the Bocas del Toro section without a shower. As a consequence, the tropical foliage is always vivid and glorious. There is none of the monotony of weeks and months of cloudless skies, with their inevitable concomitant of parched and dusty verdure. Sunshine is a splendid thing, but it never is appreciated so fully as when it breaks through clouds and turns into diamonds the billions of raindrops clinging to vine and leaf.

Those who are of the opinion that the Central American tropics are afflicted with abnormally high temperature will find the official statistics interesting in refutation of that impression. It is extremely rare that the mercury mounts to 90 in the shade, a temperature which is exceeded annually by from five to ten degrees by most of the cities of the United States. Here is the official record of the temperature and rainfall in Bocas del Toro for the fiscal year 1911-1912:

TABLE SHOWING OFFICIAL RECORD OF TEMPERATURE AND RAINFALL IN BOCAS DEL TORO FOR FISCAL YEAR OF 1911–12

TEMPERATURE (Fahrenheit)

Year	Month	Maximum	Minimum	Mean	Rainfall Inches
1911	October	86	72.64	79.32	10.44
	November	85.95	72.35	79.15	7.99
	December	84.43	71.09	77.76	8.26
1912	January	83.90	70.71	77.30	.93
	February	83.00	70.45	76.72	5.55
	March	84.23	72.00	78.11	4.68
	April	84.70	71.57	78.14	7.61
	May	87.71	72.94	80.33	17.41
	June	85.17	73.37	79.27	8.49
	July	82.23	73.71	77.97	11.45
	August	83.28	73.61	78.45	7.85
	September	85.13	73.40	79.26	8.19
	Averages	84.64	72.32	78.48	Total 98.84

That is what I call a "temperate climate." I lived for many years in an Illinois town where the range was from 40 below zero in the winter to 103 degrees in the shade in the summer, and my school books assured me that I was an inhabitant of the "temperate zone," which, in our locality, had a fluctuation of about 143 degrees. Down in the "torrid tropics" in the Bocas del Toro section the records indicate a range of from 70.45 in February to 87.71 in May, a fluctuation of a matter of 17 degrees in the year shown, and which never much exceeds 20 degrees, or less than one-seventh that of my former location in the Illinois section of our alleged temperate zone. We learn many things in geography which are not so.

The rainfall indicated in the above table is below the normal, which runs from 100 to 130 inches, or from three to four times that of the average community in the United States. These tropical rains are beautiful to watch if you are safely under cover on high ground. They are not protracted rains with intervals of mist and drizzle, such as we have to endure in the United States. The tropical rains usually come as showers of marked intensity. When it

Typical cottage in Panama banana plantation

rains it makes a business of it, and when it quits the sun flashes out with a glorious rainbow spanning the opposite horizon. Two hours' of storm in Central America will result in more precipitation than a week of dismal weather in New York or Chicago.

The early history of the town of Bocas del Toro is shrouded in mystery. It is the only populated centre of banana cultivation which was on the map of Central America when the founders of the United Fruit Company set about the cultivation and exportation of this fruit. The population of Bocas del Toro when Mr. Keith discovered its banana possibilities was almost exclusively negro, and they spoke English with a smattering of Spanish and local Carib. There are records which indicate that the ancestors of these negroes settled on this low and sandy spit of island fully 250 years ago.

There is every probability that these negroes came to Bocas del Toro from Jamaica. The present negro inhabitants have all of the characteristics of their Jamaican brethren. The original migration must have taken place when the negroes were enslaved in Jamaica, or in some other British possession. Who was the black Moses who escaped and found this asylum? Who was the slave who conceived and executed the crusade which brought these African pioneers to this refuge of freedom? Did these negro Pilgrims make peace or war with the wild Caribs who frequented these coasts? Not even tradition has an answer to these questions.

It was a miserable village before the banana industry developed and brought prosperity to Bocas and other sections along the Caribbean coasts of Central America. There was plenty of high ground on the island, but the negroes built their huts on stilts along the edge of Almirante Bay, following, perhaps, the example of their African progenitors. The sanitary conditions were awful. In the early years of the United Fruit Company not less than 80 per cent of its employees in Bocas del Toro were on the annual sick roll. The percentage is now the normal one of a healthy community. I shall treat of this phase of the company's work in a later chapter.

The original banana plantings were near Bocas del Toro, some of them on the island itself, with other plantations along the shores of Chiriqui Lagoon. The dreaded banana disease invaded these plantations and eventually destroyed them. This disease is known to come from a soil parasite, and no means for its eradication have yet been discovered. The only remedy was to abandon this naturally fertile district and set new plants elsewhere. Fresh cultivations were initiated farther west on Almirante Bay, and the new town of Almirante established.

Almirante is the base of one of the most interesting and successful of the great creative enterprises of the United Fruit Company. Leading from it are nearly 250 miles of well constructed railway which link areas belonging to the company of 109,000 acres, with cultivated tracts with a total acreage approximating 40,000. About 35,000 acres of this are devoted to bananas, and here are raised the largest and choicest bananas in all of the world. The famous "Changuinola" banana is the highest priced fruit on the market, and it comes from a district which was an untouched wilderness only a few short years ago. It derives its name from the Changuinola River, which flows for more than sixty miles with the banana plantations of the United Fruit Company on both sides of its banks.

I rode one February afternoon nearly 100 miles through the banana plantations of the Changuinola and Sixaola districts. In my study of the enterprises conducted by the United Fruit Company I have travelled by rail a distance certainly exceeding 400 miles with banana plants on both sides of the tracks, their fronds often forming a semi-tunnel through which we swiftly passed. This trackage is far less than half of that employed by the company in transporting its fruit from the fields to the wharves.

If the reader possessed an imagination capable of comprehending a banana plantation one-third of a mile wide and extending from New York City to Chicago, with this wilderness of bananas bisected by a well constructed and equipped railroad, he will begin to obtain a conception of what has been created from a virgin tropical wilderness.

Residence of a banana plantation official

We crossed and recrossed the Changuinola and Sixaola rivers and their numerous branches. The rivers looked low and peaceful on this occasion, but there were pointed out high-water marks of floods which have swept away expensive bridges and ballasted tracks. But these floods are not without their compensations. They bring down from the upper valleys their loads of fertile silt and deposit it around the bases of the banana plants.

The bananas which grow in this favored district average 64 pounds in weight per bunch, and the local officials of the United Fruit Company proudly assert that this is fully ten pounds more than can justly be claimed for any other division in which the company or its competitors operate.

There are many independent banana growers in Panama and in all of the countries in which the company has interests. There is keen competition to secure contracts with these growers. In every instance the importing concern obligates itself to accept all the bananas which pass a fair inspection. It frequently happens that this arrangement works to the decided loss of the importing concern. Large quantities of fruit are offered for which there is no profitable market in the United States or abroad, but it must be accepted and paid for at the contract price.

Newspaper stories have been printed to the effect that the importing companies hold the independents at their mercy by declining at times to accept banana offerings except at ruinously low prices, the unfortunate growers being forced to accept the price tendered or see their bananas rot on the wharves. There is not a word of truth in such tales. The competing importers are alert to secure and retain contracts with the independents, and good business policy, to say nothing of business fairness, insures to the grower a rigid compliance with the terms of all contracts

From conversations with independent growers in various parts of Central America, I am of the opinion that capably conducted banana farms of small size yield the independent growers from forty to sixty dollars an acre under fairly favorable conditions, this assuming that the owner performs most of the manual labor. This is in excess of the profits per acre on staple products in the United States, but the risks and the hardships are greater.

Like most tropical enterprises, that of banana cultivation is subject to grotesque exaggerations and misrepresentations. The promoters of banana companies are responsible for some of these false statements, and writers who draw on their imaginations are equally guilty. I ran across a clipping recently from a newspaper of excellent standing and usual reliability. The article purported to give a summary of the growth and importance of the banana industry, and it would be difficult to mass in a newspaper column a more fantastic array of "facts which were not so." The article was widely circulated in the western farming sections, and the following extract was copied in scores of newspapers:

"The profits from a banana plantation per acre are estimated at as high as $1,000 a year net."

It is very likely that this and similar statements have induced many of our farmers to sell their holdings and risk their savings in an attempt to take advantage of this alleged opportunity. For the benefit of those who may be deluded by similar statements I will explain that an acre of developed banana plants will yield annually from 150 to 300 bunches of bananas, with 200 bunches as a high average. After these bananas have been transported from the tropics to New York or Chicago they do not command much more than $1 a bunch, which includes freight charges, insurance, jobber's profits and other fixed charges.

The independent grower of these 200 bunches of bananas on his acre of land is fairly treated by the importing buyer when he receives from 30 to 35 cents a bunch for his fruit, which yields him from $60 to $70 gross an acre, and, of course, a smaller net profit, most of which would stand as his own wages. This is far removed from the $1,000 an acre blithely assured by the author of the article mentioned. If writers realized that such false statements inevitably mislead and wreck many lives they would be less careless in giving them the authority of the printed word.

In a carefully prepared article dealing with the question of banana profits recently published in *Tropical America* a

United Fruit Company's hospital at Bocas del Toro

yield of 290 bunches per acre may be expected to return a net profit of $68.75 in Mexico, $66.84 in Honduras, and $58.97 in Jamaica. This, of course, assumes that no damage occurs to the growing crops. It certainly would be conservative to reduce these figures by not less than 25 per cent to cover losses which naturally may be expected from winds, floods, and other climatic disasters.

Modern banana production, as I have already explained, must be conducted on a very large scale, which means the employment of vast capital and a complicated and expensive equipment. In its Panama Division alone the United Fruit Company employs between 6,000 and 7,000 men scattered over plantations which cover more than 170 square miles of land.

Most of these men are negroes from Jamaica or other islands of the West Indies. The labor question is a vital one in the American tropics. It is almost impossible to tempt the average native of Central America to work, and many of them are physically incapable of sustained manual abor. The wages paid by the United Fruit Company and by other concerns engaged in productive enterprises in the tropics are practically as high as those commanded in the United States, which means that they are many times the rate ever before offered to labor in Central America.

When an individual or a corporation decides to undertake development work in most parts of the American tropics the fact must be kept in mind that outside capital and outside labor must be provided. There is an educated, landholding and official class in all of the Central American countries which constitutes its aristocracy, but most of them decline to interest themselves in business or in modern methods of agriculture. There is a small middle class containing men of various salaried occupations and professions. Between this middle class and the one below it there is a vast social and economic gulf. The lower classes are Indians of innumerable tribes and varying customs, but a considerable portion of them obey the latent instinct of hatred for physical labor. In this particular they differ in no essential respect from the Indians with whom we are familiar save that the Central American Indian lives in a land whose soil and climate removes much of the incentive to work.

When the French began work on the Panama Canal they met their first rebuff when they learned that there was practically no native labor which could be lured to work for wages. They loved what money would bring, but physical exertion was too high a price to pay for the comforts of the white races. It was because of the refusal of the Indian natives to work at any price that the Jamaican and other West Indian negroes were called on, and they have responded by the tens of thousands to the high wages offered by the Americans, British, Germans, and others who have undertaken the huge task of developing the neglected wilds of Central and South America.

CHAPTER X

In Beautiful Costa Rica

COSTA RICA is an oasis of progress in that long reach of country which extends from the Rio Grande to the equator. It is the one Central American nation which has lifted itself fully out of the anarchy of mercenary revolutions and of semi-savage internal warfare and intrigue. Costa Rica is the existing proof that there is nothing climatic or elemental in Central America which precludes its people from sharing in the benefits of advancement and governmental stability.

Years ago the French writer Laferriere, in his picturesque description of the Central American republics, had this to say of Costa Rica:

"The Costa Ricans dislike wasting their resources in wars or war materials, preferring the arts of peace and to welcome those bringing wealth from other countries."

In other words, these strange Costa Ricans deliberately invited the investors of the United States and of the world to "exploit" them. They opened their national doors to the foreign builders of railroads, to the delvers of mines, to the developers of agricultural wealth, and to all others who had the money and the energy to undertake creative enterprises. And when this invitation had been accepted, the roads constructed, the wastes cleared and cultivated, the strange people of Costa Rica did not deem it necessary to indulge in revolutions which would determine what faction of politicians would enjoy the multiplied official perquisites which accrued from an enhanced national revenue. They have voted their officials into and out of office, and their small regular army has been their tool and not their master — all of which seems so strange that it demands an explanation.

This explanation is a simple one. Costa Rica is a white man's republic. Fully 80 per cent of the population of the highlands is pure Caucasian, mainly of Spanish descent, with an admixture of French, German, British, and other white

A church in San José

races. There is a real middle class in Costa Rica. There is a real farmer class in that happy republic, but best of all there is real love of country and a patriotism which defends it against the plots and wiles of military adventurers and mercenary "generals."

The native Indian tribes have absorbed some of the attributes of Caucasian civilization — which is the only way an Indian can acquire the first veneer of civilization. Each succeeding generation of Costa Rican Indians has sloughed off some hereditary tribal trait and substituted for it an energetic habit of the dominant white man. Thousands of them have acquired the working and saving habit, and the stern enforcement of peace has dulled and almost subdued the instinct to take the warpath at the instigation of the first ambitious revolutionist who provides guns, ammunition, and a promise of loot.

There has been no effective or lasting progress in all of the vast domain from the Rio Grande to Cape Horn which was not the result of Caucasian initiative and eventual supremacy, and the hope of the disturbed sections of Central America lies in an influx of the race which has the intelligence and the courage to fight only for peace.

The part played by the United Fruit Company in promoting the development and insuring the progress of Costa Rica is one which reflects credit both to the government and to this American enterprise. In all of the long forty-four years since Minor C. Keith obtained the permission of the Costa Rican Government to begin the construction of a railroad from the Caribbean coast to the city of San José, there has been nothing approaching friction between the enterprises then founded and the successive officials of this progressive republic.

It may not be amiss at this place to call attention to the fact that the United Fruit Company and its original constituent corporations have, for more than a generation, executed their vast activities without coming into conflict with any of the many nations in which they have operated. There never has been a time when the interests of these American corporations have so clashed with those of the various governments that official protest has been made by any party to these relations. Wars have been waged between these nations, strained relations have existed between some of them and the United States, revolutions have succeeded revolutions, our troops have been landed on these soils to protect American lives and property, but in all these years and amid all these happenings the United Fruit Company has continued its creative work without voicing complaint or having one made against it.

This is a record to be proud of when it is taken into consideration that the United Fruit Company and the Keith interests have expended in these years a sum exceeding $200,000,000 in the American tropics. There are possibili-

Scene in Puerto Limon's beautiful park

ties of a number of wars and scores of official protests in the expenditure of that sum of money, and with every dollar of it beyond the immediate jurisdiction of the laws and authority of the United States. If the Nobel Peace Prize could be awarded to a corporation, the United Fruit Company would have valid claims to recognition. It has done more to pave the way for peace and prosperity in Central America and in the Caribbean countries than all of the statesmanship and oratory which have vainly been directed to the same purpose. Chester Lloyd Jones, in an article entitled "Bananas and Diplomacy," appearing in the North American Review of August, 1913, makes these pertinent observations:

"If the present banana development continues, it will raise the Caribbean region from its dependence on foreign

On the way to San José, Costa Rica

markets for food to one of the regions from which an important part of the world's food-supply will be drawn. The wheat-fields of the Dakotas and Manitoba will meet as one of their competitors in feeding the world, the banana plantations of the American Mediterranean.

"But the development will have consequences not alone economic. Plantations represent capital which will demand protection from disorder. Their introduction will emphasize for the countries of Central America and northern South America, the importance of protecting life and property if they expect to avoid international complications that may threaten their independence. The world is becoming impatient of the nations which insist on the divine right to misrule themselves. The introduction of capital, however, besides increasing their duties in the keeping of order, contributes to the solution of that problem. It increases the national wealth, furnishing a larger basis for the creation of national income by which orderly progress can be assured. Further, with steady work and larger, stabler income, the wants of the people will expand, giving them greater interest in the maintenance of the order which makes the satisfaction of those wants possible. . . .

"Great as the blessings of the Panama Canal will be to the trade of the world and to that of the United States in particular, we must not let the new markets which will develop beyond the Isthmus make us forget that region so rich in possibilities which lies this side of the continental divide and so much nearer our own markets. Friendship with our near neighbors is no less important than the good will of people over wide seas. One of the most important, and from our past experience let us remember, one of the most delicate problems with which our men of state have to deal, is the diplomacy of the Caribbean."

Let us resume our imaginative trip and visit Costa Rica. It is only a few hours' sail from Bocas del Toro to Puerto Limon, and in a direction almost due northwest. The entrance to Limon is picturesque and romantic. To the west rise the Cordilleras of Costa Rica towering ridges of purple blending to tender shades of green in the foreground. Through a glass we make out the white houses of Puerto Limon, and see the gleaming line of the surf as it beats against the sea wall which protects the park and the hospital buildings belonging to the United Fruit Company.

The twin towers of the wireless station owned and operated by the company trace their steel lacework hundreds of feet against a sky of wonderful blue. To the left is a crescent sweep of beach whose white sands are framed in nodding cocoanut palms. And then we land at one of the company's docks in Puerto Limon and go ashore.

You will, of course, make the trip by rail to San José and possibly to Puntarenas on the Pacific Ocean. This railroad from Limon to San José is the one which Mr. Keith began to construct when he was a boy, the road for which 4,000 men laid down their lives in the struggle to penetrate the first twenty-five miles of the jungle.

The ride from Puerto Limon to San José is one of the most beautiful in the world, and there is no city in North America which can vie with San José in certain of its charms. Its

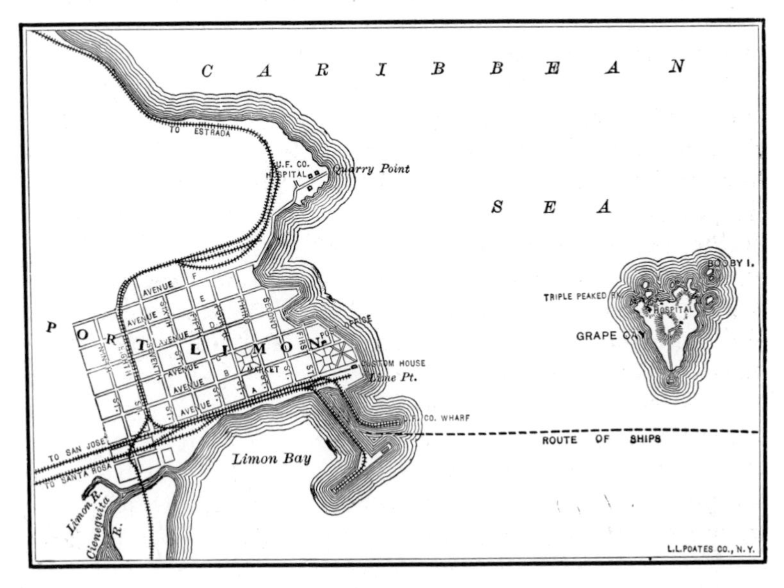

PUERTO LIMON, COSTA RICA

climate is perfect, its streets clean and well kept, its shops attractive and filled with luxuries from all the world, and its opera house so far surpasses anything in the United States that comparisons are odious. And its women — artists and poets and others who can lay no claim to authority rave over them.

But it would take a book to begin to describe the beauties and attractions of this gem of tropical cities, to say nothing of the country and towns of which it is the capital. Let us return to Puerto Limon and see what has been accomplished since Mr. Keith selected it as the base of a railroad which would penetrate the jungle and give access to the populated highlands surrounding San José.

To the west, north, and south of Puerto Limon are tracts of land covering 249,779 acres, or almost exactly 380 square miles, which the United Fruit Company has acquired by purchase, and it holds an additional 5,338 acres under leases.

On the Reventazon River, Costa Rica

It thus operates a tract of land exceeding 390 square miles in Costa Rica, or the acreage of 1,560 farms of a quarter section each, which is the acreage of the average Western farm in the United States.

Not all of this huge tract is under cultivation, and some of it is unfitted for such purposes, but the most of it will some day be utilized for new tropical products which are bidding for Northern favor.

This is by far the largest of the banana developments conducted by the United Fruit Company, and, independent of all of the other properties owned by that company, constitutes one of the great agricultural enterprises of the world.

Within this district are 47,723 acres of growing and bearing banana plants. There is an average of 400 banana plants or trees to the acre, which means that the Costa Rica Division of the United Fruit Company contains about 19,089,200 bearing banana plants! Of course no one, not even the men who supervised the work of their planting, has any comprehensive grasp of what such figures mean. You may ride hundreds of miles through these parallel rows of trees, but instead of obtaining an idea of the magnitude of such an undertaking you glean only that there are human achievements beyond the grasp of the human imagination.

An apple orchard with 100 trees is far larger than the average, but the Costa Rican banana orchard multiplies this unit by 190,000. There are hundreds of negroes in Jamaica who derive most of their annual money income from an acre of bananas, and an army of more than 47,000 of them could eke out an existence if they could divide this Costa Rica plantation and sell its product.

It is because of such plantations and of the transportation equipment for handling their products that bananas sell for retail in the United States at all seasons of the year at from 10 to 25 cents a dozen. If human stupids who imagine that an enterprise is wrong because of its size had their way they might compel the United Fruit Company and its competitors to abandon these modern plantations to the ownership and care of lazy Indians, and these stupids would later be rewarded by being compelled to pay 5 cents for a single banana or go without.

Where these plantations now stand, and where the beautiful city of Puerto Limon now thrives there was not a sign of a human habitation forty-three years ago. There were only the swamps and the jungles reaching back to the mountains which hold on their shoulders the plateau dotted with San José, Cartago, and other historic towns. The numerous rivers which had their rise on the eastern slopes of these mountains had for the natives unknown outlets. They were

Headquarters of United Fruit Company at Puerto Limon, Costa Rica

aware that there was a sea far beyond the jungle, and those who climbed the mountains could see its silver line on a clear day, but nothing would tempt them below the 1,000-foot altitude where coffee cultivation ceases.

To-day Puerto Limon and the former jungles surrounding it contain a population of fully 35,000 people, nearly all of whom are engaged directly or indirectly in the banana trade. The once unknown Puerto Limon is now one of the leading ports between Vera Cruz and Colon, and it is the leading place of banana export in the world. The United Fruit Company alone sends from Limon more than 400 shiploads of bananas a year, or fully 10,000,000 bunches of this fruit. This great industry demands in this district the services of an army of 7,000 men, who, with their families make up the bulk of the population of the Caribbean coast of Costa Rica.

Most of the workers on these plantations are Jamaican negroes who are directed by white superintendents, mainly American. The tradition that it is impossible to live in the lowlands still prevails among the working classes of Costa Rica, but this will be overcome in time. The wages paid by the company average more than double that paid by the coffee planters of the highlands, and the drainage of the swamps and the rigid enforcement of scientific sanitary measures has rendered this section as safe and healthful as any part of the republic.

Most of the manual labor on a banana plantation is what may be termed "piece work," the laborer contracting to perform certain duties on a certain tract of land. He may, for instance, contract to keep clear of weeds and dead fronds or leaves five or ten acres of bananas, or he may contract to cut and deliver to the railroad platforms the bananas grown in a similar tract.

As a rule the workman on a banana plantation selects his own time for the performance of the duties he assumes. Little or no work is done in the heat of the day. Much of it is done in the early morning hours, the men setting out from their cabins at daybreak and working until nine or ten o'clock. Others prefer to do their stint at night, especially when the splendid tropical moon gleams through the rustling banana leaves. Under this system a worker can set his own pace and earn as much as he cares to attempt, but none is assigned to work who cannot perform a reasonable minimum, the pay for which exceeds a dollar a day. There are skilled and sturdy negroes who have no difficulty in making two and three times this amount, and the task is far less arduous than that done by the average white laborer in the United States.

Their rent is nominal, and every occupant of a house or cabin has, rent-free, a garden patch on which he can raise at all times of the year the vegetables which respond to almost no attention. You may search the world over and not find a more happy and contented class than those who work in the banana plantations. The lot of the average American negro is pitiful compared with that of those who still regard Jamaica as their home, but who can win more money and greater comfort along the coast lands of Central America.

The banana plantations of the United Fruit Company in Costa Rica follow the valleys of three rivers which take their source in the mountains to the west and south. These rivers are named the Estrella, Banana, and Reventazon, the last emptying into the Caribbean a few miles north of Puerto Limon. More than 400 miles of railroad and tramways traverse these plantations and link them with the wharves at Puerto Limon. This railroad system also serves many independent growers of bananas who have contracts with the United Fruit Company. These independent growers are entitled to have their fruit collected and accepted twice a week, and in the "heavy" or rainy seasons they are entitled to four weekly cuttings and collections of their bananas. There are times, as I have explained, when this arrangement occasions heavy losses to the importer, who is compelled to accept large consignments for which there is no profitable market.

Scattered through this banana empire are a number of picturesque settlements, some of which have arrived at the dignity of towns, with churches, places of amusements, well-kept streets, electric lights and most of the accessories of advanced civilization. It seemes strange to reflect that all of these towns, railroads, bridges, docks, steamships, and the

THE FIRST INSPECTION

These bananas have arrived at the loading platforms from the plantations, and must pass inspection before transportation to the docks where a ship awaits them

bustling city of Puerto Limon itself are merely parts of a giant banana farm, and that this is only one of the farms in a series which dot the Caribbean coast from Guatemala to Santa Marta, Colombia.

Everywhere the observer sees the manifestations of a carefully designed machine calculated to yield the greatest possible result from a given application of endeavor. Here is an industrial army engaged in a constant battle with the forces of tropical nature. There is no telling when nature may strike an unexpected and dangerous blow. I crossed one railroad bridge whose predecessors had been swept away in floods thirty-one times, but it will take a record-breaking deluge to topple the huge steel structure which now spans this part of the Rio Reventazon. Corps of skilled engineers are constantly at work repairing defects and meeting new problems. Trained physicians keep watch and guard over the health of this army and hold in check any threatened invasion of contagious disease. The wireless telegraph flashes its instructions or warnings out into all parts of the Caribbean, and keeps in close and constant communication with the Great White Fleet which bears to the north the fruits raised by the various divisions in this industrial army.

Sixty thousand trained men are working in the American tropics under the command of skilled generals of the United Fruit Company, and to what end? To the end that the most perishable of tropical luxuries shall be produced so economically and handled so carefully and swiftly that it reaches the consumers of another clime in perfect condition and is offered for sale at prices lower than those charged for home-grown fruits! There is a task which would have daunted Hercules, but it is one within the easy power of the modern industrial miracle worker. Yet to me this mastery of time and space and flood and sea has all the spell of the romantic, and the subject should command the genius and melody of a poet rather than the halting comments of a worker in prose.

I shall never forget the first night I spent in Puerto Limon. I was on board the SS. *Sixaola*, one of the ships of the Great White Fleet, and she lay at her dock ready to take on a load of bananas. Four other great ships were docked at this water front, two of them crowded with passengers, most of whom were taking their first view of the American tropics. Bands played in the cool of the afternoon. Out in the bay the surf lazily caressed the shores of an island where once the pirate Morgan beached his ships and planned for new plunderings of defenseless coast towns. Kipling's lines to the "South Wind," in his poem to the English flag, suggested themselves:

"Over a thousand islands lost in an idle main,
Where the sea-egg flames on the coral and the long-backed breakers croon
Their endless ocean legends to the lazy, locked lagoon."

Less than half a century ago this was a lazy, island-locked lagoon, but the inspiration of American enterprise woke it to life.

Word had been telegraphed and telephoned hours before out to various districts of the great plantation that the *Sixaola* at seven o'clock that evening would take on board 50,000 bunches of bananas. Instantly the complicated machinery of the plantation was set in motion. Over miles of territory the cutters were instructed to deliver a certain quota of bananas to the railroad loading platforms. The *Sixaola* was to sail for New York. It was essential that the cutters should know this fact and keep it rigidly in mind. It meant that they should take from the trees only such fruit as would be in proper condition for the New York market at the end of the seven or eight days' run from Puerto Limon.

It would have been entirely another matter if this fruit had been destined for New Orleans. The field superintendents would then have to know if this particular banana cargo was for consumption in and near New Orleans, or if it was for shipment by rail to Chicago, St. Paul, Omaha, Kansas City, or other centres of banana distribution. The banana must be cut from its parent stock at such a stage of development that it will arrive at the place of its consumption in a condition fully to ripen within forty-eight hours of the time of its delivery.

There must be no mistakes, no delays, no accidents. A fog in the Gulf of Mexico, a strike of handlers on the docks of New Orleans, a freight wreck south of Cairo, a snow blockade in Illinois — all of these possible happenings and many others mean that a part or all of the 50,000 bunches of bananas

Vargas Park, Puerto Limon, Costa Rica

placed on board the *Sixaola* will ripen before their time and become a total loss.

The problem is much the same as if Havana, Mexico City, Guatemala City, San José, Colon, Panama City, Buenos Aires, and Rio de Janeiro were dependent for their ice cream on a product manufactured and packed in Chicago, the condition being that no ice or other cooling substitute could be obtained after the shipments left Chicago. Each receptacle would, therefore, be packed with a sufficient amount of ice to insure its delivery in proper condition at the various cities named, and any considerable delay would mean that instead of receiving ice cream the consignee would reject a substance which had been melted to flavored sweetened cream and sugar.

Even this comparison does not indicate the difficulties which beset the banana importer. He faces risks from both heat and cold, and time itself means deterioration of the highly perishable banana. The ice cream which melts because of insufficient ice does not menace that which is properly packed, but the bunch of bananas which ripens prematurely in the hold of a ship or in a banana car spreads the contagion of its condition to hundreds of stems about it. This is a strange freak of nature, but it is so. All of us who were brought up on farms know that one rotting apple or potato in a barrel will communicate this infection to most of its companions, and when one bunch of bananas changes from green to yellow all of the bunches in the neighborhood seem frantic to adopt the new color fashion. I suspect that bananas are feminine.

Thus it is that the men who direct the cutting of bananas for the *Sixaola* or any other ship must know just what community is to eat them. If they are for London or any other trans-Atlantic port they must be cut to conform to the speed of the ship which carries them, and must, of course, be taken from the trees at a stage of development much earlier than those shipped to our ports.

So much for the field operators. The railroad superintendent must also be on the alert. The bananas for the *Sixaola* may come from tracts ten miles away, or they may be cut in places fifty or sixty miles away. Independent growers scattered over a wide territory may have bananas due for acceptance by the United Fruit Company under the terms of their contracts. There must be no delay in the steady arrival of this cargo at the docks. From out a spreading radius train after train must converge to the dock where lies the *Sixaola*, and feed an unceasing stream of bananas to the men who place them in the cool recesses of her hold.

Let us go out into the plantation and watch the work at one of the platforms. The railroad lines traverse the plantation through its main centres of production. Connecting these railroads are hundreds of miles of tramways on which run flatcars of various types. Some of the independent growers are provided with such tramways, and they propel the cars by hand or with mules or oxen, according to the nature of the tract in which they operate. Other small growers bring their bananas in by mule-back or by wagon. The United Fruit Company depends almost entirely on tramways, many of which use steam traction.

The platform is in charge of an employee officially known as a "receiver," but his duties are also those of an inspector. Along one of the tramways comes a small train of loaded banana cars hauled by a team of mules, the entire equipment in charge of a grinning Jamaican negro. He is an employee of the company and he gets paid so much for each bunch of bananas he cuts on the particular tract placed in his care. He is a qualified expert and is presumed to know just when to cut bananas. If he cuts one out of its proper time he not only destroys a bit of property belonging to the company but he also does work for which he receives no pay. The latter is the only way in which he is penalized, the company standing the loss for the underdeveloped or overripe bunch.

Laborers unload the bananas and pile them carefully on the long wooden platform. The "receiver" keeps careful watch and count. Suddenly he darts toward a negro carrying a bunch of bananas and waves his hand. The negro knows what this means. The bunch which he was about to deposit on the platform has been rejected. It is tossed to the ground beyond the platform and becomes the nucleus of a pile which will grow steadily as the hours pass.

We examine this "reject," which is doomed to rot or to be fed to the cattle on distant pastures. There may be very little to distinguish it from its fellows who have passed the first stage of an examination which may insure them a trip to New York. But the keen eye of the receiver-inspector

ONE WAY OF TRANSPORTING BANANAS
These primitive methods are usually employed by the smaller growers of bananas

discovered some fault of age or some blemish not discernible to our untrained eyes. He knows, or has a very accurate idea, just when this bunch of bananas will ripen, and its period of development must not be too great or too little.

The darky who delivers this instalment of bananas receives from the receiver-inspector a slip of paper which serves as a receipt, and on this printed slip is a record of the number of bunches of bananas delivered, classified according to the number of "hands." This slip enumerates the number of bunches which contain seven hands, eight hands, and all containing nine hands or above that number, these being the three trade grades.

The standard market bunch of bananas is one with nine hands, and one with this number or more is known to the trade as a "count," and a bunch of this description constitutes the basis on which bananas are purchased. Bunches of less than nine hands class as "seconds," and command less prices. The United Fruit Company does not export bananas containing less than seven perfect hands, the smallest to have at least ten fingers. It has been learned from years of experience that bananas of less size are also deficient in quality, and it is the policy of the United Fruit Company to spare no effort and expense to maintain the highest possible standard of excellence.

Other instalments of bananas come rolling to the platform, and among them some which have been cut by the independent growers who have contracts with the company. Exactly the same treatment is accorded these bananas. There is seldom any protest against the rejections, the growers knowing from experience that every exportable banana will be promptly accepted and paid for. The representative of the grower is given a receipt which serves later as a check which may be cashed at the designated headquarters.

Later the trains will rumble along and pick up the huge pile of bananas which have been covered with leaves to protect them from the rays of the afternoon sun. Let us return to the dock and see them go on board.

Gangs of men are already at work placing the huge loading machines into position. There are various types of these machines, but all of them are constructed on the principle of the endless-chain conveyor, with corrugated surfaces on which the bunches are placed, or pockets into which they drop and are thus carried to the main deck of the ship. The height of this deck depends on the size of the ship and the stage of the tide, and the construction of these devices meets these conditions. They are run by steam or electricity, and four of them are used to load ships of the *Sixaola* class.

As early as six o'clock in the evening the small army of men who are to do the loading begin to arrive. They know that there is nothing for them to do until seven, but they come early because they love the fun and excitement. Most of them are Jamaican negroes, black as the ace of spades and care-free as the birds who sing in the adjacent park. Fat negro "mammies" trudge in with handcarts loaded with food and sweetmeat delicacies dear to the negro taste, and the passengers who later timidly sample their wares find most of them appetizing or toothsome. When the dusk falls these Amazonian purveyors light torches and Chinese lanterns. Powerful clusters of electric lights flash out in the vast covered shed which protects the docks, and the myriad lights of the ship add their glow to the general effect.

The docks now swarm with life. It is a riot of color and of movement. Nearly every tropical race and nation has its representatives in this mingling of humanity. Among the laborers or loiterers are Mexicans of various types, Aztec in features and swarthy in hue; exiled revolutionists from Honduras and Nicaragua, looking with suspicion on all who regard them closely; Indian laborers from Guatemala who have wandered thus far from their own country; turbaned Hindoos who are coming into Central America to take the places of the natives who fear the lowlands; German merchants and planters who have made Costa Rica their home and are prospering; tourists from New York, London, Paris, and all the world, cool in white flannels — all mingled and touching elbows with an *insouciance* which goes far to prove the inborn democracy of mankind.

It is a few minutes to seven o'clock when the first banana train backs into the loading shed on one of the tracks which

Feeding the banana-loading machines

run parallel to the length of the *Sixaola*. A whistle blows and the various gangs scramble to take places at their stations. The engines which work the conveyors are set in motion. The doors of the freight cars are thrown back revealing the deep green of serried rows of bananas — bananas which only a few hours ago gleamed in the sun below the nodding plumes of fronds. Again a whistle blows. It is seven o'clock and the long night's work has begun.

There are eight cars ready to be unloaded, two cars for each of the four machines. Two of these machines feed into the ship forward of the cabins, and two of them feed aft. In each of the cars are six workers called "car-men," whose duty it is to lift the bananas carefully and place them on the shoulders of the "carriers," the laborers who cover the 40 or 50 feet from the cars to the conveyors. There are from twenty to twenty-six men in each of the four gangs which thus serve the swift travelling conveyors. A negro foreman is in charge of each of these gangs.

Two men stand at the receiving end of the conveyor and take the bananas from the carriers, who press forward in an unbroken line. The work of these two men is the most arduous of all in the loading of a ship, and they are frequently relieved. It is not a difficult feat to lower one end of a bunch of bananas weighing from 50 to 80 pounds, but when you have done this thirty or more times a minute and have kept it up two or three hours it ceases to be an attractive form of exercise.

Standing near the conveyor is a negro with a pencil and pad of paper, a "checker" who keeps count of the bunches as they climb up the sides of the ship. Opposite him is another checker operating a machine. If I could receive sufficient compensation, this is the sort of a job I should seek. This counting machine has a single key and the operator presses it every time a bunch of bananas leaves the shoulders of the negro carrier. The pressing of this key not only automatically does the counting, but it also jingles the most musical sort of a bell — the kind of a bell that Dickens would have loved to describe.

And on the deck above is another man with the same sort

of a counting machine, save that it has a bell in a different key, half an octave higher, but just as musical and in perfect harmony with the one below. The rhythmic hum of the conveyor provides the bass, and all about is a laughing,

The beach north of Puerto Limon

shouting, singing, and chattering chorus, garbed in a hundred shades of the colors of the rainbow. The roar of the surf as it strikes the sea wall; the silver path of a full moon on waters seen through cocoanut palms; the strains of a military band in the near-by park rendering "La Paloma"; the crackling of the wireless from the *Sixaola* as some message spreads in an instant over every foot of the tumbling waters of the Caribbean and the Gulf of Mexico — such is a dim word picture of some of my impressions when I saw 50,000 bunches of bananas off on their first and last trip to New York.

Inspectors scurry along the lines of the carriers to make sure that no bunch of bananas gets on board under false pretences. Two experts have already passed on them before they reached the docks, but every precaution must be taken to see that a bunch does not ripen before it reaches its journey's end. Squeeze a green banana which normally would ripen in two weeks, and it will turn yellow in three days and induce a thousand others to do the same thing. A slightly crippled "hand," a dent visible only to an eye uncannily keen, and a score of other minute defects will cause an inspector to dart at a carrier and grab the offending bunch from his shoulder.

In a few hours the docks are piled high with these rejected bananas. A New York or Chicago push-cart man would weep bitter, scalding tears at the sight of this seeming wanton destruction of perfect fruit. In the single shipping point of Puerto Limon the United Fruit Company rejects annually an amount of bananas which must cost it to raise or purchase not less than $75,000, but the officials insist that it is worth more than this to keep their product to a rigidly high standard.

The indications are that the day is at hand when valuable commercial use will be made of this enormous quantity of rejected bananas. Science has perfected the art of making banana flour, and there are other products already on the market, such as "Banan-Nutro," a substitute for coffee, prepared by the Panama Banana Food Company of New York, which also sells banana flour. There are still other products on which chemists in the employ of the company are experimenting with confidence.

On the deck and in the hold are other gangs of men who take the bunches from the conveyor and pass them down from hand to hand to the successive decks in the bowels of the ship. Devices are being perfected which will carry the bananas all the way from the docks to any part of the hold.

Each machine requires the services of from eight to fourteen "stowers," who are charged with the skilled task of so standing the bananas on end in the refrigerator apartments that they will make the long sea voyage without suffering bruising or abrasion even in the most violent storms. They are placed erect in two layers, and it is quite a trick to deposit the top layer so that it will rest firmly on the smooth and rounded surfaces below it.

William Fawcett, author of "The Banana, Its Cultivation, Distribution and Commercial Uses," gives this description of the general arrangement of the SS. *Barranca*, one of the ships which carry United Fruit Company's bananas to Europe:

"The refrigerating machinery and cooling appliances are in deck-houses on the upper deck, thus leaving the spaces below as clear as possible for the cargo. There are three decks for fruit forward and aft respectively, and each deck has a run of about 130 feet between bulkheads, making six fine chambers, each taking about 10,000 large bunches, the total of 60,000 being about three times the number carried by the *Port Morant*, which initiated the service in 1901.

"The fruit comes on board within a few hours of cutting, and is stored without covering of any kind, the lowest bunches being arranged with the stems vertical, with a final layer placed horizontally, this giving the best results both in utilizing space and freedom from damage. Every cargo space is divided into bins by portable horizontal sparring fitted into vertical posts, thus checking the movement of the fruit in rough weather. Sparred gratings are laid on the steel decks to carry the fruit clear of the plating, and to allow the air to circulate below and up through the fruit. The ship's sides and bulkheads and the highest and lowest decks are insulated with granulated cork and wood boardings, forming a complete envelope about seven inches thick. Along each side trunks conveying the cool air are formed by boarding, in which are a number of openings fitted with adjustable slides, and spaced at suitable intervals and levels.

"Powerful fans of the centrifugal type, arranged in pairs and coupled with electric motors, draw the air from the fruit chambers through the suction chambers on one side, pass it over closely nested brine piping, thereby cooling and drying it, and returning it through the delivery trunks on the opposite side. The cooler pipes are electrically welded into grid form, there being no screwed joints except those on the headers, the brine flow being regulated by valves controlling a number of separate groups of grids. The cooling surface is

Mysore cattle in Costa Rica

properly proportioned to the work to be done, and the cooler with its fans is completely insulated. Ventilators are provided, enabling the air in the fruit spaces to be changed in as few minutes as may be found desirable from time to time, the fresh air passing through the cooler before reaching the fruit, and the vitiated air being discharged to the atmosphere. The brine pumps are of the vertical duplex type, two in number, either one capable of performing the full duty in emergency.

"The machines and fans are run during the last day or so

of the outward voyage to cool down the spaces in readiness to receive the fruit. Stowage is rapid, owing to the use of power-driven conveyors, and discharges even more rapid, some of the fruit in the square of the hatches being stowed in special cribs, which are lifted out by the ship's derricks immediately the hatches are off, leaving space for the discharging elevators, which are promptly lowered into position. During the first two days of the homeward voyage the plant is run continuously to extract the sun heat from the fruit and to retard ripening. The condition of the fruit is kept under close observation, temperatures being taken at regular intervals day and night, the captain, assisted by the ship's officers — all carefully trained men — personally attending to these duties. After a few days at sea the temperatures are generally well in hand, and care then has to be taken to avoid the risk of chilling, the machine being slowed down, and probably one of the compressors disconnected, just sufficient power being developed to maintain the temperature at about 55° F."

Thus we see that it is far from a simple task to bring a banana from the tropics to its temperate market. Scores of details require constant care and unceasing vigilance, and a single mistake in the adjustment of temperatures may work great damage to a cargo of from 40,000 to 65,000 bananas. The system which has been perfected by the United Fruit Company has demanded a tremendous amount of study, care, and money, with the result that the public is benefited by a fruit luxury at astonishingly low prices.

It is a fascinating sight to stand on the decks of a ship and watch the loading of a cargo of bananas. This is seen at its best in Puerto Limon, where the setting and the environment give the scene all of the illusion of a magnificent stage picture. Train after train pulls in, and its cars are quickly emptied. It took forty trainloads of eight cars each, or the contents of 320 freight cars, to fill the yawning capacity of the hold of the *Sixaola!*

The four machines elevated these bunches of bananas to the deck of the ship, and the men stored them away in the

Hospital buildings and wireless masts in Puerto Limon, Costa Rica

hold at the rate of eighty-three a minute, or about 5,000 an hour. There are slight delays from various causes, but the system in use in Puerto Limon insures that a full cargo of 52,000 bunches for the 5,000-ton *Sixaola* can be placed in her hold in twelve hours or less.

Almost from the start the Jamaican negroes began to sing at their work. All of them are religious, and most of them sincerely so. The United Fruit Company has erected churches for them in various parts of Central and South America, and has aided the more permanent classes to acquire actual ownership of such edifices. I should judge from their songs that the majority of them cling to the Methodist denomination. Most of their voices are good, and some of them excellent. The young negro who led the singing of one of the deck gangs had a rarely sympathetic tenor voice, and scores of passengers crowded about the rail and applauded the rendition of "Blest Be the Tie That Binds," "Sweet Hour of Prayer," "Nearer, My God, to Thee," "Rock of Ages," and other songs familiar and loved by all, irrespective of religious inclinations, but most often sung by the Methodists.

On the opposite end of the ship was a rival concert, but at times some singer with a powerful voice would sound a strain which would ring clear above the hum and racket of the conveyor machinery and the shunting of trains, and the workers from end to end of ship and dock would join in. On the night which I am attempting to describe, a huge Jamaican negro took artistic advantage of a slight lull in the noise. He was black as night, with huge shoulders and massive torso. For hours he had been handling seventy-pound bunches of bananas as if they were bouquets. In a splendidly modulated baritone voice he suddenly began the second verse of "Nearer, My God, to Thee":

> "Though like a wanderer, the sun gone down,
> Darkness be over me, my rest a stone;
> Still in my dreams I'll be,
> Nearer, my God, to Thee —
> Nearer, my God, to Thee, nearer to Thee."

There were few passengers who did not join in the melody. I wonder what Morgan, the buccaneer, later Sir Henry Morgan, would have thought had he stumbled on such a scene in the days before he purchased respectability with his plunderings?

It is true that these negroes are "wanderers" from their beautiful native island of Jamaica, but they are free and able to come and go, and thousands of them make the trip back to their island home annually. It is to be doubted if any body of colored men anywhere in the world receive as high pay, enjoy as much comfort, freedom, and happiness as the 60,000 or more Jamaican negroes who make possible the giant activities of the United Fruit Company and competitors.

CHAPTER XI

The Awakening of Guatemala

CRUISING up the shores of Central America we will make no stop until we reach Puerto Barrios, Guatemala. About ten years ago Minor C. Keith began operations to provide Guatemala and Salvador with railroad communication to the Atlantic coast. This was in furtherance of his plan to connect the United States by rail with the Panama Canal Zone. He had completed the main lines of the railroad system in Costa Rica, and now assumed, with his accustomed energy, the task of opening two more nations to the commerce of the world.

Guatemala and Salvador are the two most populous nations in Central America. The total population of Panama, Costa Rica, Nicaragua, Honduras, British Honduras, Salvador, and Guatemala is roughly 4,600,000, of which Salvador contains about 1,040,000, and Guatemala 1,900,000 — all of Central America containing much less than the population of New York City, but vastly more potential wealth. Little Salvador, with its area of 7,225 square miles, has a density of population not touched by any nation in the New World. Its showing of 144 inhabitants to the square mile is fully five times that of the United States and surpasses that of well-settled Pennsylvania. Salvador has no coast on the Atlantic side and is therefore cut off entirely with direct communication with the great outside markets for its agricultural products.

Only 5 per cent of the population of Salvador are Caucasian, and nearly all citizens of this small fraction are of Spanish descent. Fully 55 per cent of the population are pure-blooded Indians, members of several tribes, most of which have displayed progress compared with the average native Indian population of Central America. Comparative immunity in recent years from revolution and internal strife is largely responsible for this outcome. Nearly all of the soil

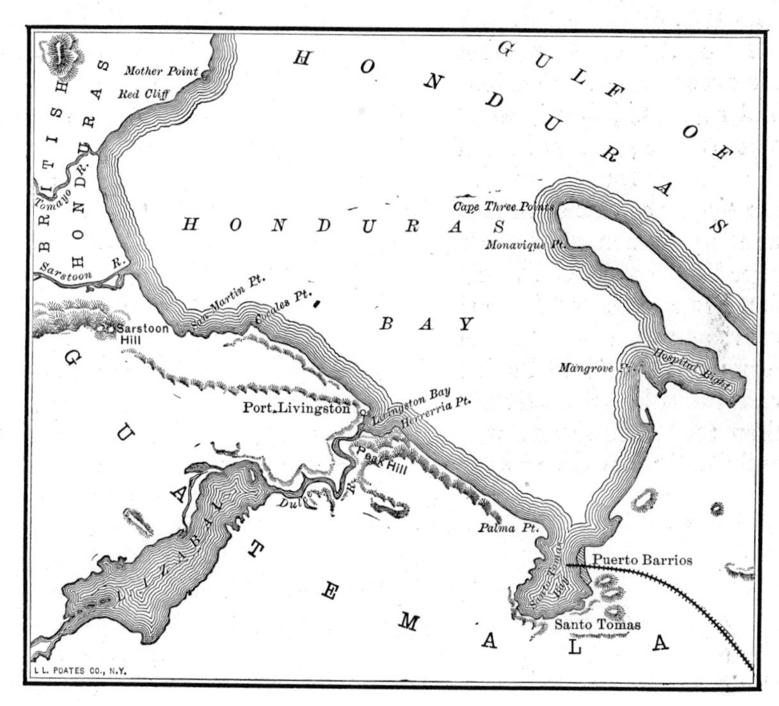

PUERTO BARRIOS, GUATEMALA, AND VICINITY

of Salvador is under cultivation. The Pacific slopes of Salvador and Guatemala are ideal for the cultivation of a score of tropical products, among which are coffee, indigo, sugar, tobacco, rice, cotton, cacao, pineapples, and all kinds of tropical fruits.

On the great plateau of Guatemala are scores of towns and cities, including Guatemala City with a population of 100,000 or more, the largest city in Central America. It was for the purpose of giving these populous and productive districts an outlet to the Atlantic and communication with the trade of the world that Mr. Keith planned a railroad which would connect Puerto Barrios with Guatemala City, capital of the Republic of Guatemala, and San Salvador, capital of the Republic of Salvador, with branches touching various ports on the Pacific, also eventual contact with Mexico and South America.

Like all other Central American countries, with the possible exception of the colony of British Honduras, Guatemala had neglected and ignored its Caribbean lowlands. To the mass of the people of Guatemala, who lived in the highlands, the coasts were dreaded. They were the feared sections of the *tierras calientes*, the fever-stricken hot lands. When the wealthy citizen of Guatemala went to Lisbon or Paris he escaped by way of the Pacific coast, and thence to Panama or San Francisco, and from there to New York. It is only six years ago that he had the choice of any other route, and the American who had business in Guatemala City or San Salvador first bought a ticket for San Francisco or Panama City, then took a long and weary voyage along the Pacific coast, and finally was dropped from a sling to a lighter which rolled perilously in the swell which surges into the open roadsteads that take the place of harbors on most of the west shores of Central America.

It seems strange, does it not, that the Guatemalan railroad was not constructed years and years ago? It seems such an obvious thing to do, yet our American tropics are filled with obvious opportunities and with political problems for which there are obvious remedies. We of the United States spend tens of millions of dollars on huge engineering plants intended to bring our deserts to cultivation, but our statesmanship declines to glance south of the Rio Grande and of Tehuantepec, where uninhabited empires of rich soil are already provided with water and with the climate which must have existed in the Garden of Eden.

When Mr. Keith and his associates decided to build a railroad from the Caribbean through these neglected countries the United Fruit Company agreed to undertake the banana development of sections of the uninhabited eastern lowlands. The Motagua River empties into the sea on the border line between Guatemala and Honduras, and is the longest and most important river in Central America. It has a broad and very fertile valley reaching more than two hundred miles toward the Pacific, and scores of branches are also natural centres of cultivation.

For seventy miles or more back of its mouth the Motagua flows between lands well suited to banana cultivation, and in 1906 the United Fruit Company acquired by purchase

Typical scene at Guatemala railway station

tracts with a total acreage of 50,000. There was at once developed an experimental plantation of 1,250 acres. The test was successful, and an additional 747 acres were planted in 1907. In the following year the banana plantings were increased to 5,080 acres, but the company had not acquired any additional tracts of land. It had demonstrated that banana cultivation in the Motagua Valley was practical and profitable, but it did not attempt to take advantage of this knowledge and of its position to monopolize all or any considerable part of the natural banana lands.

It was not until 1910, five years after the original purchase of 50,000 acres, that the United Fruit Company increased its holdings by the purchase of an additional 30,549 acres, and since that year it has gradually acquired other tracts which gave it in 1913 a total of 126,189 acres, of which 27,122 were devoted to banana cultivation. The annual report of President Preston for 1913 places the cost of the Guatemalan development at $3,884,807.27, thus placing it fourth (in money invested) in the list of tropical divisions of the company, Costa Rica, Panama, and Colombia leading in the order named, with Jamaica in fifth place. Guatemala, however, stands third in the production of bananas.

Puerto Barrios has deep water and an excellent natural harbor, lying well within the shelter of an island which forms the Gulf of Amatique, but at the present time Puerto Barrios is the least attractive and sanitary of all of the ports largely used by the United Fruit Company. Work is now in rapid progress which will change all this. The low site of the native town of Barrios will be raised and protected with a sea wall. The squalid huts which line the beach will disappear, and in their place will rise a fine hotel and office structures for the company. All of the adjacent swamps and lowlands have been reclaimed and made sanitary, and the reconstruction of the small native town will solve the only remaining sanitarv problem which has harassed the company.

A few miles across the gulf is the attractive town of Livingston, situated at the mouth of the Rio Dulce, which connects Lake Izabal with the Caribbean. Lake Izabal is, next to Lake Nicaragua, the largest body of fresh water in Central America, and is navigable for small steamships nearly fifty miles inland. The Rio Dulce is a winding, narrow canyon of great height and surpassing tropical beauty. There is nothing else of this nature in the American tropics, and those who can spare the time will not regret a trip through the wonders of these overhanging cliffs crowned with palms and graced with clinging vines, the voyager finally emerging to the placid surface of Lake Izabal, its far shores fading into the deeper blue of distant mountains.

Leaving Barrios by train, we plunge almost immediately into the most perfect jungle I have ever seen in the tropics. On both sides of the track for miles is a tropical display of trees, plants, flowers, ferns, vines, and shrubs, all woven into an impenetrable network of a thousand hues so delicately blended that it would seem that some horticultural genius had spent a lifetime in arriving at this perfection. A Newport millionaire would give a fortune for an acre of this splendid but worse than useless jungle. For miles it crashes its

ANTIGUA, GUATEMALA
With the famous volcanoes Agua (water) and Fuego (fire) in the distance

pulsating beauty in the face of the beholder. Orchids which would drive a connoisseur to frenzy flame their delicate colors from thousands on thousands of trees. Other towering trees are veritable masses of huge flowers, some of them purple, others tantalizing shades of red, blue, orange, and violet. Why has no artist ever painted such a jungle? He could not do it justice, but he might try. I have never seen on canvas any creation which even pretended to depict in form and color the representation of this native tropical jungle.

We leave the jungle and strike the Motagua River and the banana country. For fifty miles or more we run west and fairly parallel with the Motagua, with bananas on both sides of us most of the time. Some of these belong to the United Fruit Company and others are the property of independent growers. Many natives of Guatemala are owners of such plantations. The people of this republic stand in less fear of the coast lowlands than do the natives of the rest of Central America, but the trustworthy Jamaican negro does the most of the physical labor.

For fifty miles we stop at town after town which had no existence prior to the advent of the banana industry. Some of them betray their newness and their American origin by their names, for instance the town of Dartmouth and the thriving town of Virginia. The latter is in the heart of the banana district, and is modern in every respect. It is a railroad division point. Here are well-equipped railroad shops, an electric lighting and power plant, an ice plant, steam laundry, and up-to-date stores with supplies fresh from the United States and abroad. The residential district contains streets and dwellings which would be a credit to any community, yet all this was a wilderness only a few short years ago. The same is true of Dartmouth and of Quirigua. In the latter is located the wonderful new hospital erected by the United Fruit Company, which will be described elsewhere.

The Guatemala Division of the United Fruit Company is in charge of a manager who maintains headquarters in Puerto Barrios and branch offices in Virginia and Guatemala City. The Guatemala Division is divided into three districts, El Pilar, Quirigua and Los Andes, each under a superintendent, and each district divided into plantations of about 1,000 acres each. These plantations are conducted by "mandadors," or foremen, who are assisted by two timekeepers. All of these officials are white, and most of them are Americans. It is the duty of the mandador to give out and supervise the execution of the contracts with the workmen.

In this district, as in all others conducted by the United

Fruit Company, the labor of clearing new lands, keeping plantations in order, cutting bananas, etc., is done by contract, as I briefly explained in the chapter on Costa Rica. Only a theorist would dream of employing Jamaican negroes and Central American Indians to work on banana or other plantations by day wages. To quote a current phrase: "It can't be done." These toilers lack that altruism which impels some men to work when they are not watched, and you cannot watch negroes and Indians scattered in a wilderness of banana plants which extends for miles in all directions. Hence a contract system which is absolutely fair to all concerned, and which operates to the complete satisfaction of the men, who make a good living from it.

Guatemalan Indian musicians

William Joseph Showalter, in the *National Geographic Magazine* of February, 1913, writes entertainingly of "The Countries of the Caribbean," and has this to say concerning the United Fruit Company:

"It is in Guatemala that one begins properly to appreciate the great civilizing influence of the United Fruit Company. That corporation has many thousands of acres of banana plantations along the lowlands of the Motagua River and extending to the Caribbean Sea. It pays its laborers a dollar a day, eleven times as much as the laws of Guatemala say shall constitute a day's wage. One can readily imagine what a boon this is to poor Indians who have formerly been paid only nine cents. Yet the United Fruit Company voluntarily pays this wage, and is able to give work to every Guatemalan Indian who applies for a job.

"It is the advent of such organizations as these—powerful enough to protect their own interests when disputes arise with the local governments — that spells the economic salvation of these countries and promises an honest wage to the laboring classes. I hold no brief for the United Fruit Company, but it must be said that that great corporation has done more for Central America than all other agencies combined."

There are tasks in the Guatemalan banana industry in which the wage system prevails and in which, as Mr. Showalter states, the natives receive pay many times that dreamed of before the United Fruit Company undertook the development of these neglected tracts of land, but the contract laborer who has a fair degree of intelligence and is willing to work from six to ten hours a day is in receipt of an income which ranges from \$1.25 to \$2.50 a day — the latter figure representing what the average Guatemalan Indian formerly received for a month's hard work.

Guatemalan Indian dandy

There is every likelihood that the payment of good wages, coupled with sanitary surroundings and civilizing influences, will breed in Guatemala and in all of Central America strong, self-reliant, and progressive races of people, and with these traits will come that sense of responsibility and real patriotism which ever serves as the foundation for orderly government and national advancement. Men who are forced to work for nine cents a day or any small multiple of that wage have no interest in government and nothing to arouse a sentiment of national patriotism. Having nothing to lose and all to gain — they naturally turn to revolutions and anarchy. This is the secret of the sad conditions which inevitably lead to political lawlessness in many sections south of the Rio Grande. Central America needs an influx of more corporations that are able and willing to "exploit" her natives by paying them eleven or more times the prevailing legal rates of wages, and whose productive operations will pour a flood of revenue into impoverished national treasuries. There is no other peaceful solution of this problem, and most unbiased critics agree with Mr. Showalter that the United Fruit Company "has done more for Central America than all other agencies combined."

The view from the roof of the hospital in Quirigua is the most impressive in Central America from a banana standpoint. The hospital is on a hill, with the railroad at its base. Beyond the tracks is the front rank of a row of bananas which extends as far as the eye can reach to the east and west. Miles away to the south is the Motagua River, swinging in a curve almost to the Honduras line, but it is buried in a forest of bananas which extends to our south in an unbroken mass a distance of ten miles or more. Beneath the rays of a tropical sun this vast reach of vivid green banana fronds is an impressive sight. Here and there a spiral of steam or smoke indicates the location of a railway train on tracks which place all parts of this plantation within easy access of the workers.

To the south frowns the jagged skyline of a Honduranean range of mountains, with extinct volcanoes rearing ugly cones into a clear sky. Their fertile lower slopes would grow the tropical output for a million of the consumers of the United States, but they are practically uninhabited, unexplored, without any authorized name, and known only to the few Indians who roam about them. They are a part of the unused and neglected assets of a world which complains of the increasing cost of food products, and which does not know enough to utilize the lands which a generous nature has provided.

Centuries ago a mighty race of people lived in the valleys of the Motagua and for hundreds of miles along the now deserted coast lands of Guatemala and Honduras which the United Fruit Company is quickening to step with the new civilization. There are no legends, no traditions, and no understandable records of this people, but within the tangle of the jungle and partly buried beneath its dead fecundity are the ruins of cities, temples, and monuments which declare more vividly than printed words the tale of their progress and achievements.

The lowlands, which now hold such terrors for the ignorant and physically deficient Indian tribes of Guatemala, did not deter their worthy predecessors of centuries ago from master-

Indian marimba, drum, and flute (Guatemala)

ing the sanitary problems of these valleys. They knew that these fertile lands were perfectly fitted to support in comfort and luxury large masses of people, and it was here that they lived and wrought, and finally faded from memory and history, without leaving behind any translated sign of what caused their disappearance.

In a jungle belonging to the United Fruit Company are the famous ruins of Quirigua, only a few miles from the town of that name. In the extension of its banana development the United Fruit Company acquired the tract on which the centre of the ancient metropolis was located, and the company has extended substantial financial aid to archæologists who have performed the work of exploration and excavation under the direction of the School of American Archæology.

It is the aim of the United Fruit Company to clear all of the seventy-five acres which contain the wonderful ruins of temples and the scores of huge and superbly carved monoliths which rise out of the encroaching jungle. This will result in the creation of a tropical park distinct in its attractions from any in the world.

The March issue of the *National Geographic Magazine* of 1913 contained well illustrated articles on the ruins of Quirigua by W. F. Sands, formerly United States Minister to Guatemala, and also one by Sylvanus Griswold Morley, Assistant Director of the Quirigua Expedition of 1912, which executed most of the work of bringing the buried temples to light. I quote passages of their interesting observations and deductions. Mr. Sands expresses this theory:

"With the opening of the Quirigua ruins in Guatemala a most important addition is being made to the material now available for study of the races which once occupied the low, hot, coast land between Copán, in Honduras, through the Guatemala littoral, Petén, and Quirigua Roo to Yucatan.

"Master races they were, as were once the Brahmans of Indo-China. They conquered in easy battle the fever-ridden natives and lived thenceforth upon the country and its population.

"They taught them nothing of their higher civilization, but ground them back to the earth, until inbreeding, idleness, and fever took their toll, and in their turn they were overthrown and perished, leaving nothing but the elaborate monuments and massive buildings which, covered with the mould of centuries of quick-springing and quick-decaying tropical forest, form the 'Indian mounds' so plentiful in this region.

"The theory of an alien sacerdotal aristocracy, claiming

Glimpse of the ruins of Quirigua

divine descent because of superior development, and ruling an untutored, conquered race, while it offers no suggestion as to origin, may at least explain why no memory of their rule remains among the inhabitants of these regions to-day. Knowledge of every kind was kept from the subject races, and with the downfall the slave fled from the ancient holy places, and the symbols of arrogance, cruelty, and power were shunned for centuries as an abomination.

"It is not necessary to hold with Brasseur de Bourbourg that all these countries (the 'Hinterland' of Atlantis) were submerged when the island-continent was destroyed — although his theory is immensely attractive — and that after remaining under the sea for an unknown period they rose once more and were peopled from the highlands.

"It is simpler to imagine, so long as we have nothing definite to go on, and one man's tale is as good as another's, that some such catastrophe took place as is so charmingly told in Sir Hugh Clifford's 'Tragedy of Angkor,' and that the degenerate rulers of the coast were suddenly shown to their subjects by some attack of the hardier mountain tribes no longer to be irresistible, no longer divine, but only very feeble men, and so were wiped out utterly and effectually, as would have been the first weak settlement on our own shores without succor from the mother country. . . .

"In the spring of 1910 the tract of land surrounding the monuments, on the left bank of the Motagua River, was opened for planting by the United Fruit Company, and a park left about the principal ruins. The company generously supplied labor and many other facilities for clearing this park of underbrush and cleaning the stones, so that at last an organized study was made possible under the guidance of Prof. Edgar L. Hewett, Director of the School of American Archæology, and of Mr. Sylvanus Griswold Morley. Both of these gentlemen have spent many months in exploration and detailed examination, and under Mr. Hewett's direction the institute has an opportunity for study hardly paralleled in the history of American archæological research. . . .

"The ruins lie on low, flat land, flooded and renewed each

Uncovering the ruins of Quirigua

rainy season by the Motagua's overflow — rich, inexhaustible alluvial soil and ideal for banana planting. A more inspiring spot can hardly be imagined. Under the immense ceiba and other coast trees (70 and 80 feet to the lowest branches, each branch as big as a thirty-year-old maple and hung with orchids and Spanish moss) has grown up a thicket of palms and fern trees, forming, when the underbrush is cleared, arched forest galleries impossible to describe.

"From the ceiba and mahogany trees drop long, leafless, snake-like black vine stems — one, the 'water-vine,' containing a quart of clear, pure water to every foot, which spurts forth in a refreshing stream when cut. It is a real, thirst-quenching water, drawn up from the soil and filtered through the pores of the plant; not a sap, as one might suppose.

"Through the arches of the palms suddenly appears a group of mounds, still overgrown with masses of foliage, and beyond these an avenue of great stones, carved monoliths leading to some — as yet — invisible altar or temple. From each pillar stares — impassive, gloomy, or sullen — a gigantic face. Each figure is crowned with a tall feather head-dress; is belted with a short, embroidered skirt like the sacrificial apron worn by Korean eunuchs in the Heaven sacrifice — naked, with heavy ornaments at wrist and ankle.

"On the sides of the stones are columns of glyphs, until now undecipherable, but nearly all plain and well preserved, and, when the cue shall have been found, easily legible. The faces are well carved, of a heavy, full type, with thick lips, narrow eyes, and thin, carefully pointed Egyptian beards, like the Sargent Pharaoh in the Boston Library. Several show a remarkably cruel strength, which lessens with each set of pillars to a weak, purposeless, degenerate type — loose-lipped, chinless, and imbecile. Among them are to be found the most perfect pieces of carving I have yet seen among American antiquities.

"It is not to be supposed that either this place or Copán was an isolated group of temples. It is more likely that they were centres, and that similar remains will be uncovered in the near future in the course of deforestation preliminary to banana planting."

One of the superb monoliths of Quirigua

It is thus known that the banana plantations surrounding the park were once the site of a great and populous city, of which these ruined temples and towering monuments were the centre. Beneath the rustling fronds of this wilderness of bananas lie the ashes of a race whose rise and fall are lost to history, and the people of our day gaze with lack of comprehension on the mighty works of men who had risen to a high civilization in an age when our Saxon ancestors were still members of savage tribes — tribes which did not come in contact with civilization until it was beaten into them by the all-conquering Roman Empire.

And we, in our pride and folly, vainly imagine that our works and our boasted progress may not some day be obliterated by flaccid, pampered idleness and degeneracy, and we decline to entertain the thought that some future race will uncover the ruins of the Woolworth Building and speculate on what occasioned the depressions caused by the caving in of what now are New York's subways.

Protest it as we may, we have no assurance that it is within our power to rear or create anything which will convey to the people of the coming ages the story of our petty achievements and of our boasted triumphs. Destruction may come from within or from without, from this earth of ours or from the unknowable forces of the nether universe, but the ruins of great cities which antedated buried Babylon and Nineveh, the crumbling débris of mighty cities which crowned the plateaus of Peru, the pyramids of Mexico, which were old before those of Egypt were begun, the magnificent wreckage of palaces where once lorded the rulers of Yucatan, and the orchid-festooned temples of Quirigua all warn us that "we too shall pass away," and that we shall leave behind no understandable sign of why we encumbered the earth.

Mr. Morley has another theory to account for the ruins of Quirigua, and he thus expresses it in his article in the *National Geographic Magazine* of March, 1913:

"Quirigua was one of the older centres of the great Maya civilization, which flourished in southern Mexico, Guatemala, and Honduras during the first fifteen centuries of the

Christian Era. Judging from the dated monuments which are erected in its several courts and plazas, this ancient American metropolis was abandoned during the first half of the sixth century A. D.

"Toward the close of the sixth century the Mayas moved out from the older centres of their civilization in the south

An ornate carving in Quirigua

and migrated northward into Yucatan. Here in the stress of colonizing a new and unfamiliar land, the remembrance of their former homes gradually faded, until Quirigua, along with many another southern city, became only a memory, a tradition. Finally, long before the discovery of America, even the tradition of its former existence had passed from the minds of men."

I cannot readily subscribe to this theory. Races do not abandon a metropolis because of the founding of relatively adjacent colonies, and the ruins of Yucatan are only a few hundred miles from the remains of the presumably deserted Quirigua. Taking courage from Mr. Sands' frank confession that "we have nothing to go on, and one man's tale is as good as another's," I take this opportunity to exploit a theory of my own.

Scattered all through Guatemala and Mexico are tribes of so-called Indians who speak dialects which contain many words of Japanese origin. There are tribes in Mexico with languages in which more than half of their vocabulary is Japanese. It is a fact that a native of Japan can enter villages of such tribes and converse readily with their inhabitants in their own tongue. Even more significant is the fact that there is a marked physical resemblance between them and the modern Japanese.

What is the logical deduction from this unquestioned fact? It is that parts or all of Mexico and Central America were once settled from Japan, or — which is equally possible — Japan was originally settled by some great migration or conquest originating from Central America.

Mr. Sands speaks of the Egyptian characteristics of the faces and the figures carved on these monoliths, but he and other students will be compelled to admit that all of these carvings depart from a conventional rule seldom violated by Egyptian artists or sculptors. On this point I quote the New International Encyclopædia as follows:

"The main attempt (of Egyptian artists) was to show as much as possible to the beholder. Therefore, in relief, figures were spread out as on a map: the head in profile (but the eye in front view), the shoulders full front, the arms and hands in profile, the trunk three-quarters, the legs and feet in profile."

Now the carvings of human faces and figures as displayed by the monoliths and temple decorations of Quirigua *do not conform to a single one of these specifications of Egyptian art.* That art knew nothing of perspective and little of proportion.

It was confined almost entirely to distorted profiles. *In all of the carvings recovered from Quirigua there is not a one which is executed in profile, all of them being in full or three-quarter face.* More than that, the faces are far more Japanese than Egyptian

One of the mysteries of Quirigua's ruins

in expression, and several of them have the inwardly tilted eyebrows peculiar to the Japanese and Chinese races.

Having proved this much, I might as well explain the mystery of the abandonment of the capital of Quirigua and of its surrounding empire. Some Napoleon of this tropical empire learned of the existence of the island of Japan, and went forth with a vast army to conquer it. Whether he went by land up the warm coasts of the present United States and Canada into Alaska and thence by ships to the Asiatic mainland, or if he went by ships or steamers from some lower Pacific port, or if he went by flying machines is a matter of slight consequence in the determination of the truth of my

Getting ready for a fiesta

theory. The main point is that these people were kin to the Japanese, and they went there either to fight or because they were dissatisfied with their former tropical surroundings. In any event they left and did not come back, and that is the reason that the United Fruit Company found the ruins of Quirigua inhabited with baboons, herds of peccary, tapirs, jaguars, and other denizens of a deserted wilderness.

Having settled this momentous question to my own satisfaction, if not to that of those who hold other theories, we will leave the ruins of Quirigua to the ghosts of an unknown race, and step out into the light of an age which is so busy trying to make a living that it has little time to solve the mysteries of vanished ages.

There is every reason to believe that the enterprises set on foot by Minor C. Keith and his associates in coöperation with the United Fruit Company will pave the way for the lifting of Guatemala and Salvador to the plane made possible by their varied natural resources. It is the settled policy of the heads of these enterprises to lend every reasonable aid and encouragement to Americans who are attracted to these countries, but it is only fair to warn the intended agriculturist that an undertaking in any part of Central America requires much more capital than does farming in the United States.

Let us glance briefly at the countries in which the operations of the United Fruit Company are of lesser importance at the present time.

The traveller from New Orleans who takes the boats of the United Fruit Company makes his first stop at Belize, the capital and only town of consequence in British Honduras. This little British possession is an oasis of peace in a desert which for centuries has been swept by storms of revolution and lawlessness. The happy and prosperous inhabitants of British Honduras do not have to worry over the problem of "working out their own destiny," this detail devolving on the officials of the political party which happens to be in power in London.

Most of the inhabitants of Belize and a majority of those of British Honduras are negroes, whose ancestors migrated there from Jamaica and other islands of the West Indies. If they are denied any of the rights of freedom, political and otherwise, they are utterly unconscious of it, and there is no more likelihood of a "revolution" in their country than there is in Massachusetts. When the student contrasts the conditions which exist in Spanish Honduras with those which prevail in British Honduras he is likely to regret that England did not grab most of Central America a century and a half ago and bequeath to it the order and prosperity for which our British brothers are so willing to fight.

There seem to be no opportunities for banana development on a large scale in British Honduras. The United Fruit Company has about 1,500 acres of banana cultivations in the southern part of the country, the product being exported from Puerto Barrios. British Honduras is fitted for many other profitable kinds of agriculture, but its development has

Street scene in Guatemala City

been retarded by the bad reputation which has been given to all of the vast section south of the Rio Grande through the successive outbreaks which have harassed Mexico and the revolution centres of Central America. When peace is enforced on her neighbors, little British Honduras will come to her own.

Nicaragua produces about 2,500,000 bunches of bananas annually, but these are all imported and handled by competitors of the United Fruit Company. The latter owns a tract of 193,000 acres of land in Nicaragua, but has not as yet extended its plantation development to this rather ebullient republic. Nations with natural resources prosper about in proportion as they maintain stable conditions of government, and the sole reason why Costa Rica is more prosperous than Nicaragua is that she deserves to be so.

The United Fruit Company has about 49,000 acres of land in Honduras, and holds 17,000 acres under lease, 9,000 of which consist of banana plantations. These plantations are near Puerto Cortez, which has one of the finest harbors along the coasts of Central America. Puerto Cortez is in the extreme west of Honduras, not more than forty-five miles from Puerto Barrios, Guatemala. The Caribbean coast line of Honduras extends east and west, and this republic is almost shut off from the Pacific shores, having only a few miles of frontage on Fonseca Bay.

Honduras is the least developed of all of the Central American countries, and this is true despite the fact that it has wonderful natural resources and possibilities. It has had six so-called revolutions in the last fifteen years. That is the principal reason why its population is less now than it was fifty years ago. No railroads connect her interior cities with her coasts, and her capital, Tegucigalpa, less than 250 miles from Puerto Cortez, is one of the least known, most isolated and inaccessible places of political importance on the face of the globe. It requires three weeks for mule trains to cross from the Caribbean to the Pacific, over trails and comparatively low mountain passes which a railroad train would negotiate in twelve hours or less.

But the United Fruit Company is displaying practical confidence in the future of Honduras. It has faith that the completion of the Panama Canal will prove the means of calling the attention of the world to the possibilities which long have lain dormant in such nations as Honduras. It is inevitable that the pressure of population and of capital seeking investment will not halt at the handicaps which have been reared by weak and inefficient governments. There is no room for hermit kingdoms or military despotisms north of the Panama Canal Zone.

Honduras has had no chance to show what she can do. Without railroads penetrating her fertile interior plateaus there is no incentive to raise crops which cannot reach the seacoast. Years ago Honduras authorized a huge bond issue for the purpose of constructing such a railroad from Puerto Cortez. The bonds were sold. Fifty-seven miles of narrow-gauge road was constructed over fairly level land south from Puerto Cortez. The actual cost should not have exceeded $30,000 a mile, but corrupt public officials in conspiracy with equally corrupt English contractors pocketed nearly $1,000,000 a mile for this wretched bit of railroad construction — one of the most audacious, stupendous, and criminal specimens of public robbery in all of the history of plunder.

A later chapter on the sanitary work conducted by the United Fruit Company includes a description of the work now in progress in Spanish Honduras.

CHAPTER XII

Along the Coast of South America

HE northern coast of South America was practically unknown to modern travel and commerce until the productive activities of the founders of the United Fruit Company awakened its picturesque cities to life and ambition. There is no section along the American Mediterranean richer in historic associations. These waters floated the fighting ships of British sailors, adventurers, and buccaneers whose prowess and crimes established the prestige which deposed Spain and made Great Britain the acknowledged mistress of the seas. Morgan, Drake, Vernon, Captain Kidd and a score of other hardy and reckless commanders of equally desperate men raped the coast towns of northern South America of their richest treasures, and some of them were knighted for acts which now would send them to the gallows. These glistening waters, ancient cities, and mountain-buttressed shores still hold the glamour and the spell of the romance which ever will invest the Spanish Main.

In our imaginative trip we will now retrace our water paths and return to Colon, sailing from there to Cartagena and Santa Marta. The traveller must be warned to give Cartagena its proper Spanish pronunciation, in which the syllable "ge" has the English sound of "ha"; the letter "a" in all Spanish words taking the sound it has with us in the word "father." Cartagena is too famous and alluring to be mispronounced, and the Spanish way is musical and preferable:

"Cah-tah-hāy′-na." Try it.

It is less than a day's sail on one of the fast steamers of the United Fruit Company from Colon to Cartagena, and the voyager must not miss a minute from the decks after the mouth of the outer harbor is sighted. Here is where you realize that the makers of the wood engravings of tropical ports, which appeared in the ancient school geographies, were not such bad artists after all. There is a sea tang about the old-fashioned engravings which escapes the camera and

Street scene in historic Cartagena

defies the painter in oils. The best picture of Cartagena I have ever seen is contained in an encyclopædia which was published nearly half a century ago.

Cartagena is the most fascinating city along the winding reaches of the Caribbean. Its origin is lost in history, but there is every indication that it was a centre of Indian population long before we have any record of London. The Spaniards took possession of it in 1533, and fortified it at an expense of $29,000,000, which meant an expenditure in labor value ten times that of the present day. The fortifications included a huge wall which entirely surrounded the city, and this wall was spaced with forts which still stand as a testimony to the skill of those who supervised their construction.

In 1544 Cartagena was seized by the French, who won the temporary fealty of the native population, but it soon reverted to the Spaniards. In 1585 Sir Francis Drake captured Cartagena after one of the most reckless exploits in his romantic career as an aristocratic pirate and adventurer. In order to understand the audacity of this attack it is necessary to explain how Cartagena is approached from the sea.

The famous old city lies squarely abreast to the Caribbean, but its waves beat up against rocks and reefs, and no landing is possible except by small boats at rare intervals. Ships must approach it by a winding lagoon which opens in two places from the sea, but only one of these has deep water. These are called the Boca Grande and the Boca Chica — the "Big Mouth" and the "Little Mouth" — but it is the latter which was used centuries ago and now.

At the entrance of Boca Chica stands a massive and moss-covered fort of white stone, the Fort of San Fernando. Opposite San Fernando is the ancient Fort of San José, these two guarding a fairly narrow channel between the mainland and Tierra Bomba Island, whose intrusion forms the two mouths which open into the broad but generally shallow inner and middle harbors. From Boca Chica to the docks in Cartagena is fully ten miles via the winding channels which are bounded by saw-toothed coral reefs, and it was along these channels that Sir Francis Drake sailed with his gentlemen adventurers, and it is over the same route that we enter the shelter of the inner harbor.

Near Fort San José is a lighthouse — one of the kind you see in picture books but never expect to see with your eyes. It clings to slimy rocks, the salt spume of the Caribbean lashing its polished stone surfaces, and from base to lantern dome it fairly oozes the mystery and charm of the sea. These forts and this lighthouse were not there when Sir Francis Drake sailed in with virtuous intent to despoil

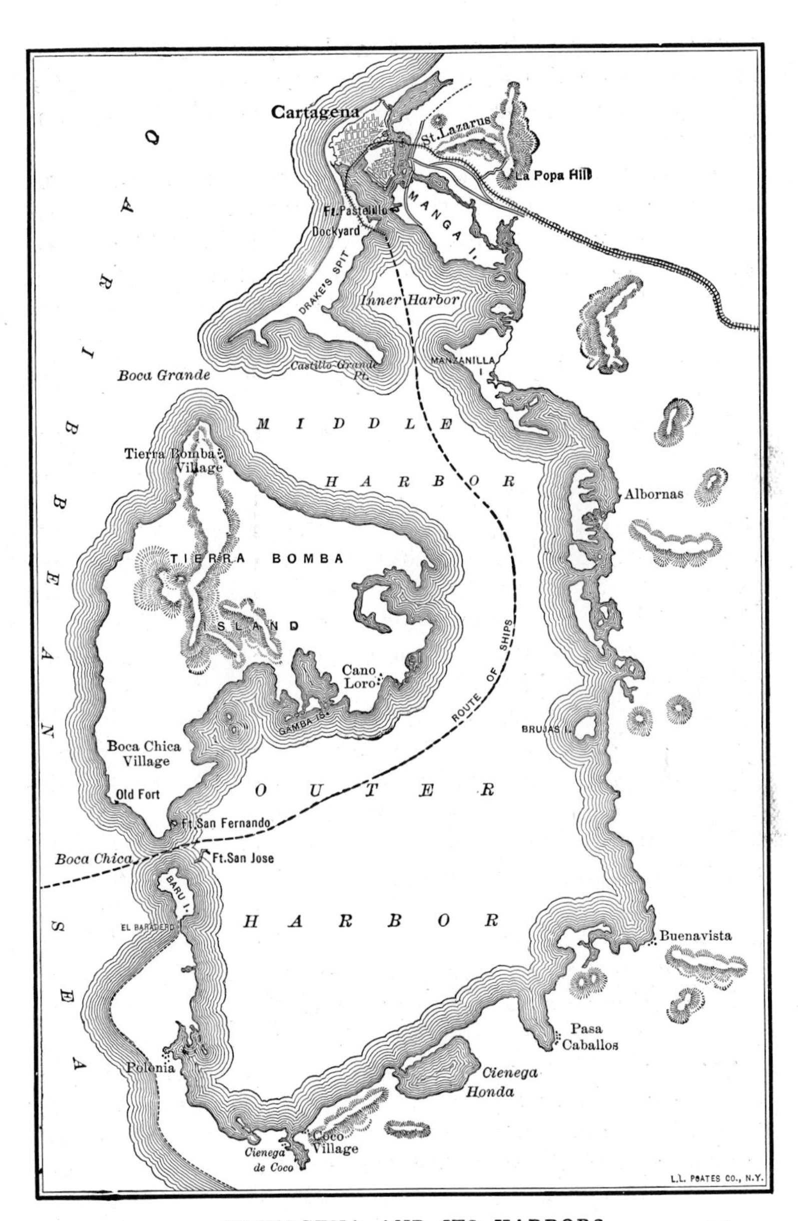

CARTAGENA AND ITS HARBORS

Cartagena, and their erection and use might have saved these people much loot and bloodshed.

Cartagena rises out of the sea like some illusive mirage. It seems to float half in air. Beyond the white of houses and the green of palms rises La Popa, a once sacred acropolis, now marked with the crumbling ruins of a convent whose walls join with precipices, over which tradition relates that the soldiers of Sir Francis Drake tossed the nuns to show

CEMETERY AND CITY WALL OF CARTAGENA
The convent in the distance is on the summit of La Popa, a most picturesque landmark

their contempt of the anathemas which had been hurled against them. I should hate to believe that there is historical authority for this tradition. Once a year the devout people of Cartagena make a pilgrimage up the easier slopes of La Popa, but I much doubt if they pray for the repose of the soul of Sir Francis Drake and the men who slew and looted their ancestors.

Inner Harbor is not reached until Middle Harbor has been passed. The latter is formed by what is known as

Drake's Spit and by Manzanilla Point, a projection of an island which lies close to the mainland. In times of attack by pirates or other foes the Spaniards would sink ships across this space, and they did this despite the fact that they never had heard of Hobson.

More than three centuries ago Sir Francis Drake captured San Domingo and sacked its towns. Having nothing more exciting to do he planned to levy tribute on Cartagena. He entered Boca Chica at four o'clock in the afternoon and later made a pretence of attacking Fort Pastelillo, which then stood and still stands at the mouth of Inner Harbor. This fort was very strong and Drake had no intention of taking it at that time. His attack was a feint and an effective one.

Under cover of darkness Carliel, one of Drake's officers, led a detachment of buccaneers along the narrow and uninhabited strip of sand and brush which now is known as "Drake's Spit." Sir Frederick Treves, in his masterly book on the West Indies entitled "The Cradle of the Deep," gives a spirited and historically verified account of what ensued:

"The last half mile of the spit, where it comes between the Inner Harbor and the sea, and where the railroad from the pier now runs in peace, is very narrow. As the English neared this point they were discovered by some mounted scouts, who promptly galloped off to alarm the garrison. Across the narrow path the buccaneers found that a wall had been built, with a staked ditch in front of it. There was a gap in the wall to allow the horsemen to pass in, but the entry was already blocked by gabions in the form of wine butts filled with earth. Behind the wall were six demi-culverins and sakers, and a force of men armed with muskets and pikes. Moreover, two great galleys, drawn up on the harbor beach, were manned by a company of soldiers who could command the passage with their firearms. Every gun was trained on the spit.

"As Carliel advanced, the Spaniards poured a torrent of shot upon the narrow way. The British kept silent and

The Cathedral of Cartagena

never fired. They crawled along the water's edge so as to be out of range until they were close under the wall. Then, at a given signal, they made a rush for the gap through a blizzard of bullets. Down went the wine butts like ninepins. A volley was fired in the very face of the horrified defenders of the breach, and with a yell the English fell on them with pike and cutlass. Carliel with his own hand cut down the standard-bearer. The Spaniards without more ado turned heel and fled, helter-skelter, for the city. As Thomas Cates, who wrote a chronicle of the fight, modestly explains, 'our pikes were longer than theirs.'

"The British tore after them like a pack of baying wolves. The flying crowd made an attempt to stand but were swept down, so that the men with the long pikes had to leap over their bodies. 'We gave them no leisure to breathe,' says Master Cates with great relish. In a moment the market-place was gained, but every street leading to it was blocked with earthworks. Over these mounds went the Spaniards, and the buccaneers after them, as if it were a hurdle-race. Behind each barricade Indians were posted with poisoned arrows, but Drake's men jumped on their backs or their heads as they crouched, and gave them a taste of the long pikes if they had the heart to stand. Poisoned stakes had been driven into the ground 'to run into one's feet,' but as the Spaniards stumbled over them in their terror the pursuers had something soft to tread upon.

"Women hurled stones, pots, and jugs out of windows; a musket would blaze through a loophole in a gate; figures in night attire crouched in archways or fled in the gloom shrieking wildly. Every dog in the town was barking as if possessed, while drums beat without ceasing. Whenever a stand was made by the garrison the pikes charged, and the breathless Cartagenians, scattered and bleeding, bolted down dark alleys or hid under carts.

"The town was taken and taken handsomely; the fort that had defied Frobisher was seized and blown up, and, after a pleasant stay of six weeks — during which time Drake entertained the governor and bishop at dinner — that officer departed with 110,000 ducats in his pocket."

It was all very wicked and improper, no doubt, but I would go a long way to see a verified moving picture of the English buccaneers as they tore through that gate, and I would listen eagerly to a phonographic record of the conversation when Sir Francis Drake entertained the governor and the bishop at dinner — at their own expense.

Our historians make little mention of the fact that the men of the American colonies in 1741 helped make an impressive but disastrous attempt to capture and loot Carta-

In ancient Cartagena

gena. It is true that this plan to ravish the Spaniards was conceived by a British king, who ordered his American subjects to furnish 4,000 foot soldiers and as many sailors as might be required by the English fleet. Forty-five hundred soldiers volunteered or were pressed into service by various methods, and history does not record how many sailors were "induced to volunteer," but it is known that very few of them came back. This was one of the things to which our historians devote scant space.

Virginia and Massachusetts each sent 500 men. The

Virginians were commanded by Lawrence Washington, a mere boy from Hunting Creek, and the half-brother of George Washington. The naval end of the expedition was in command of Admiral Vernon of the British navy, and Lawrence Washington so admired the "Hero of Porto Bello" that he later gave to his Virginia estates the name of Mount Vernon, and the immortal George Washington retained this name when he came into possession of the property on the death of his half-brother.

Entering the harbor of Santa Marta

The death of Lord Cathcart threw the command of the land forces to General Wentworth, an English officer, and from the start there was constant friction between Admiral Vernon, otherwise known as "Old Grog," and the inefficient Wentworth. The great fleet sailed with more than 25,000 men on board, of whom probably 7,000 were Americans. None of these colonists has left behind any written account of the disasters which befell them. In a most pitiful sense the colonial dead of Cartagena are the American "Lost Legion."

The vast fleet which bore the combined hopes of England and its American colonists sailed its slow way to the Isthmus of Panama. Not far from the present site of Colon is the beautiful Cape of Manzanillo, and within a lagoon is what remains of the once famous and dreaded Porto Bello. In those years it was presumed to be heavily fortified and possessed of much treasure. No place on the Spanish Main made so strong an appeal to the romantic in man's nature.

Small-pox and yellow fever had swept the Spanish garrison and they neither expected nor were prepared for an attack. Admiral Vernon captured the famous Iron Castle and Stone Fort with the loss of only four men, and when the news reached London there was wild rejoicing, and medals were struck off in honor of "The Hero of Porto Bello." This was the first engagement in what is known in English history as the "War of Jenkins' Ear," and it had its pretext in an allegation made by Robert Jenkins, master of the British trading brig *Rebecca*, that a Spanish pirate had cut off his ear, which member Captain Jenkins displayed for years before its picturesque loss was made the excuse for a war to despoil Spain.

The victorious fleet next sailed for Cartagena, expecting to duplicate with ease the exploit Drake had executed a century before with a handful of men. The forts at the entrance of Boca Chica were dismantled by bombardment and captured by the land forces with slight loss. When the news reached England that Fort San Fernando had fallen, the nation again went wild. Vernon was dubbed "The Scourge of Spain."

The fleet moved up into Middle Harbor. The soldiers landed, and the long and disastrous siege of the city began. Attack after attack was made on the fortifications, but with slight success. Yellow fever broke out and killed thousands of men in a few days. Admiral Vernon and General Wentworth kept up their wrangles, but finally agreed on one thing, which was that Cartagena could not be taken, and that a longer stay would result in the death of all by disease. What was left of the fleet sailed back for America, but of the 25,000 men who left Porto Bello in triumph only 12,000 stumbled or were carried aboard the ships. Among the 13,000 who perished in this ill-fated attack on Cartagena there were not less than 4,000 Americans, and the horror of their experience seems to have struck the survivors dumb. Lawrence Washington soon died from diseases contracted before the walls of Cartagena.

The volcanic cliffs of Santa Marta

Bolivar wrested Cartagena from Spain in 1815, but was forced to surrender it the same year. It was finally taken and held by the republicans in 1821, and has since been free from foreign domination.

For these and many other reasons Cartagena possesses a peculiar interest to well-informed American visitors. The ships of the United Fruit Company remain at their docks long enough to permit passengers to spend the time required for a comprehensive ride through the famous old city and to view the points of historic interest. As one winds through the narrow streets, with their doorsteps worn deep by the bare feet of scores of generations, he can imagine the fright of those who lived in Cartagena when the savage buccaneers under command of Drake rushed into the fortified market-place, knives in their teeth and bloodstained pikes in their hands.

In the cool of the evening our ship glides from her dock and heads down Middle Harbor. The rays of the declining sun seem focused like a searchlight on the white façades of the dead convent which crowns the heights of La Popa. To the left are the lower levels of Fort San Lazar, where in a last desperate attack a thousand unknown American colonists perished in a fight for a monarchy with which the next generation went to war. The black mouths of the cannon of Fort Pastelillo are on our port quarter, and the sound of a bugle rings clear and in harmony with the deep-toned bells in the cathedral within the walled enclosure of Cartagena. The weeds and stunted jungle must look the same as when Drake's men crawled through them that eventful night centuries ago.

Out we swing into the broad expanse of Outer Harbor, picking a cautious way between red-painted buoys. Tierra Bomba Island is to our right, and in the shelter of one of its bays stands a leper village, the sad abode of living human beings who are already dead to hope and ambition. Ahead of us are Forts San Fernando and San José, and as we look the lighthouse flashes forth its friendly gleam. A boat rowed by strong Indian oarsmen bobs over the waves, our pilot climbs down the swaying ladder, tumbles into the cockleshell, we give him a cheer, and a moment later are past the forts and into tumbling billows kicked up by the invigorating trade winds.

We are headed for Santa Marta, and all the next fore-noon are in sight of the lofty mountains which slope down almost to the Caribbean along this coast. The entrance to the protected harbor of Santa Marta is rugged and grandly beautiful. Volcanic rocks form a bristling palisade along the mainland, and towering above them is a range of mountains with their deserted crests mantled in clouds. Still back of them is an unseen wilderness of still mightier mountains, the snow-clad and mysterious Sierra Nevadas, which reach out from the Andes in a gigantic spur a thousand

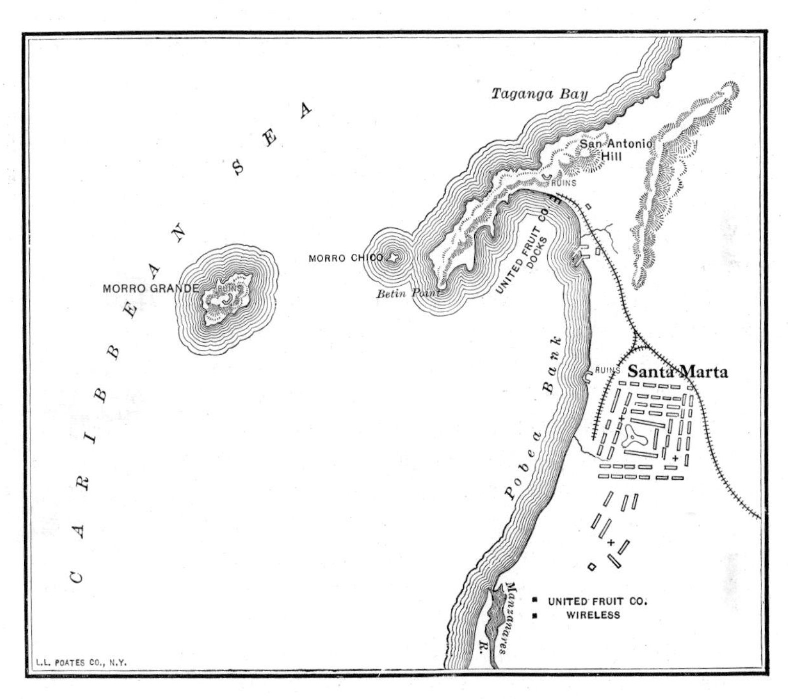

SANTA MARTA, COLOMBIA

miles or more across Colombia and Venezuela. One must climb the lower mountains nearer Santa Marta to obtain a view of the glistening fields of snow which have ever defied the rays of the equatorial sun.

It is this stupendous and practically unknown range of mountains which bequeaths to Santa Marta and its vicinity their agricultural advantages. There is practically no rainfall along these coasts. There are years in which there is a total absence of rain, and there are intervals of heavy precipitation, but no one depends on this phenomenon for water. A hundred miles or more back through the impenetrable jungle flow streams of clear, cold waters which take their rise from the melting snows on the flanks of the Sierra

Harbor of Santa Marta, Colombia

Nevadas. This supply never ceases, but it varies according to the frequency and intensity of the storms which rage in mountain fastnesses never seen by the eyes of white men who have lived to return and tell the tale of the explorations.

None of the natives of Santa Marta and of other coast towns pretends to know anything of these snow-crested giants to the south and west. The few explorers who have ventured into their foothills have failed to discover even scattered inhabitants, to say nothing of tribes. Here is an empire which has rebuffed even the most primitive and savage of mankind, and yet we humans prattle of having extended our dominion over the world and imagine that we have about exhausted its resources. We know as little about the heart of South America as we do of the geography of Mars, and more than half of Mexico is still uncharted and unexplored.

The mysterious Sierra Nevadas have given to the banana industry an added insurance against the depletion of supply through climatic disasters. The melted snow which flows down from their summits provides for the irrigation of great plantations which furnish an excellent quality of bananas. There is slight chance of destructive winds back from the coasts, and there is no chance that the dreaded banana disease incident to cultivation in humid lowlands can ever afflict these districts. The only handicap is an occasional failure of the rivers to meet the demands of the plantations, such failure meaning lessened production.

Santa Marta lies on a low and narrow plain between angry volcanic hills which would be called mountains in New York or Pennsylvania. The sea once occupied this space, but the beaches gradually receded and created this site for a city fronted with a deep and natural harbor, one of the best on the Caribbean.

Here is the ideal combination of sea and landscape, with a broad bay buttressed by abrupt cliffs and peak piled on peak, shaded and softened by sun-colored clouds. Storm-beaten islands and headlands guard the harbor approach. On one of the islands is a deserted fort, its rusted cannon affording nests for seafowl. With the changing hours this bay and its mountain frame thrills the lover of nature with ravishing color harmonies in blue, green, orange, and red. I saw a sunset that — but it is useless to attempt to describe that sunset. I should class it as a Wagnerian sunset, and let it go at that.

The steamer makes a stay of a day or two in Santa Marta,

and the passengers are afforded a chance to journey by railroad back into the tropical beauties of an irrigated country. By far the larger plantations in the Santa Marta district are owned by the United Fruit Company, but there are many independent raisers, most of them native Colombians. Bananas were cultivated in this section long before Mr. Keith or the United Fruit Company entered the field, but this cultivation was conducted on a small scale and for

United Fruit Headquarters at Rio Frio, Colombia

home consumption. These planters used crude methods of irrigation and knew little of the scientific methods now in vogue.

When the United Fruit Company purchased its Colombian property it included 12,547 acres of banana plantations, a larger acreage than that of any other country in which it then operated. Since then these plantations have been increased to 22,790 acres, which places this division fourth in banana acreage and only slightly behind Guatemala.

As has been stated, the available acreage is limited by the water supply, and this is about all utilized in the vicinity of Santa Marta.

Five rivers help to give life to the naturally fertile soil. The largest of these is the Rio Frio (Cold River), and the plantations along its banks extend thirty miles back from Santa Marta. The smaller rivers are the Sevilla, Tucurinca, Aracataca, and the Fundacion, all of which rise in the Sierra Nevadas from peaks which climb 16,000 and 17,000 feet into the tropical sky.

The gravity system of irrigation is used exclusively, and water is let in between the banana rows twice a week. This insures a uniformity of height, quantity, and quality not possible in places where dependence is placed on rainfalls. The Santa Marta banana commands a high place in the banana trade, and it is to be regretted that a larger acreage cannot be planted.

Here is the one place in the tropics where the Jamaican negro does not dominate the labor field. Most of the 2,500 workers in the banana fields and along the irrigation ditches are native Colombians, most of whom have been attracted here from higher altitudes by a certainty of good wages. They are an excellent class of workmen, strong and active and of good habits. Many of them have acquired from their earnings small tracts of lands of their own. The company has repeatedly extended money or credit to natives who have indicated a capacity to develop into independent producers of bananas. Those who have displayed an aptitude for banana agriculture have succeeded, and some of them have become rich from original investments of a few hundred dollars.

It is not in Colombia alone that the United Fruit Company has extended financial aid to independent growers of bananas. Almost from the inception of this enterprise the policy has been followed of giving substantial encouragement to those who had acquired lands fitted for the production of bananas. It is easy to understand why a corporation engaged in a competitive industry might deem it expedient to pursue a policy exactly opposite one which involves the lending of money to independent producers of its leading articles of commerce. The United Fruit Company could not have been justly criticised had it employed every legal effort to acquire and hold all promising banana lands near the tropical ports from which it operates, but the facts show that it did nothing of the kind.

On the contrary, the United Fruit Company has loaned tens of millions of dollars to those who otherwise would not have been able to use their lands for banana cultivation. These loans have ranged from a few hundred dollars to loans of hundreds of thousands of dollars. Such loans have been made to residents of Guatemala, Costa Rica, Panama, Colombia, Jamaica, and have also been made to citizens of the United States, of Germany, Spain, and other countries.

It has been explained that the prevailing rates of interest in Central America, South America, Cuba, and most of tropical America range from a minimum of 12 per cent to 20 per cent and even higher. No bank in any of these countries could be induced to lend money on any terms to an individual on the prospect that he might convert a tract of jungle land into a banana plantation. It costs from $40 to $60 to bring such lands to banana bearing. Again, the owner of the land would be unable to satisfy a bank that he would have a purchaser for his bananas after they were ready to cut. He might find the money to bring banana trees to bearing, but he lacked the money to buy and operate ships. How has the United Fruit Company treated these tropical land owners?

It has encouraged American citizens and others to buy banana lands adjacent to its own plantations. It has encouraged native landowners to undertake the cultivation of bananas on as large a scale as their circumstances would permit. It has offered to lend, and has actually lent, millions of dollars to such native landowners. This money was not advanced by the United Fruit Company at 12, 20 or 25 per cent interest, which rates are eagerly paid by borrowers with good security in most parts of these sections, but at low and reasonable rates of interest.

Here is something worth considering by those who assume that all corporations are swift and eager to take extortionate advantage of opportunities.

Under this broad and liberal plan the United Fruit Company had deservedly won the loyalty and coöperation of thousands of planters who have shared in the prosperity which always accrues when men of energy deal fairly one with the other. This plan has been in frictionless opera-

Headquarters of United Fruit Company in Santa Marta

tion for years; it has enriched men who thus were permitted to take quick advantage of an opportunity to obtain access to a fertile soil, and it has also contributed to the success of the United Fruit Company by creating a corps of independents who are trained and skilled in their avocation, and who give to the banana industry that wider source of supply which insures added protection against the climatic disasters from which no single plantation has sure immunity.

More than that, these independent producers constitute a training school from which graduate the men who are called on to accept high positions in the broader fields of the activity of the great corporation which founded the banana industry.

On a slight elevation above the plain on which lies the city of Santa Marta rise the graceful masts of the wireless station installed and maintained by the United Fruit Company. These twin masts are 310 feet high, and the powerful plant with which they are equipped places Santa Marta in constant communication with New Orleans, all of Central America, and the wide ranges of the Caribbean and the Gulf of Mexico. All of the passenger ships of the United Fruit Company are provided with the most up-to-date wireless equipment, with the result that the great producing sections on the land are linked with the ships of the fleet which convey freight and passengers to and from the tropics.

A novel and very important feature of the wireless system developed and in operation on the ships of the United Fruit Company is that of an auxiliary power plant. This consists of storage batteries of sufficient power to take the place of the regular generating plant in the event of an accident. The storage batteries thus held in reserve are of power adequate not only to operate the transmitting and receiving wireless instruments, but also to furnish electric lighting for the ship during a period of from six to eight hours. This gives ample time to repair any ordinary defect in the system regularly employed, and gives absolute protection against a class of accidents likely to put a wireless equipment out of commission, and affords this protection at a time when the services of auxiliary power are most needed. The time will doubtless come when public sentiment or international law will force the general use of this plan of insurance for wireless efficiency, an expedient which has been successfully developed and installed by the United Fruit Company.

No private enterprise in the world has made such an impressive use of this wonderful invention. It is not generally known that the United Fruit Company was one of the pioneers not only in the use but in the development and perfection of wireless telegraphy. Experts in its employ have made valuable contributions to this almost uncanny science. The public and the world of finance and commerce have profited immeasurably from the installation of a system of communication which places most of the American tropics within instant communication. In the furtherance of this work the United Fruit Company has expended a very large amount of money, which has provided an asset of safety and progressive efficiency which is certain to yield benefits not to be calculated in dollars and cents.

Houses built of fibre of banana plants

Land wireless stations of high efficiency have been established at New Orleans, Cape San Antonio, Cuba; Swan Island, off the coast of Honduras; Cape Gracias á Dios, at the border line of Honduras and Nicaragua; Bluefields, Nicaragua; Puerto Limon, Costa Rica; Bocas del Toro, Panama; and Santa Marta, Colombia, with others planned for the near future.

From the powerful Santa Marta station messages have been received from along Cape Cod and even as far as the coast of Maine, and it is the expectation of the company that promising improvements will make communication possible with London and the Continental centres of banana consumption. Here is a typical illustration of the demands made by the humble banana on the capital which undertakes its production and distribution. The investment of the United Fruit Company in wireless telegraphy alone is probably more than that incurred by the Boston Fruit Company in the days when it was providing all of New England with the bulk of its banana supply.

The visit to Santa Marta ends our investigation of the great chain of banana enterprises conducted by the United Fruit Company. This chain links Guatemala, Honduras, Costa Rica, Panama, Colombia, and Jamaica, and speeding to and from its units are nearly a hundred ships which bear its products to most parts of North America and Europe. And over all this vast land domain of plantations rescued from the tropical wildernesses, and over seas and bays and harbors dotted with the ships which bear the flag of the United Fruit Company, dart the invisible currents which direct the movements of an industrial army of 60,000 men who are toiling in a successful attempt to help meet the fruit and food hunger of a world.

CHAPTER XIII

Exploring the Sugar Bowl of Cuba

ANTILLA is a new and growing Cuban town located at the head of Nipe Bay, which, fifteen miles away, opens into the Atlantic along the upper coast of the east end of that island. A spur of land, fairly narrow in most places, separates Nipe Bay from the smaller one of Banes, and back from the shores of these two protected bodies of navigable water is one of the great centres of sugar production of the world.

In the fourteen years since its organization the United Fruit Company has been instrumental in converting the once neglected wildernesses surrounding these bodies of water into sugar plantations which, in the fiscal year of 1912–13, produced 261,326,640 pounds of sugar and 5,600,025 gallons of molasses. This includes the output of the Nipe Bay Company, listed as one of the investments of the United Fruit Company. Possibly the average reader might be able better to comprehend the amount of this sugar production if expressed as 130,663 tons, and was informed that a ton is a fair wagonload for a team of horses.

In this, as in all of its undertakings, the company did not seek to make a success of the sugar business by buying established properties and deriving profits by economies and the skilled use of large capital, but it launched its enterprise in new fields and engaged in a struggle with the unsolved problems raised by a section in which sugar cane had never been planted except on a very small scale. I was fairly familiar with the sugar industry in Cuba twelve years ago when the United Fruit Company was constructing its great mill in the Banes district, and I remember well the comments of the recognized heads of the leading sugar concerns who laughed at the attempt to raise sugar cane along the east coasts of Cuba. According to these prophets, none of the requisites of soil, rainfall, labor, or any other requirement was at the command of the inexperienced fruit men who had dared engage in the sugar industry.

But the prophets were wrong. The region which the experts ignored and rejected has become one of the world's important sources of sugar supply, and has been made a steady and conservative field of revenue to the company which had the courage to undertake its development.

The Boston Fruit Company was the founder of the present prosperity of the Nipe and Banes districts. It originally acquired a section of land near the little Cuban town of Banes and devoted part of it to banana cultivation. A year or so prior to its purchase by the United Fruit Company the Boston Fruit Company decided to engage in sugar cultivation, experiments having proved that an excellent quality of cane could be raised in fields adjacent to its banana plantations. It thus came about that in the first year of the life of the United Fruit Company President Preston was able to report that the company had 7,803 acres of growing sugar cane in its Banes plantations and a mill rapidly approaching completion. This was in 1900.

At about this time the Dumois-Nipe Company was formed and began extensive operations at Saetia, a favored spot along the southeast shore of Nipe Bay, and fifteen miles or so from Banes. This company devoted its activities largely to fruit, and raised large quantities of bananas, oranges, grape-fruit, and other tropical products. The United Fruit Company was the largest purchaser of these fruits, and continued so until it decided to abandon banana cultivation and handling in Cuba, which was in 1906. From that year until 1912 the Dumois-Nipe Company disposed of its fruits to various concerns, but in that year it was decided that

In the great Cuban Sugar Mill, the "Central Preston"

sugar could be raised to greater advantage and to more profit, and the Saetia Sugar Company was formed, the United Fruit Company furnishing most of the capital and owning control of the stock.

The success of the United Fruit Company at Banes soon led to the formation of the Nipe Bay Company, a concern largely financed by investors who had learned to have faith in the judgment of the heads of the United Fruit Company, and this new company purchased a large tract of undeveloped land along the south coast of Nipe Bay and reaching almost

Loading sugar cane in Cuba

to the town of Antilla. It thus came about that three American enterprises were located in a sweeping semicircle about the waters of Nipe Bay and Banes Bay, with modern sugar mills at Banes and on the property of the Nipe Bay Company. The latter mill is known as the "Central Preston," and the pioneer mill near Banes as "Central Boston." Both of these great mills are fitted with every device and employ every scientific process necessary for the speedy and economical extraction of sugar from the raw cane.

Early in 1907 the United Fruit Company purchased a majority of the common stock of the Nipe Bay Company, and in that year the latter harvested and ground its first crop, which yielded 32,000,000 pounds of sugar and nearly 1,000,000 gallons of molasses. This company still maintains its corporate entity, but its operations are conducted by the United Fruit Company in coöperation with the other two great divisions in this locality. In 1913 the United Fruit

United Fruit Company park in Banes, Cuba

Company acquired by purchase the remaining outside stock of the Saetia Sugar Company, with its 35,000 acres of land near the Nipe Bay Company, more than 6,000 of which are already planted to cane.

The Banes, Nipe Bay, and Saetia districts contain a total acreage of 255,000, of which 58,000 acres are now planted to sugar cane. The Nipe Bay Company has about 25,000 acres of cane under cultivation, with additional tracts of 82,000 acres, much of which is available for cane. There are also 12,500 acres devoted to pastures, the feeding places of the thousands of oxen, mules, and other live stock required on a modern sugar plantation. The original, or Banes division, has a total acreage of 92,000, of which 28,000 acres are planted to cane and 20,000 acres used for pasture.

These three divisions of Banes, Nipe Bay, and Saetia are not contiguous plantations owned by the two companies which possess and operate the mills. Reaching out for miles in three directions from the Boston Central are fields of cane planted years ago by the Boston Fruit Company, but intersecting and interlacing these fields are others owned by individual producers, and still other fields which are untilled and are the property of outsiders who decline to sell or cultivate.

The detailed maps of the Banes and Nipe Bay divisions, with the various land holdings painted in colors, look like a puzzle picture. In the subdivision of Cuban lands there is not that uniformity and rectangular accuracy which distinguish our real estate holdings, especially in the Middle and Western States. The Cuban heir to land traces his inheritance by following winding creeks and along lines with startling angles. It thus comes about that there are hundreds of independent cane growers with their lands completely surrounded by the more comprehensive development of the American enterprises.

These independents sell their cane to the mills. This cane is ground and a careful record made of the amount of sugar extracted from it. The independent receives in pay the market value of 5 per cent of the sugar extracted from his cane. In other words, he becomes the owner of 100 pounds out of every ton of 2,000 pounds extracted, and the mill takes this 100 off his hands and pays him the quotation price of raw sugar on the day of the sale. This is the system in vogue in all Cuba, and is one which is fair to the independent producer and to the owner of the mill.

Under favorable conditions of crop and prices the independent will obtain from his cane an amount which will

SCENE IN "CENTRAL PRESTON" SUGAR MILL

The machines disclosed are "centrifugals," in which the sugar is extracted by high rotative speed

yield him a net profit as high as $100 an acre, and even this figure has been exceeded. Under the reverse conditions of poor crops and low prices — the latter due to bumper crops of beet sugar abroad — the independent sugar grower is compelled to share with the mill in actual losses for the year; but under average conditions the small sugar grower is fairly well assured of returns which will range from $30 to $60 an acre annually, which figure is considerably in excess of that obtainable from standard crops grown in the United States. However, the Cuban grower runs more risks, has less comfort, and not as congenial surroundings as his brother agriculturist in northern climes.

Leading out from the huge Central Boston — "Central" being the technical expression of a sugar mill which grinds the cane raised by all producers within reach of its capacity — are 110 miles of railway owned and operated by the company. Nineteen locomotives and more than 800 freight cars are employed in bringing the cane from plantations, some of them thirty miles away from the mill. Bear in mind that this impressive transportation equipment is used on the Banes division alone. It has no identity and not even connection with the railroad systems employed at Nipe Bay and Saetia. The transportation equipment which feeds the Central Preston of the Nipe Bay Company has about 70 miles of track and 387 freight cars. The Saetia division has a smaller railroad system which transports the cane from the fields to the docks at Entre Casco, where it is lifted by steam power to barges which are towed by tugs to the Central Boston, where it is ground. Three tugs and a fleet of lighters are employed in this work. The Saetia cane makes a water trip of about eight miles, but it is probable that the future development of that district will warrant the construction of a third mill.

Crossing the railroad lines at frequent and regular intervals are broad roads which serve the double purpose of permitting cane-loaded wagons to arrive at the railroad switches and also of checking the sweep of flames in the event that fires start in dry weather. These roads are called "guarda rayas," which translates as "protective spaces" or "fire lines." A considerable percentage of a plantation is occupied by these broad but necessary roads.

Reference to the map on this page will give the reader a clear idea of the geographical setting of the 255,000 acres included in this wonderful centre of sugar production. Those who are inclined to ignore or decry the part played by American capital in the development of adjacent tropical

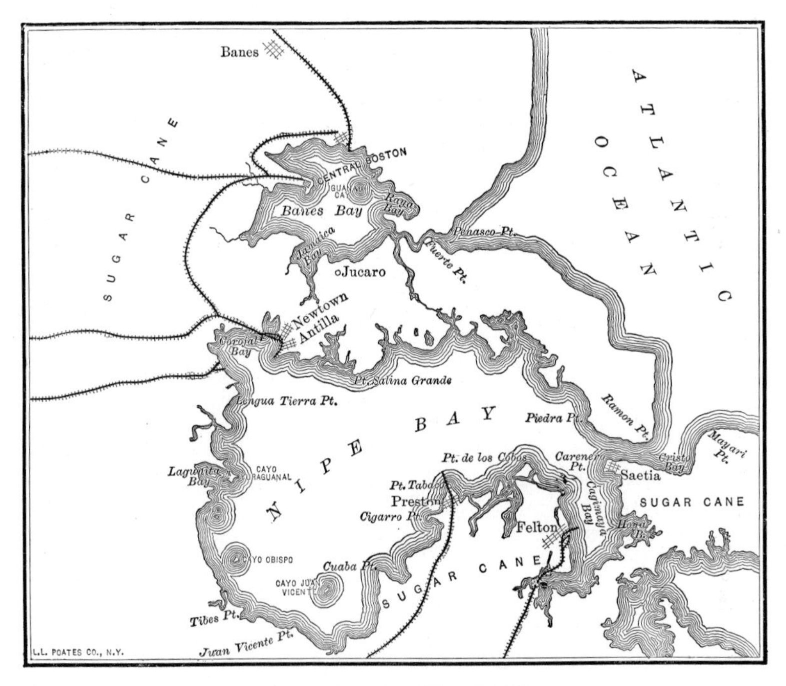

NIPE AND BANES BAYS

sections are now reminded that within the immediate scope of the operations of the United Fruit Company in the Nipe Bay country is a population of fully 25,000 people, all of whom are enjoying a measure of prosperity and a standard of living much higher than obtains in any manufacturing community in the United States or any in the world.

It is doubtful if any large body of unskilled labor anywhere on this wide earth of ours receives compensation equal to that awarded the men who work in the fields about these great Cuban sugar mills. When it is taken into consideration that the activities of these men bring from formerly unused soil a vast product which enters into general consumption in the United States, and cheapens the price of commodities imperatively required by all classes of our people, it is obvious that the rearing of this enterprise by the United Fruit Company means something far more important than an attempt to derive dividends.

When we have other private corporations, or public corporations, or any sort of a system of production, which will insure that all the food necessities of life compare with sugar at 4 to 5 cents a pound, and bananas at from 10 to 20 cents a dozen, there will be an end to the complaint of the high cost of living.

There is not the slightest chance that this happy condition of affairs will obtain until all possible food products are brought from the soil and transported from their sources of supply and distributed to the consumer under some such system as has been applied by the United Fruit Company. The eager advocates of Socialism claim that they could do it if they had a chance. Possibly they could, but the United Fruit Company has done it and is doing it, and it is a grand and a worthy thing to do. It is a splendid victory over Nature, the stern but fair giantess who enforces the decree that the soil of this earth shall yield its treasures only to those who battle with her, but who smilingly submits to the ardent and intelligent trespasser on her domains.

Twelve years ago there were squalid little native settlements at Banes, Antilla, and Saetia. There were a few cultivators of small cane plantations, and they extracted enough sugar for their own needs by primitive processes. You could search the average map of Cuba in vain and not locate Antilla, Preston, Banes, or Saetia. There were no docks worthy of the name at which steamships could load, and the surrounding country produced nothing of consequence to lure a ship into these beautiful waters. For a hundred years Cuba had been desolated by wars and revolutions, but the strong arm of the United States had reached out and the mandate had been given that anarchy should end and that industry would be protected. This was an awful blow to the professional revolutionists, but it meant prosperity for Cuba and cheaper food products to the United States.

No railroad then connected the Nipe Bay country with Havana or Santiago. Then another revolution broke out,

SCENE IN THE "CENTRAL PRESTON"
The powerful appliances by which a carload of sugar is lifted and conveyed to the crushers

but of a type new and startling to devastated Cuba. It was an industrial revolution, fomented and headed by American investors and officered by engineers, mechanics, and men skilled in agriculture. They cut a wall through the guinea grass and the jungles of central Cuba and connected the head of Nipe Bay by railroad with Havana and Santiago. They dredged a harbor beneath the bluffs of Antilla and projected docks out into the clear waters of Nipe Bay. They offered the ragged veterans of a score of uprisings and revolutions good wages to use the machete as a tool of agriculture instead of as a weapon of war and loot, and when the word went out that these crazy Americans were in earnest and kept their promises the Cuban natives and the negroes responded.

Square miles of fields, untouched since the island was heaved out of the sea, were reclaimed from swamps and jungles. An army of men raised the massive steel spans of the sugar mill. Ships from all parts of the world ploughed the waters of Nipe Bay and unloaded the materials necessary in the prosecution of this giant undertaking. The cleared fields were planted and bore a bounteous harvest of cane. The cane was cut and fed into the maws of the tearing and grinding crushers — fifteen hundred tons of cane a day yielded up its juice under the impact of this machinery.

The first three years showed a loss of about $60,000, and the prophets of disaster took great credit for their forecasts, but the company did not deviate in the slightest from its original plan to develop this section to sugar cane. In 1904 the tide turned, the Banes mill turning out a product which netted a profit of $345,000, and there has been no year since that time when Cuban sugar has not helped the United Fruit Company meet its dividend responsibilities.

To-day, all of this district is dotted with towns and villages which owe their inception and progress to the extension of the sugar industry. Antilla has a growing population of 4,500, and boasts of the best hotel in the east of Cuba. Saetia, out near the mouth of Nipe Bay, has a population in the busy season which mounts to 2,000 or more. Where a few years ago was nothing but waste land and fever-breeding jungles there has arisen, as if by magic, a flourishing and attractive little city — Preston — named for the man who was chiefly responsible for this magic. Preston is a beautiful town of 5,000 population, with broad streets lined with palms and flowers, electric lights, churches, public and private schools, and all of the comforts and luxuries of a town of equal size in the United States.

Macabi is the model little town which has been built up

GENERAL VIEW OF A SECTION OF PRESTON, CUBA

Only a few years ago this was an unbroken tropical wilderness. Now it is a part of one of the great sugar producing districts of the world, and one of the centres of activity founded by the United Fruit Company, and giving employment or livelihood to 25,000 persons. This picture was taken from the roof of the "Central Preston"

about the Central Boston. Banes is the metropolis of this section, and has progressed from a miserable little settlement to a city with a permanent population exceeding 7,500. I shall describe these larger centres of population more fully in the following chapter, which deals with the sanitary work of the United Fruit Company.

The process of manufacturing sugar and the systems of conveying the cane from the fields to the mills are so well known that I shall not enter into a description of them in this book, which is designed to present facts which are novel to the average reader. But the United Fruit Company is the pioneer in a system of sugar extraction and handling which is entirely new, and the probable success of which will completely revolutionize the entire industry. I refer to what is technically known as the "Simmons Process" of dealing with sugar after it has been cut and delivered to the "Central."

The great expense of manufacturing raw sugar is incurred by two acts in the present process, viz., the enormous power required to drive the rollers which crush the cane and extract the juice by rotative pressure, and, second, the large amount of fuel required to boil the water from the juice in order to precipitate sugar by high centrifugal motion.

The most powerful crushers yet devised still leave a considerable percentage of juice, and, consequently, sugar, in the mutilated fibre, which is called "bagasse."

Now comes a peculiar and interesting consideration. It has been known for many years that the fibre of sugar cane possesses the inherent qualifications for the manufacture of paper. Fine grades of white paper, some of them exquisite in texture, have been made from the fibre of sugar cane, but — and here is a monumental "but."

In the first place, the severe crushing of cane required to extract a high percentage of its juice destroys some of the qualities of the fibre which make it valuable in paper manufacture. The cells are broken down, and while the resultant pulp will produce a paper, it is one lacking in the tenacity and texture of a fibrous compound.

In the second place — and here is a stickler — Cuba is

A PART OF THE GREAT SUGAR MILL, THE "CENTRAL BOSTON"
This mill is in the Banes district, and was the first one erected by the United Fruit Company

deficient in coal, oil, wood, or other fuel usually employed in generating power or heat. The pioneers in the sugar industry discovered that it was possible to feed the bagasse into the furnaces, and it thus came about that the crushed body of one stalk of cane furnishes the fuel by which his brother is crushed and the juice boiled and the sugar extracted. Hence it makes no difference, under this system, whether the tissue and cells are destroyed or not. They are demanded as fuel.

But inventors and scientists have long looked askance at this process. They have denounced it as wasteful, uneconomical, crude, and improvable. I do not know who was the first to suggest and experiment on the "desiccation" and "defibrication" of sugar cane, but the first plan to yield practical results is known as the "Simmons System," and it has been given a comprehensive test at Preston, Cuba, under the direction of experts in the employ of the United Fruit Company. The first mill ever erected for this purpose was destroyed by fire in the summer of 1913, but not until it had demonstrated certain very important matters beyond doubt. It is obvious that water can be evaporated from such a substance as cane quicker than it can be removed from the juice by boiling. A temperature of 212 F. is about the maximum which can be obtained by boiling. Years ago the experiments were made of applying heated air at a higher temperature to shredded cane, but it was learned that temperatures between 200 and 400 destroyed the sugar. It was deemed folly to experiment with higher temperatures, it being natural to assume that if 200 or 400 degrees of heat would burn the sugar crystals a higher temperature would precipitate that disaster more quickly and surely.

It remained, however, for the experimenters to make the rather remarkable discovery that the sugar crystals were immune to a sudden plunging into a temperature of from 1,600 to 1,800 degrees of heat. The sugar seemed to like it, but the water hurriedly quit its company in the form of steam. I don't know why this is so, but it is a stubborn fact. I have never been able to explain why fog does not freeze into small and hollow hailstones when the mercury drops below zero, but it

Scene in Preston, Cuba, with the "Central Preston" in background

floats in air and seemingly is as warm and comfortable as if it were a balmy summer day. The scientists tell us that this is because the fog globules are filled with "latent heat," but when you ask them to explain why the zero temperature cannot disturb this latent heat they have no reply. And the sugar crystal that shrivels in a heat of 250 and is cozy and contented at 1,800 is no more of a mystery than a thousand other things which we fool mortals pretend to explain, but don't.

When this was discovered the rest was comparatively easy.

Tennis courts in Banes, Cuba

Instead of crushing the cane it is shredded in this process. The cane is fed into revolving knives which cut and tear it, but which do not crush and lacerate the cellular tissue. The cane and such juice as has escaped are conveyed to a series of drying chambers. The initial chamber has a temperature of about 1,800 degrees. In the successive chambers through which the shredded cane passes the temperature is gradually reduced to 200, and the plunge into the first chamber renders the sugar immune to lower ones which otherwise would have been destructive of its good qualities.

All save an insignificant percentage of the water is exhausted in this process, and this important result is attained with an expenditure of only a fraction of the heat units employed in the present method of extracting sugar by boiling.

When this combination of shredded fibre and dried sugar emerges from the last heated chamber it is conducted down a vertical flume about 18 inches square. At the lower end of this flume it is subject to pressure and baled in a manner very similar to that used in compressing hay. A cubic foot of this baled and desiccated cane weighs about 50 pounds, making the weight of the bales approximately 150 pounds.

Under the present process a mill which will extract 90 per cent of the sugar and syrups is deemed a model of efficiency. By a simple method of treating this desiccated cane it is possible to extract 92½ per cent of sugar and 6 per cent of syrups, a total of 98½ per cent extraction, which closely approaches the sugar producer's dream of perfection.

But this saving in sugar and syrup is not the most important factor. In the first place, the plant required for the desiccation of cane will cost much less than the one now required to handle a given amount of cane, and the power required is slight compared with that now necessary to operate the stupendous machinery of crushing the cane, boiling the juice, and actuating the centrifugals. In the second place, there is saved a fibre which can be manufactured into grades of high-class white paper, and the inventors of this system confidently claim that *the rescued fibre is worth more than the sugar.* They even go so far as to assert that sugar will become a by-product of sugar cane, and that the latter will be raised for the principal purpose of supplying the world with all grades of paper.

This also implies that the rapid depletion of forests for the manufacture of paper pulp would cease. Here is one of the problems which has dismayed and appalled the earnest advocates of forest conservation. If the experiments just described, and others now being conducted on a large scale by the United Fruit Company, shall demonstrate that the cane fibre which now is burned for fuel is capable of meeting a large portion of the paper demand of the world, the outcome will be a blessing not to be measured in the dollars which may accrue to those who have stood the risks and costs of this quest.

The view from the deck of a steamship traversing Nipe Bay is of surpassing interest to one who is familiar with the history of this beautiful part of Cuba. It was my privilege to sail these waters nearly twenty years ago. At that time there was hardly a sign of life or industry along these shores. Where the modern and progressive town of Preston now stands our party camped one night not far from where the

Type of residence in Preston, Cuba

huge sugar mill now shakes the very earth with the shock of its machinery. In every direction were the swamps and jungles, a seemingly worthless wilderness and one reserved for all time for those like us who were on an adventurous hunting and fishing jaunt.

To-day one looks out from the deck of a ship and sees to the south an unbroken line of deep and velvety green, darker in spots where the cloud shadows drift from fleecy sky-ships overhead. This ocean of growing sugar cane extends east and west as far as the eye can reach. Its vast carpet of verdure undulates back into the lower foothills of a range of purple mountains — the mountains within whose depths were discovered the greatest iron ore deposits which ever rewarded the search of American prospectors, and which have a verified capacity capable of supplying the world with iron and steel for one hundred years!

As we sail out past Saetia, with its white houses almost lapped by the swell which heaves in from the Atlantic, we take one parting glimpse of Loma Cristal — the mother peak which overlooks these valleys and Santiago as well — and the jutting hills gradually draw their curtains of tropical verdure across the distant carpets of cane; we pass a steamer hurrying in to collect the day's sweet output of Central Preston, we exchange salutes, our prow rises to meet the thrust of a roller which has circled a hundred miles through the Bahamas, and we pass the lighthouse and set a course for climes where trees are laden with snow and not with orchids flaming from a lacework of Spanish moss.

CHAPTER XIV

HEALTH CONQUEST OF THE TROPICS

THE first record of a great sanitary triumph which has been handed down by legend makes the mighty Hercules the hero. One of the labors imposed on him was to clean the stables of Augeas, King of Elias, which feat the mythological hero of the ancient Greeks easily accomplished in a day by changing the course of a river to flow through the stalls which had been occupied for years by 3,000 oxen. This was the only practical and sensible task ever set for this capable giant, and it has always seemed to me that Hercules should be made the conventional deity of all who are engaged in making this earth clean and sanitary. It is and ever has been a Herculean task.

It is generally believed and understood that not until the United States Government assumed full charge and responsibility for the construction of the Panama Canal were the problems of tropical sanitation attacked and mastered. Without desiring to detract in any way from the merit which is due Col. W. C. Gorgas and his staff and army of sanitary workers, it must be recognized that the United Fruit Company and the companies which preceded it in Costa Rica, Colombia, Cuba, and elsewhere antedated the Panama Canal Commission in successfully combating tropical disease on a large scale.

The mere establishment of the fact that these American concerns were able to conduct large operations and to find armies of men ready to continue working on these plantations is ample proof of this assertion. If ten men, a hundred men, or ten thousand men undertake to-day to clear and cultivate any of the coastal lowlands of Central and tropical South America, and in doing so use only the precautions which would be observed in clearing an equal tract in any part of the United States, most of them will be dead in a very few years and the others will be incapacitated for mental or physical work.

The head of the Tulane School of Tropical Medicine of New Orleans has this to say on the same point:

"The magic touch of tropical sanitation introduced by the United Fruit Company has transformed this deadly climate into a habitable zone. The vast improvements there do the genius of American medical men a credit that only future ages will appreciate. Every one knows what great sanitary work the American Government has accomplished on the Canal Zone, but few realize that a similar improvement has been worked in the rich fruit centres of every country to the south of us, and that the United Fruit Company is entitled to the credit for this great achievement."

The United States did not take over the Panama Canal and establish and begin the work of the sanitation of its Zone until 1903. In 1900, three years prior to this event, the United Fruit Company had an industrial army of more than 15,000 men at work on cultivated tracts covering more than 60,000 acres of normally disease-breeding coastal lands in Costa Rica, Cuba, Honduras, Jamaica, San Domingo, and Colombia. Had there been any high degree of mortality in this army of men, there would have gone up a cry of indignation from all of the civilized world against a corporation which was willing to sacrifice lives in order to derive profits from bananas and other tropical fruits. But no such cry went up, and the plain and sufficient reason was that the United Fruit Company had already mastered and applied the basic principles of the system which later made possible the completion of the Panama Canal without awful sacrifice of life.

When Colonel Gorgas began his work of cleaning up the Canal Zone, in 1904, the United Fruit Company owned or leased 324,889 acres of tropical lands and had nearly 20,000 men on its pay-rolls. The company thus had a total acreage

Conditions before United Fruit Company began its sanitary work in Guatemala

of 500 square miles, over all of which it exercised sanitary precautions, and this 500 square miles was *in excess of the area included in the Panama Canal Zone.*

But Colonel Gorgas and his assistants had to meet a

problem not so much in evidence with the United Fruit Company. Colon and Panama City were old and established cities with fixed prejudices against the *Americano* with his strange nonsense about mosquitoes and open sewage. Their inhabitants had been bitten so many years by disappointed *stegomyia* and *anophelinæ* that they were fairly immune from yellow fever and malaria, and they resented all attempts to eradicate the pests responsible for these and other diseases. True, the United Fruit Company was handicapped by contact with such unsanitary towns as Santa Marta, Bocas del Toro, Banes, and a few smaller towns, and it had the more severe handicap that it did not possess the legal authority vested in the Canal Commission enabling it to enforce sanitation, but as a rule the towns grew with the growth of this great private enterprise, and the heads of the company had the foresight to install and execute health protective methods.

Deadly as was the Canal Zone when the French conducted their ill-fated attempt to connect the two oceans, Costa Rica was worse when Minor C. Keith dared its jungles and was helpless to prevent the death of 4,000 men in the construction of the first twenty-five miles of his railroad. He was young then, but the bitter experience which cost the lives of three of his brothers taught the grim lesson that more than mere courage and physical stamina were required in the conquest of the tropics.

The natives of these countries were practically immune from diseases contracted by and often fatal to outsiders, but the natives would not work on plantations, and most of them still have an unconquerable aversion to sustained physical toil. The reason is not far to seek. The mosquitoes, the hookworm, and other insects and parasites fond of human flesh have so inoculated them with their virus that they have neither the ambition nor the strength to compete with workers not thus afflicted. It is entirely possible that a generation of Central American natives of the laboring class might, if forced or persuaded to conform to modern sanitary science, surprise the world by displaying none of the laziness inherent in those who now inhabit mosquito-ridden sections.

But the laziness and physical inability of these natives compelled Mr. Preston and Mr. Keith and their assistants to seek for labor in other lands, and the Jamaica negro responded. He was not immune from Central American pests or from the miasmal emanations from undrained swamps and fetid lagoons and jungles. His life had to be protected and his energy conserved, and the men who employed these negroes were faced with the responsibility of doing this.

It was impossible to call on American experts on tropical sanitation, for the good and more than sufficient reason that there was none. We knew nothing about the tropics at our gates, commercially, medically, or otherwise. The cultured people of Central America knew nothing about the sanitary problems of their lowlands, for the good and ample reason that they did not deem them a fit place in which to live, and they kept as far away from them as possible. Mr. Preston and Mr. Keith had no expert medical knowledge on the tropics, but both knew that the Asiatic tropics had the general characteristics of the ignored American tropics.

Scientists and physicians with experience in Java, India, the tropical sections of Africa, and elsewhere responded to the call to assist American enterprise in this pioneer industrial invasion of the tropics. It was this paucity of our knowledge concerning tropical diseases which impelled the United Fruit Company to suggest and later to give substantial financial assistance to the founding of a department in Tulane University for the exclusive study and investigation of maladies peculiar to the coastal regions of the Caribbean, and much of the advancement since accomplished has been due to the discoveries made and the remedies applied by those sent out by this university.

Almost from the very beginning the development of these great fruit plantations was carried forward under health conditions far superior to those which the Jamaican negroes had left in their native island. In the selection of sites for new towns and settlements careful attention was given to the requirements of drainage. All adjacent swamps were cleared, and the grass and underbrush kept cut about the

One of the smaller hospitals of the United Fruit Company

houses. The laborers were verbally instructed how to take precautions against the known dangers of these districts, and the medical employees of the company made regular inspections of their places of living and enforced strictly the basic regulations of sanitation. Hospitals were erected and prompt measures taken to isolate any victim of contagious disease. Strict quarantine was enforced against unsafe foreign ports, the various governments coöperating with the fruit companies in this important detail.

In the former swamps and jungles of Costa Rica, Mr. Keith was conducting extensive banana cultivations during most of the years when the French were attempting to build the Panama Canal. With an average working force of 10,200 men the French lost 22,189 in the nine years inclusive of 1881–1889, with an annual death-rate which, according to Colonel Gorgas, reached the astounding figure of 240 a year out of each 1,000, or nearly one death a year to each four employed in this region of terror.

Nothing of this kind took place in the banana plantations of Costa Rica. While the health conditions did not begin to compare with those of to-day, they were fully as good as those which prevailed in Jamaica and other established centres of tropical population. There was more or less malaria, but no epidemics of yellow fever, cholera, small-pox, and other contagious diseases were permitted to obtain a foothold and decimate the workers on the banana plantations. Fairly accurate statistics indicate that the death-rate in these banana communities was less than 50, or about one fifth of that which cursed and disgraced the Panama Canal region.

As a matter of fact, the death-rate in the banana producing sections of Costa Rica, Cuba, San Domingo, and other districts operated by Mr. Keith and the Boston Fruit Company was decidedly less than that which existed in Havana, Santiago, and Vera Cruz, the three larger cities in the American tropics. And this worthy result was attained prior to the organization of the United Fruit Company, but the credit belongs to Mr. Preston, Mr. Keith, and others who laid the broad foundations for the present corporate leader in the banana industry.

United Fruit Company hospital buildings at Puerto Limon, Costa Rica

It was in 1898 that medical science positively established the fact that yellow fever is transmitted by the bite of the *stegomyia* mosquito. It was already a generally accepted fact that the *anophelinæ* mosquito was the pest responsible for the spread of malaria, and the medical heads of the banana companies mentioned were prompt to take systematic advantage of these important discoveries. The efficiency of the use of petroleum as a thin covering of stagnant water was proved at about the same time.

The United Fruit Company was organized in 1899, or just about the time that experiments and study had solved the deeper mysteries surrounding the deadly character of tropical lowlands. This company had a more direct interest in availing itself of these discoveries than any other private enterprise. The United States Government was deeply concerned in the eradication of yellow fever in Havana and other parts of Cuba, for the reason that New Orleans, Mobile, and other Gulf ports were menaced by the contagion which came from commercial contact, but our Government was not then much interested in the health of the Isthmus of Panama.

The sanitary work and the experiments conducted by the pioneer banana companies in Costa Rica and elsewhere in the years between 1873 and 1899 were invaluable in aiding those medical scientists who were finally able to announce to the world that the mysteries of yellow fever and malaria had been solved.

On the organization of the United Fruit Company prompt steps were taken to enlarge the scope and efficiency of its medical department. In every section of its activities relentless war was declared on the mosquito. The use of copper wire gauze had already been made, but one of the first steps was to insure that all houses used by employees not immune to mosquito bites should be screened, and, in some cases, double screened. Petroleum was used unsparingly in stagnant pools and slow-running streams. Large sums were expended in drainage and in all of the proved expedients for eliminating tropical menaces to health.

It was not until March 1, 1904, that Colonel Gorgas was

called to the Isthmus, after having completed his wonderful work of redeeming Havana as a plague spot. The United Fruit Company had then been applying for fully four years the sanitary methods developed in Cuba by Colonel Gorgas and others. But the problems of Havana were far different from those presented by the jungles of Costa Rica and Panama, and the records undisputably show that the United Fruit Company was the first to apply to the Central American coast lands important features of the system later perfected by Colonel Gorgas along the Canal Zone. Proper credit has not been awarded to this progressive private corporation for its pioneer work in tropical sanitation. The fact that it has not asked for it is no reason why it should be withheld.

From the time that Colonel Gorgas began his crusade in Panama there has been hearty coöperation between the medical staff of the United States Government and that directed by the United Fruit Company. The members of the latter have been in a position to take immediate advantage of all details of proved efficiency in producing the desired health results.

During all the years of rigid quarantine maintained by the United States in favor of the Isthmus against tropical ports, it has rarely happened that such restrictions have been enforced against the Central American harbors from which sail the ships of the United Fruit Company.

GUATEMALA

Beginning with Guatemala on the north, I will briefly sketch the nature and progress of the work conducted by the medical department of the United Fruit Company.

There are three classes of laborers in the Guatemala Division: the West Indian negro, the Carib, and the Central American natives. The Carib Indians are the best workers. They are strong and well-nourished men, keep excellent health, and are cleanly in their habits. These exceptional Indians rarely appear in hospitals except as the result of accidents.

The West Indian negroes are mainly from Jamaica, and

most of them readily conform to sanitary regulations, with resultant good health. The native laborers are poorly nourished and have very little disease-resisting power. They drink large quantities of vile native rum and are quarrelsome and vicious under its influence. They are dirty in their habits and fall an easy prey to malaria. Much progress, however, has been made with this class, and the coöperation of the Government in suppressing the sale of alcoholic liquors would be a blessing.

Guatemala is a comparatively new division and has had the benefit of what has been learned from others. The camps for laborers, the houses for the white employees and officials, and all of the structures erected have carefully been constructed with the safeguarding of health in view. The miserable native shacks in Puerto Barrios and elsewhere have been done away with. In their places have been built neat wooden houses raised from the ground and set on concrete pillars to a height of from five to six feet.

All low-lying, pest-breeding places about Puerto Barrios have been filled in or flushed with salt water, and all danger spots above high tide have been drained. The camps out on the plantations have been located on high ground, and every effort has been made to insure perfect drainage. All grass and other vegetation is kept low for 150 yards about these camps, and no garbage, bottles, tin cans, etc., are permitted about the houses. The water supply throughout the district is rain water, which flows from the zinc roofs of the houses into tanks which are thoroughly screened and mosquito-proof. All surface water is oiled at stated periods.

In order to make Puerto Barrios not only perfectly sanitary, but attractive as well, the company has under way extensive improvements. Puerto Barrios is a native town of about 3,000 population, and is the only Central American port in which the company is interested that is not properly safeguarded. It is proposed to pump sand in from the sea and raise the level of the town eight or ten feet. A new hotel and office building will follow, and it is expected that the Government of Guatemala will coöperate in redeeming the town.

Quirigua Hospital in process of erection

The medical headquarters of this district are at Quirigua, whose picturesque ruins have been described. Here are administrative offices, railroad yards, machine shops, electric light and ice plants, all grouped in a busy hive of American efficiency.

On a hill to the north of the railroad stands the recently completed hospital, a splendid monument to the care and foresight of those who have accepted the task of stamping out tropical diseases. This steel and concrete structure has been erected and equipped at a cost exceeding $100,000, and is the finest institution of its kind between New Orleans and the progressive capitals of South America. As a purely tropical hospital it is to be doubted if its equal exists in the world, and it is interesting to reflect that it was projected and executed by private capital and is a part of a great private enterprise.

This structure is 340 feet long and has two connecting wings. It has standard accommodations for 150 patients, with reserve for fully 100 more. There is an administrative building, with quarters on its upper floors for a staff of doctors. There are public and private wards, laboratories, convalescent quarters, bathrooms of various kinds, and all of the conveniences which modern medical science can suggest. A large single building is devoted entirely to surgery. There is also a separate service building containing a modern kitchen, bakery, cold storage plant, laundry, and other accessories.

The whole structure is designed as a unit, and all of its parts are connected by screened corridors, so that attendants may pass from one building to another without possibility of permitting the ingress of mosquitoes and other insects. Powerful elevators are provided, and the heat, light, and power all are generated from a central plant.

Here is the capitol of a medical empire which reaches out more than sixty miles, and has as its subjects 6,000 employees and an extra population exceeding 10,000 people dependent on the skill and vigilance of its executives. At night its electric lights illumine a district which only a few years ago was deserted and dark save for the glow of fireflies and the phosphorescence of fallen and rotting trees.

UNITED FRUIT COMPANY HOSPITAL IN QUIRIGUA

This magnificent hospital, erected and fitted at an expense exceeding $100,000, stands in what was an uninhabited wilderness only a few years ago. Not far away are the famous ruins of Quirigua, whose rise and fall are shrouded in mystery

Dispensaries and sick-camps are scattered throughout the district. This field work is an important part of the medical service in all of the divisions in which the United Fruit Company operates, and a description of the one in Guatemala will serve for Costa Rica and all others.

The Guatemala Division is portioned into conveniently worked districts, and a dispenser is stationed in each. All of these dispensers are pharmacists and are well qualified to treat minor surgical and simple medical cases, and are able to determine when a laborer is so ill as to require hospital attention. Each camp is visited by a dispenser at least every other day, and at times he makes daily calls and a house-to-house inspection. All cases of dysentery are immediately sent to the hospital. The medical superintendent and his assistant make frequent trips to all of the dispensaries and inspect the camps at short intervals.

This system of camp patrol is effective in insuring that sick laborers receive prompt treatment, whether they call for it or not. Before the company assumed responsibility for their medical care the average native would not go to a hospital voluntarily until in the last stages of some dangerous malady.

The efficacy of the medical supervision of the Guatemala banana districts is eloquently shown by results, which indicate that out of the 1,634 hospital cases during 1913 only 42 died, a remarkably low rate of 2.57 per cent. The dispensary and sick-camp services treated 14,745 cases.

Not a case of quarantinable disease appeared in Puerto Barrios or in any port in which the United Fruit Company operated during 1913, nor did any case appear on any one of the ninety or more ships which sale under its flag.

This happy result was attained despite the fact that plague entered western Cuba, Porto Rico, Venezuela, Ecuador, and even the Canal Zone. There were outbreaks of yellow fever in the Canal Zone, Venezuela, and Trinidad, and Mexico was infected with small-pox and other highly contagious diseases, but the medical department of the United Fruit Company ended the year with a clean record. This was not an exceptional feat. It has been duplicated in other years, and here is the absolute proof that it is thoroughly practical to accomplish the complete eradication of such diseases on both sides of the Canal Zone.

SPANISH HONDURAS

It was not until 1913 that the United Fruit Company began the planting of bananas on a large scale in Honduras. This country has been a large producer of this fruit for years, but most of it is grown by the natives, the various importing companies bidding for this product.

When the United Fruit Company decided to make the attempt to become a banana producer in Honduras it acquired a tract of land bounded by the Colorado River to the east and the Ullola River to the west, and extending back into the foothills of the Montanas de Poco (the Little Mountains). This tract lies between Puerto Cortez and Ceiba, the present shipping points of the 8,000,000 or more bunches of bananas exported annually. The port of the new district is Tela (pronounced as if it were "Tailer"), a town of 2,000 inhabitants. The coast area also includes Colorado village, a town at the mouth of the river of that name.

Tela has a fine location both from a commercial and sanitary consideration. There is deep water and good harbor possibilities. The town lies well above the Caribbean, has natural drainage and an easily available water supply. It is open to the direct winds which ever sweep in from the sea, and has many other advantages as administrative and medical headquarters. The Tela River divides the town into two parts. The Government of Honduras has granted the company certain exclusive rights on the west side of the river, and here are its railroad yards, shops, office structures, hospital, and other buildings.

Here was a chance to illustrate on a large scale what modern scientific sanitation can accomplish in what is practically a virgin tropical wilderness. The location of these plantations is in what even the most hardened natives have denounced as a pest-hole and an impossible agricultural proposition. There are prosperous banana holdings to the

HOSPITAL AT SANTA MARTA, COLOMBIA, WITH A DUPLICATE AT TELA, HONDURAS

Model hospitals of this type are now nearing completion, each with accommodation for 100 patients. The facilities of these modern tropical institutions will equal those of Quirigua and Puerto Limon

east and west of it, but these growers would not accept this land as a gift. What has happened?

In a period of less than a year the planting of 50,000 acres of bananas is well under way, the building of 250 miles of railroad is being rapidly pushed, temporary piers have been constructed, and the office and other structures completed — and the health of the thousands of men employed is as good as that of the average farming community in the United States. Not only has the health of these employees been preserved, but that of the surrounding community as well. How was this miracle accomplished?

The medical staff were sent out ahead and placed on the firing line. They pushed into the wilderness with forts of mosquito-proof houses. They tested the soils and the water, and applied remedies whose worth had been proved by years of experience. It was not necessary to create a new corps of medical experts, doctors, dispensers, and nurses. These were drafted from the older divisions, and there descended on the swamps and jungles of Spanish Honduras a battalion of veterans before whom the mosquito and his breed of diseases had no more chance than had the breath of the Arctic frozen these coasts.

This is how the tropics are being conquered. This is War, and it is Magnificent! It has all the dash, the brilliancy, the courage, the organization, the discipline, the generalship and the strategy of war, and it has its heroes, dead and living. And it is a fight to create and not to destroy. Man will not have accomplished his mission on earth so long as a pestilential swamp remains to menace his fellows, and those who work to transform swamps and jungles into food-producing gardens have not lived in vain.

COSTA RICA

This is the oldest and largest of all of the great divisions operated by the company, and sanitary improvement has kept pace with agricultural and mechanical progress. The Republic of Costa Rica long since relieved the company of responsibility for the health of Puerto Limon, but the government does not extend its work to the outlying plantations.

It therefore devolves on the United Fruit Company to give sanitary attention to a population of about 11,500, of whom 5,200 are on its pay-rolls. This is the size of a populous town in the United States, but it must be considered that these plantation workers are scattered over tracts containing nearly 250,000 acres, or 390 square miles, and this is more than the combined municipal areas of Chicago, Philadelphia, Boston, and Omaha.

The company has constructed and maintains a chain of hospitals, dispensaries, and sick-camps extending from Puerto Limon to San José, and the work of the medical department has resulted in health conditions which would be considered normal in most parts of the United States. The hospital in Puerto Limon is second only to the newly completed one in Quirigua, and it has the marked advantage of a site on the seashore. The records handed down by the pirate Morgan and his men prove that the place where the hospital now stands was one of their favorite haunts. The grounds are guarded from the sea by a massive wall which swings in a deep crescent from the hospital to the gem of a park on the water front of the town. Parallel rows of graceful and nodding cocoa palms follow for miles the indentations of the coast. In the ocean foreground are islands which rise sheer out of the water, their precipices meeting the unceasing brunt of the swell, and their crests bedizened with tropical foliage. A more ideal and poetic location for a hospital could not be imagined.

The Puerto Limon hospital has accommodations for 175 patients, and its service and comforts are not excelled by any in the tropics. The company generously accepts many charity patients from Puerto Limon and thus renders effective coöperation with the local health authorities.

There is nothing pretentious about the scores of camps where the workers live, but they are clean, neat, and sanitary. All of the houses are raised from the ground and rest on concrete pillars. The average Central American native lives in bamboo huts with dirt floors which become areas of mud in the many severe storms. Well-constructed wooden houses have taken the place of these, and each

Hospital grounds in Puerta Limon, Costa Rica

family has a garden plot which they are encouraged to cultivate. A nominal rent is charged for these houses, and the sole restriction imposed on these thousands of tenants is that they are compelled to obey the orders of the medical inspectors who make regular and frequent visits.

In what sort of camps do our home American workmen live? Did the reader ever make a visit to a railroad construction camp and investigate its "sanitary" provisions? Despite the fact that all of the natural conditions usually are favorable to health, it is the rule that such camps are constructed and maintained as pest-holes, and that naturally strong men sicken and die because the contractors have not the decency or intelligence to safeguard the health and strength of the men on their pay-rolls. And the local or state health authorities usually do nothing to compel obedience to the laws of health or of humanity.

The laboring camps in our lumbering districts have been a menace and a disgrace for years, and this scandal has grown to such proportions that congressional action is demanded. Here are thousands of men working in the cold, bracing, and healthful air of pine forests, yet the disregard of the simple precautions against disease is so flagrant that hundreds die annually without forcing their employers to take steps to obliterate the criminal conditions responsible for this loss of life.

Contrast this sad condition of affairs in the United States and under its laws with what has been accomplished by an American corporation voluntarily in the tropics. The United Fruit Company has proved its solicitude for the lives and the health of the negroes and Indians who work for them in lands far removed from the jurisdiction of the laws of the United States. There are too many individuals and corporations in the United States that seem to care little whether their American workmen live amid sanitary conditions or not. The negro worker on a Costa Rican banana plantation would be appalled if forced to endure the squalor of a railroad or lumber camp of the average type in these United States.

Dr. G. C. Chandler, a well-known health authority of

Louisiana, made this public statement after a recent visit to the tropics:

"The United Fruit Company realizes that its employees are producers of wealth, and that good health is necessary to enable them to work to the best advantage. Acting on this broad view, the company spends hundreds of thousands of dollars annually to preserve the health of its employees. Everything is done in a business way. A record is kept of every square yard of weeds cut, of ponds filled or oiled, garbage removed, and cases of illness, as well a record of deaths and their causes.

"In the Bocas del Toro division there are 300 whites and 5,700 negroes employed, and the death-rate is 7.5 per cent per thousand. A novel and effective method for the advancement of sanitation used by the United Fruit Company is to build churches and furnish preachers for the negro laborers, with the understanding that they are to preach health and sanitation as well as salvation.

"The marvels accomplished in this tropical section in the way of good health make it a crime for a city or community not to be sanitary, and the cost for sanitary conveniences is so small that no excuse should be accepted. It should be the first detail looked after, for it means so much to every man, woman, and child."

The illustration which appears on the following page, and others contained in these chapters, give a hint of the beauty and tropical comfort of the residences owned or leased by the field officials and other white employees of the company. But no photograph can give an impress of the charm of color and of light and shadow which delights the visitor to these parks cut out from a forest of banana trees. The winding walks lead between masses of flowers and brilliantly colored foliage plants which would make the fortune of a New York florist. Royal palms send their smooth trunks up to the bronze-green stem from which bursts a glorious spray of drooping fronds. I have never quite forgiven Mark Twain for his humorous description of a palm when he wrote that

A branch headquarters in Panama

it was "Nature's imitation of an umbrella that has been out to see what a cyclone is like, and is trying not to look disappointed." This may be a just description of a dusty and bedraggled India palm, but it is a gross libel on the magnificent trees of which one never tires in our American tropics.

The houses in these parks could well be copied by those who believe that one should live as much as possible in the open air. Some of them are completely surrounded by broad porches carefully screened in copper wire gauze. Connecting with these screened porches are wide halls which meet in the centre, thus cutting the floor space into four parts and insuring a constant flow of pure air to the four sides of all of these sections. These halls form the reception- and living-rooms, and meals are served at the juncture of the broad and intersecting halls, the guests looking out in all directions on vistas of tropical perfection. Sleeping apartments are provided with other screens, thus affording protection against the insect which may have come in through an opened door. This system of double screening has fully proved its health efficiency.

Residences built on this and other attractive models are to be found by the hundreds in all of the countries in which the United Fruit Company operates. They are a pleasing combination of tropical architecture and sanitary perfection, and would serve as well for summer use in the United States as they do all of the year in Costa Rica and other southern latitudes.

REPUBLIC OF PANAMA

The banana-growing districts adjacent to Bocas del Toro and Almirante, in the Republic of Panama, offered to the United Fruit Company the most difficult and stubborn of its sanitary problems, but it has won a triumph which is the more satisfactory because of the seemingly insurmountable handicaps interposed.

It was not until 1903 that the company began the active work of clearing a large tract of land for banana cultivation. Prior to this various planters had developed banana properties along the shores of the Chiriqui Lagoon and else-

BOSCAS DEL TORO BEFORE SANITATION
See opposite page for illustration showing what the United Fruit Company has accomplished in this former pest-hole

Bocas del Toro after being reclaimed by sanitation

where. These planters knew little and seemed to care little about sanitary precautions, and the result was a death-rate which must have mounted to 10 per cent or more annually, or 100 out of 1,000, instead of the fraction of this which is now obtained.

The United Fruit Company did not then possess a large and fully trained and equipped medical corps, and it could not apply the precautionary measures on the start, as has recently been done in the case of opening Spanish Honduras up to banana cultivation on a large scale. The vital importance of sanitation as a preliminary to attacking a tropical wilderness was not then fully realized, and the field men and their workers plunged in first, and the medical department followed the best it could. As a result, the deadly swamps and jungles demanded and obtained their toll, and in the grim list of those who fell were many young Americans who were careless in the face of unseen but relentless foes.

Then all the energy and strategy of medical science were waged against these menaces to health and life. Screened houses took the place of tents and huts. Rigid sanitary rules were established and sternly enforced. Hospitals and dispensaries were erected and manned with capable physicians. A systematic campaign was conducted against the mosquito, and the result of this and other steps was a rapid drop in the sick and death-rate to one approximately normal.

In this initial and disastrous attack against the Panama wilderness the invaders were smitten with yellow fever, acute forms of malaria, and all the deadly tropical diseases. There has not been a case of yellow fever in this district for six years. When the work of sanitation was begun not less than 80 per cent of the men were on the sick roll some time during the year. This has now fallen to normal.

The native town of Bocas del Toro required drastic treatment. It lay on low and frequently flooded land, with many of the huts on rotting posts, and the sanitary conditions wretched beyond description. It was decided to raise the level of the town several feet, and this was accomplished by pumping sand in from the bay, the same method which was employed in Galveston after a hurricane had driven the sea over the low beaches. From an ugly pest-hole, Bocas del Toro was transformed to one of the most healthful and attractive of tropical cities.

The present centre of activity is Almirante, a town and

HOW BOCAS DEL TORO WAS RECLAIMED
Sand was pumped in by the same process used in Galveston after its hurricane

harbor at the head of the bay of that name. This also is on low land, and the company at great expense has constructed a sea wall and raised the land level by the sand-pumping process. A fine new hospital will be erected here to take the place of the beautifully situated but inadequate one on Nances Cay Island, which was described in a preceding chapter. The Republic of Panama supervises the sanitation of Bocas del Toro and Almirante, but most of the expense is assumed by the company. About 6,500 employees receive medical attention and are conforming to the rules of sanitation in force here and in all other divisions, and the total population dependent on the company for medical service is about 11,500, or nearly that of Costa Rica.

It has been possible to educate the laborer to know that his condition is vastly improved by obeying the rules intended to protect his health. He now fully recognizes that the bite of the mosquito is a serious matter and he needs little urging to assist in wiping out this pest. The company has provided churches and schools, and this has helped to secure a better class of labor. With a steady and well-paid job, a house and a garden, chickens and other fowls, the Jamaican negro is as happy and contented and much better off than on his native island.

COLOMBIA

The health conditions on the great irrigated plantation back of Santa Marta are as good as those of the other districts, but the old cities of Santa Marta and La Cienega offer a serious health problem, and one which cannot be completely solved without the coöperation of the Colombian Government. Santa Marta has a population of 8,000 and La Cienega about 15,000. While the sanitary conditions are better than in many South American ports, they leave much to be desired, but work is in progress which will bring them up to the high standard of the other cities visited by the ships of the United Fruit Company.

A large hospital, which is practically a duplication of the splendid one erected in Quirigua, Guatemala, is now under construction in Santa Marta, and with this as headquarters the medical department will supervise its line of smaller hospitals, sick-camps and dispensaries which cover the entire district. The native labor conforms readily to sanitary regulations and the death-rate is normal.

Rio Frio, a town of 3,000 inhabitants, Sevilla with 2,500, Aracataca with 3,000, and Fundacion and Buenos Aires

Types of sanitary cottages erected by the United Fruit Company in the tropics

with 1,000 each, are scattered through this vast banana district, and all of these towns enjoy good sanitary conditions. Well-equipped hospitals are maintained in all of them, and the inhabitants make a sincere effort to coöperate with the medical department of the company.

CUBA

The Government of Cuba has the official supervision of sanitation in the Nipe Bay section, but the United Fruit Company provides medical attention for all of its employees and most of those who live in Banes, Preston, and elsewhere. The company maintains hospitals in Saetia, Preston, and Banes. Sanitary and protective measures are energetically promoted and the general conditions of health are as good as in the United States.

The medical department of the Nipe Bay Company has headquarters in Preston, and the hospital service, sanitation and health measures are entirely under its supervision. This service extends to the 5,000 inhabitants of Preston and to a total population in this district of more than 12,000.

The medical supervision of Banes and its surroundings is a model of efficiency. Banes is divided into two parts, one of which consists of the municipality of Banes, under the jurisdiction of the Cuban Government, while the other section is devoted to the use of the several thousand employees of the United Fruit Company. Here are the homes of the local officials of the company, hotels, neat cottages for the laborers, parks, tennis and baseball grounds, a well-kept polo field, and other places of recreation. There is keen athletic rivalry between Preston and Banes. Both have polo teams and fine strings of ponies, and thousands witness the tournaments and cheer for their respective champions.

Here also is the excellent Banes hospital, a modern structure and efficiently conducted. From it radiate a comprehensive system of smaller hospitals and dispensaries which serve a population exceeding 15,000.

The extent of the operations of the medical department

of the United Fruit Company is indicated in the last annual report of its medical department. In 1913, 10,383 patients were admitted to the hospitals, and the deaths from all causes were 306, a proportion difficult to duplicate in any part of the world. The dispensaries treated 53,082 patients, and the total number receiving attention was 63,465. The number of employees on the pay-roll receiving treatment was 25,121, and 17,515 persons not in any way connected with the company were given hospital or some sort of medical attention.

The company has $240,166 invested in hospitals. Each employee pays a small sum per month for medical service, but this is not sufficient to meet the expenses and there is always a considerable annual loss which the company is glad to meet. It is to be doubted if any private enterprise in the world has originated or maintains any service approaching that under the direction of the United Fruit Company.

The sanitary work and discoveries of the United Fruit Company constitute a notable contribution to medical science. At a sacrifice of money and of human lives the means have been found to safeguard the health and lives of those who care to go to the American tropics to participate in the development of its hardly touched resources, or to assist in building up new and important markets for the products of their own country.

CHAPTER XV

An International Tropical Farm

THE United Fruit Company is immeasurably the greatest agricultural enterprise of which we have any record. There are individuals and corporations owning a greater acreage, but none approaches it in the extent of cultivated tracts or in the market value of output. It is a fact worth noting that this has been accomplished by American citizens operating in virgin fields in widely scattered foreign countries. In this work the United Fruit Company has had no advantage of subsidies or special favours of any kind.

The annual report for 1913, as submitted by Andrew W. Preston, president of the company, places its improved land holdings at 271,737 acres, its unimproved lands at 810,917, making a total of 1,082,654 acres owned or leased by the company. This does not include the sugar lands belonging to the Saetia Sugar Company and the Nipe Bay Company in Cuba. All of the stock of the former belongs to the United Fruit Company, and all save a small portion of the stock of the Nipe Bay Company which carries the voting privilege has been purchased by it as an investment. It is therefore proper to include these land holdings in the total owned and operated by the United Fruit Company.

Including Nipe Bay and Saetia, the company owns or leases 1,210,443 acres of land, of which 313,347 are improved and 897,096 are unimproved. The distribution of these lands as compared with its holding when the United Fruit Company was organized is shown in the following table:

COMPARATIVE STATEMENT OF LANDS OWNED AND LEASED BY THE UNITED FRUIT COMPANY ON SEPTEMBER 30, 1900 AND 1913

ACRES OF LAND OWNED BY THE COMPANY

LOCATION	IMPROVED		UNIMPROVED		TOTAL	
	1900	1913	1900	1913	1900	1913
Colombia	13,035	32,826	......	49,177	13,035	82,003
Costa Rica	18,810	65,081	70,382	184,698	89,192	249,779
Cuba	17,183	106,186	43,147	149,073	60,330	255,259
Honduras	500	10,362	300	38,391	800	48,753
Jamaica	8,235	17,329	20,802	17,487	29,037	34,816
San Domingo	3,500	......	16,500	......	20,000	......
Guatemala	......	28,233	......	97,956	......	126,189
Nicaragua	......	......	......	193,000	......	193,000
Panama	......	38,906	......	70,290	......	109,196
Total	61,263	298,923	151,131	800,072	212,394	1,098,995

ACRES OF LAND LEASED BY COMPANY

	IMPROVED		UNIMPROVED		TOTAL	
	1900	1913	1900	1913	1900	1913
Costa Rica	1,000	3,321	......	2,071	1,000	5,338
Guatemala	......	......	......	67,392	......	67,392
Honduras	......	216	......	16,892	......	17,108
Jamaica	4,031	10,887	18,776	10,723	22,807	21,610
	5,031	14,424	18,776	97,024	23,807	111,448
Grand total	66,294	313,347	169,907	897,096	236,201	1,210,443

It is difficult to comprehend the vast areas indicated by these figures. Even at its inception the United Fruit Company was the greatest of known agricultural enterprises. There were cattle ranches in the United States and Mexico with greater acreages, mostly of barren wastes, but no other concern had 66,000 acres of land under cultivation.

In the short space of thirteen years the company increased its area of cultivation from 66,294 acres to the impressive total of 313,347, and its total owned and leased lands from 236,201 to the stupendous aggregate of 1,210,443 acres. This means that its cultivated tracts extended over an area of almost exactly 500 square miles, and that all of its lands had an area of 1,891 square miles.

Expensive work in constructing a banana railroad

This area of 1,891 square miles is 641 square miles more than the size of Rhode Island, it almost equals the area of Delaware, and is about one-third of the size of the State of New Jersey. It would be about equal to a farm three-quarters of a mile wide and extending from New York to San Francisco. It surpasses the combined area of the following great cities of the United States:

CITIES	AREA IN SQUARE MILES	CITIES	AREA IN SQUARE MILES
New York City	326	San Francisco	44
Chicago	190	Duluth	67
Philadelphia	130	Denver	59
New Orleans	192	Grand Rapids	17
Boston	43	Houston	16
Washington, D. C.	69	Kansas City	26
Baltimore	31	Mobile	15
Cincinnati	43	Scranton	19
Cleveland	45	Rochester	13
Detroit	36	Atlanta	13
St. Louis	61	Columbus, Ohio	16
Indianapolis	31	Dallas	15
Milwaukee	23	Jersey City	19
Minneapolis	53	Memphis	16
St. Paul	55	New Haven	22
Omaha	24	Buffalo	42
Pittsburgh	38	Newark	23
Providence	18	San Antonio	36
Louisville	21		
		Total, sq. miles	1,887

It is thus seen that thirty-seven of the more populous cities of the United States do not cover a territory equal to the land holdings of the United Fruit Company in the American tropics. The dwellers in New York, Chicago, and New Orleans can well comprehend the stupendous extent of plantations whose areas dwarf their own vast municipal domains.

Some of this land is unfitted for cultivation of any kind, but a large percentage of it will later be utilized in an attempt to keep pace with the rapidly increasing demand for tropical fruits in the United States and abroad. The following table gives a clear idea of how the cultivated tracts are distributed in the different countries and the crops raised on them:

STATEMENT SHOWING THE LOCATION, ACREAGE, AND CHARACTER OF CULTIVATIONS ON SEPTEMBER 30, 1913, AND TOTAL FOR 1900

Description	Location and Acreage								
	Colombia	Costa Rica	Cuba	Guatemala	Honduras	Jamaica	Panama	Totals	
	1913	1913	1913	1913	1913	1913	1913	1913	1900
Fruit:									
Bananas	22,790	47,723	111	27,122	9,037	8,767	34,903	150,453	38,463
Oranges	......	52	694	......	......	88	.....	834	315
Pineapples	......	......	......	......	......	....	......	......	17
Sugar Cane	......	5	58,972	......	......	....	......	58,977	7,803
Miscellaneous:									
Cocoanuts	......	......	123	......	97	4,112	......	4,332	1,842
Cocoa	47	441	846	......	......	77	1,143	2,554	313
Rubber	......	66	......	......	21	15	......	102	307
Pastures, roads, etc.	9,989	20,115	45,440	1,111	1,423	15,157	2,860	96,095	17,234
Total Acreage	32,826	68,402	106,186	28,233	10,578	28,216	38,906	313,347	66,294

The banana and sugar plantations cover a combined area of 209,430 acres, or 327 square miles. The average western farm is a quarter of a mile square. It would require 1,309 farms of this size to contain the sugar cane and banana plants now growing on the United Fruit Company's tropical lands, most of which have been reclaimed from virgin wildernesses. This would make an unbroken farm a quarter of a mile wide extending from Boston to the Mississippi River. Those who have motored for weeks over Long Island can obtain a fair conception of the total land assets of the United Fruit Company when informed that they would cover all of that island, spanning the 112 miles from Brooklyn to Montauk Point and from the Sound to the Atlantic, and would overlap its shores with 250 square miles of surplus territory.

Those who have travelled up the broad expanse of the Hudson River from the Battery to Albany, a distance of about 150 miles, may be interested to know that its surface is less than one-half that of the banana plantations owned by the United Fruit Company, to say nothing of the plantations owned by independent banana growers who sell their fruit to the company.

A battery of banana-loading machines

Enormous as are these banana cultivations of the United Fruit Company, they are less than 29 per cent of those now being operated in the tropics. Against the 150,000 acres of banana plantations owned by the company are about 370,000 acres owned by its competitors and independent growers who sell to the various importing concerns. The United Fruit Company is simply the leading producer and dealer in this tropical product, but it exercises no control over the sources of supply or of prices charged to the dealer or consumer. It has the legitimate trade advantage of the chain of banana plantations described in these chapters, and it has the further advantages of systems of transportation, communication, distribution, and administration which have been perfected after years of study and unflagging determination to reduce this business to a science.

The American farmer who owns a dozen horses and fifty head of cattle is exceptionally well provided. A further idea of the magnitude of the operations of the United Fruit Company can be obtained from the fact that its plantations contain more than 30,000 head of live stock, as follows:

CATTLE		HORSES AND MULES	
Cows	5,261	Stallions	224
Bulls	1,506	Mares	505
Oxen	8,099	Geldings	1,199
Steers	3,668	Colts	271
Calves	3,051	Mules	4,388
Heifers	2,207	Asses	24
Total	23,792		6,611
		Total head of live stock	30,403

So far as I can ascertain, the United Fruit Company stands absolutely without a peer as an industrial exterprise in the extent of its transportation facilities. This transportation service has three general divisions, viz: (1) Means of conveying the bananas, sugar cane and other products from the fields to the docks or mills; (2) a fleet of ships to carry these products to the United States and foreign ports; (3) improved facilities by which to protect and expedite the transportation of its fruit products from the ports of entry to the consuming centres.

In conveying the products from the fields to the docks three distinct means of transportation are employed, viz: railroads, tramways, and animal traction power. Nearly 18,000 head of oxen, steers, horses, and mules are thus employed, and for their upkeep enormous tracts of pasture lands must be cleared and maintained. The mythological king who thought to dismay Hercules with the task of cleaning the stables occupied by 3,000 oxen was a puny agriculturist compared with

The Picturesque Plateau of Costa Rica

the concern which finds constant use for more than 30,000 head of live stock, including nearly 12,000 oxen and steers.

Interlacing the banana and sugar-cane plantations owned by the United Fruit Company are 907 miles of railways and 532 miles of tramways, a total steel trackage of 1,439 miles, all save a small percentage of which is the property of the company. The traction and freight equipment of this private railway and tramway system consists of 144 locomotives and 4,105 cars.

These are not toy railroads, engines and cars. There has been expended on them not less than $25,000,000. The tracks are well ballasted and the right of way is kept to a high standard of maintenance and repair. Massive steel bridges span wide rivers and resist the rushing tropical floods. These roads are equipped with the best of safety devices, and all parts of the various divisions are connected with telegraph and telephone systems, also with wireless installation at the principal operating headquarters. In a word, these railroads are modern and permanent in their construction, equipment, and administration. This is an imperative requisite. The banana must come from the fields to the docks at a certain period in its development, and the failure of the railroad to provide swift and sure transportation means the absolute loss of a valuable but perishable product.

The use of the tramways has been fully explained in a former chapter. They help serve to bring the fruit from the more remote parts of the plantation to the railroad platforms.

When the United Fruit Company had finished its first fiscal year it had 112 miles of railways, 17 locomotives and 289 cars. Its progress since 1900 is thus shown:

RAILWAYS OWNED OR OPERATED BY THE UNITED FRUIT COMPANY IN 1913

ROADS OWNED

Location	*Miles of Road* Railways	Tramways	*Equipment* Locomotives	Number of Cars Railways	Tramways
Colombia	11.46	19.15	...	....	69
Costa Rica	91.54	324.93	28	489	606
Northern R'y Co.	126.57	......	13	223	....
Cuba	183.67	......	30	1,189	....
Guatemala	43.96	113.53	3	12	273
Honduras	23.03	5.17	5	44	11
Jamaica	16.20	8.58	5	72	30
Panama	247.40	60.73	33	506	125
Total owned	743.83	532.09	117	2,535	1,114

ROADS OPERATED

Location	Railways	Tramways	Locomotives	Railways	Tramways
Costa Rica R'y	163.21	......	27	456	....
Total owned and operated	907.04	532.09	144	2,991	1,114

BRINGING BANANAS TO THE AWAITING FRUIT SHIP

Here are five banana trains where a few years ago was an unbroken and deadly wilderness

There is every reason to believe that the coming ten years will witness a growth of these railroads which will equal or surpass that of the last decade. The restoration of peace in Mexico should insure the speedy completion of the links which will complete the International Railways of Central America and thus make it possible to journey by rail from any part of the United States to Panama City, and, in the near future, to all of the great commercial centres of South America.

It is safe to predict that the railways in Guatemala, Honduras, Costa Rica, and Panama will be extended and become feeders of a comprehensive system which will open all of Central America to the development and progress possible under stable conditions of government. At the present time these roads are devoted almost entirely to the transportation of bananas and to the materials used by the United Fruit Company in the prosecution of its enterprises, but the time is at hand when the innumerable possibilities of these sections will be embraced by investors from all parts of the world. The triumphs of sanitation insure that new towns will be founded along the lines of new railroads, and that the millions who one day will live and prosper in these redeemed coast lands will realize that all this was made possible by the American citizens who were the pioneers in this Conquest of the Tropics.

These paragraphs may give the reader an idea of what has been expended in a successful attempt to carry the banana from its parent stalk to the wharves where await the ships which convey it to the ports of the United States and of Europe.

The fleet of the United Fruit Company was established primarily for the purpose of transporting its products from the tropics to the markets of their consumption. Prior to the advent of the enterprises headed by Mr. Preston and Mr. Keith there was practically no commerce with Central America. As has been explained, there were no harbors and no railway communication with the populated interiors of Guatemala, Salvador, Costa Rica, and the western parts of the Republic of Panama. It therefore followed that the original ships owned or leased by the United Fruit Company were "fruit boats" in the strict sense of the term. There was little to attract passenger traffic to the new ports, and the ships operated by the company had limited accommodations for those who dared venture such trips.

In these early years nearly all of the ships employed in the banana trade were chartered from Norwegian or other foreign owners, and the largest one in the service of the company had a tonnage of about 2,000 and a capacity of 35,000 bunches of bananas. The forty-four ships owned or leased in the first year of the life of the United Fruit Company had accommodations for only 350 passengers, or an average of eight to a ship. The present Great White Fleet has unsurpassed accommodations for fully 2,500 passengers, and the ships now building will increase this to 3,000 or more.

Most significant is the increase in the amount of general freight carried for the public. In its initial year, 1900, the forty-four small ships of the company carried about 319,000 tons of freight, of which only 51,000 tons, or 16 per cent, was general freight carried for the public. The remaining 84 per cent consisted of bananas, miscellaneous fruit, and merchandise belonging to the company and carried for its account. This insignificant 51,000 tons of freight represented the commercial possibilities of trade intercourse between the United States and Central America.

In the short space of twelve years this 51,000 tons has mounted to 359,686 tons, or an increase of more than 700 per cent. There is a practical sort of eloquence in those figures. They mean that the activities of the United Fruit Company have opened new and profitable markets to our manufacturers and to the people of Central America who had been shut off from the world of trade.

In the eleven years between 1900 and 1911 the single port of New Orleans, according to certified custom-house records, increased its exports to British Honduras, Guatemala, Spanish Honduras, Nicaragua, Costa Rica, Panama, Mexico, and Cuba from $4,410,139 to $17,909,658, and a large percentage of these manufactured exports were carried in ships which bore the flag of the United Fruit Company.

Early in its history the company decided that it must construct ships specially adapted to its purpose. The awakening of Central America stimulated travel, and each succeeding ship as it came from the builders had added conveniences and luxuries for the passenger. The steady and rapid growth of the Great White Fleet has been narrated. There are no ships afloat so skilfully designed to meet the peculiar requirements of tropical cruising. Most of them look like huge private yachts, and the service and accessories comport with their appearance.

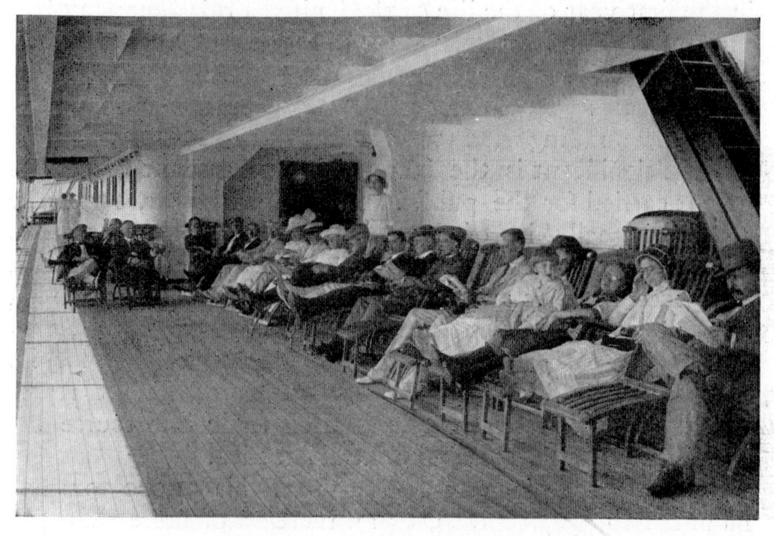

The broad decks of a ship of the Great White Fleet

Willis J. Abbot, in his entertaining book, "Panama and the Canal," has this to say concerning this great fleet:

"The United Fruit Company would welcome the opportunity to transfer their ships to American registry, except for certain requirements of the navigation laws which make such change hazardous. Practically all the ownership of the ships is vested in Americans, and to fly the British flag is to them an offensive necessity. Chief among the objections is the clause which would give the United States authority to seize the vessels in time of war. It is quite evident that this power might be employed to the complete destruction of the Fruit Company's trade; in fact to its practical extinction as a business concern. A like power existing in England or Germany would not be of equal menace to any single company flying the flag of that nation, for there the government's needs could be fully supplied by a proper apportionment of requisitions for ships among the many corporations. But with the exceedingly restricted merchant marine of the United States, the danger of the enforcement of this right would be an ever-present menace.

"It is for this reason that the United Fruit Company steamers fly the British flag, and the American in Colon may see, as I did one day, nine great ocean steamers in the port with only one flying the stars and stripes. The opening of the canal will not wholly remedy this. In all respects save the registry of its ships, however, the United Fruit Company is a thoroughly American concern, and to its operations in the Caribbean is due much of the good feeling toward the United States which is observable there. . . . To my mind the United Fruit Company, next to the Panama Canal, is the great phenomenon of the Caribbean world to-day. It has accomplished a creative work, wonderful and romantic."

The following table gives the names and the tonnage of the ships which now constitute the fleet of the United Fruit Company:

STATEMENT OF STEAMSHIPS OWNED BY SUBSIDIARY COMPANIES OF THE UNITED FRUIT COMPANY

Steamships	Gross Tonnage	Steamships	Gross Tonnage
Orleanian	2,293	Sixaola	5,018
Greenbrier	3,332	Tivives	5,017
San José	3,296	Pastores	7,782
Limon	3,298	Tenadores	7,783
Esparta	3,298	Calamares	7,783
Saramacca	3,284	Matina	3,870
Marowijne	3,192	Miami	3,762
Suriname	3,275	Manistee	3,869
Coppename	3,192	Nicoya	3,911
Cartago	4,937	Pacuare	3,891

Steamships	Gross Tonnage	Steamships	Gross Tonnage
Parismina	4,938	Zent	3,890
Heredia	4,944	Barranca	4,115
Abangarez	4,955	Chirripo	4,041
Turrialba	4,961	Reventazon	4,041
Atenas	4,962	Tortuguero	4,161
Almirante	5,010	Manzanares	4,400
Santa Marta	5,013	Aracataca	4,400
Metapan	5,011	Chagres	5,288
Zacapa	5,013	Bayano	5,948
Carillo	5,013	Patia	5,911
		Patuca	5,900

Total tonnage of these 41 steamships	187,998
Tonnage of the 49 ships chartered from other companies	60,609
Total tonnage for the 90 ships operated	248,607

Most of the names of these steamships are derived from cities, towns, rivers, and mountains in our American tropics. Four of them, viz: *Saramacca*, *Marowijne*, *Suriname*, and *Coppename*, obtain their names from Dutch Guinea. Twenty of these names are of Costa Rican origin, and I have prepared a map of this republic with the places properly located and numbered. The general map of the American tropics touched by the Gulf of Mexico and the Caribbean Sea contains thirteen other geographical originals of these steamship names. This system of designating ships was originated partly with the idea to familiarize the public with the geographical points of interest in the fields where the company conducts its operations.

In busy seasons this fleet of ninety ships is materially increased by the addition of chartered vessels, and there have been times when the total has reached and exceeded one hundred. The policy of the company, however, is to increase its fleet by the construction of new ships specially adapted to meet the peculiar requirements of a growing passenger and freight business.

With that end in view the United Fruit Company placed orders in the latter part of 1913 for fifteen new ships, seven for service to the United States, and eight for the use of its rapidly increasing European trade. It is to be doubted if any shipping interest ever made a similar increase in a given year, and it is a certainty that no industrial or agricultural enterprise ever was compelled to take similar steps to keep pace with an augmenting demand for a staple product of food consumption.

Three of the ships ordered for the United States will have passenger accommodations surpassing even those of the fine new ships *Pastores*, *Tenadores*, and *Calamares*, and will give the United Fruit Company exceptional facilities as a caterer to tropical travel. These three ships will be delivered in 1915. The other four ships for the United States are intended for freight service only.

Two of the new ships for the European banana trade will be delivered in 1914 and the other six in 1915. It is likely that other ships will be ordered before these are in commission. The banana trade, while not in its infancy, has far to go before it can meet the probable demands of a world which is seeking cheaper food products, and it is not beyond reason to predict that the coming ten years will witness the doubling of the size of the Great White Fleet.

The ships which serve the United States enter the ports of Galveston, New Orleans, Mobile, Charleston, Baltimore, Philadelphia, New York, and Boston. New Orleans is by far the leading port of banana entry in the United States or in the world, with New York, Boston, and Philadelphia following in the order named.

There is no duty on bananas — thanks to a press and the common-sense of a public which was quick to denounce and defeat a proposed clause to that end in the present tariff measure — with the result that no officials delay unloading and no custom-house brokers exact a tribute ultimately paid by the consumer. There are no warehouses for the storage of bananas, with charges mounting every day. There is no speculative exchange with an army of employees and principals, all of them depending for a living and income on alleged services later charged to the consumer. There are no insurance charges. No municipal official has an opportunity to extort graft in the transit of the bananas from the docks to the push carts and retail stores.

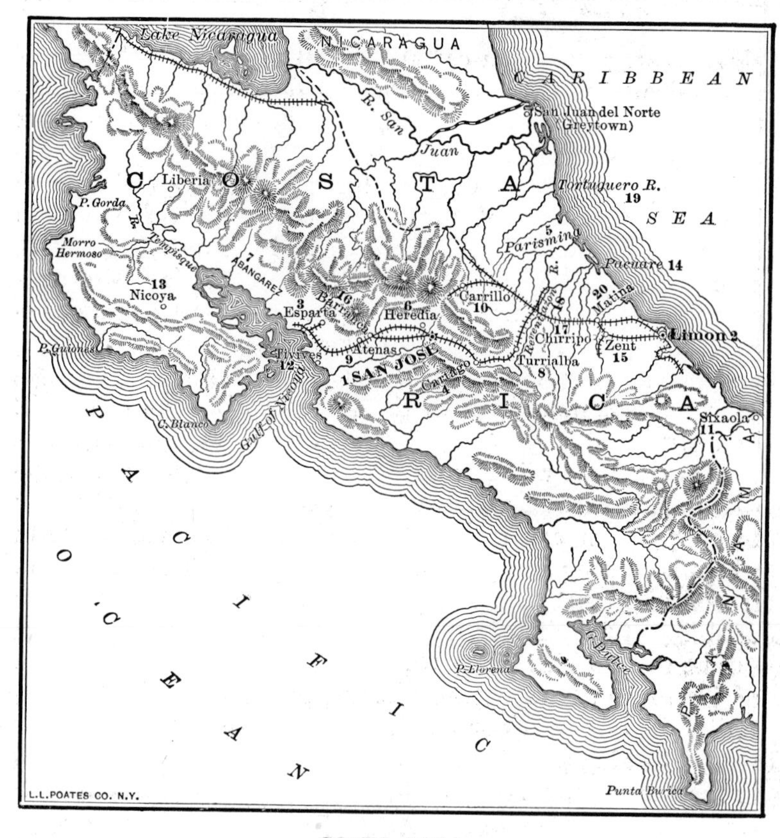

COSTA RICA

Here is the key to the above map:

No. 1, "San José," capital of Costa Rica.
No. 2, "Limon," principal port of Costa Rica on the Caribbean.
No. 3 "Esparta," a railroad town on west coast of Costa Rica.
No. 4, "Cartogo," a famous city in Costa Rica, once destroyed by earthquake.
No. 5, "Parismina," a Costa Rican river flowing into the Caribbean.
No. 6, "Heredia," a province and town in Central Costa Rica.
No. 7, "Abanquarez," a mining district in western Costa Rica.
No. 8, "Turrialba," a town in Central Costa Rica.
No. 9, "Atenas," a town in western Costa Rica .
No. 10, "Carrillo," a town in Central Costa Rica.
No. 11, "Sixaola," the river which divides Panama and Costa Rica.
No. 12, "Tivives," a village on the west coast of Costa Rica.
No. 13, "Nicoya," a gulf and town on west coast of Costa Rica.
No. 14, "Pacuare," a river flowing into the Caribbean.
No. 15, "Zent," a town in the heart of the banana plantations.
No. 16, "Barranca," a small town in the mountains of Costa Rica.
No. 17, "Chirripo," a village in eastern Costa Rica.
No. 18, "Reventazon," a river flowing into the Caribbean.
No. 19, "Tortuguero," a river in northern Costa Rica flowing into the Caribbean.
No. 20, "Matina," a river a few miles north of Limon.

WHERE THE BANANAS COME FROM

Here is the key to the above map:

No. 21, "Almirante," a bay and also a town in Panama.
No. 22, "Santa Marta," a city on the north coast of Colombia.
No. 23, "Metapan," a town in San Salvador.
No. 24, "Zacapa," an important railroad centre in Guatemala.
No. 25, "Pastores," a town in the western part of Gautemala.
No. 26, "Tenadores," the junction of two rivers in Central Guatemala.
No. 27, "Calamares," a town in Colombia.
No. 28, "Miami," a bay and town in Florida.
No. 29, "Manistee," from several sources in the United States.
No. 30, "Aracataca," a town in Colombia.
No. 31, "Chagres," the Panama River that the engineers of its canal had to harness.
No. 32, "Patuca," a river in Spanish Honduras.
No. 33, "Manzanares," a river in Colombia.

It is all very simple. The fruit steamer arrives, ties to her dock, and a few minutes later the bunches of bananas begin to pour out of her holds. In several of the larger ports they are unloaded by machinery, but in all cases the local supply goes to the trucks of the wholesale dealers and a few hours later most of it is in the hands of the retailers. Some of these dealers have limited storage capacity for surplus purchases, or for the ripening of undeveloped fruit, but the great percentage of the bananas for local consumption is in the hands of the retailers, and sold by them within two or three days from their arrival from the tropics. The importing company sells bananas to the dealers by weight, and the price varies so little that it is seldom that a rise or fall is reflected in the prices charged to the consumer.

The population thus served by local distribution from Boston, New York, Philadelphia, Baltimore, Charleston, Mobile, New Orleans, and Galveston may roughly be estimated at 15,000,000, nearly half of whom live in or near New York City, the banana-consuming metropolis of the world. There remains the more difficult problem of placing the perishable banana within reach of the largest possible percentage of the 65,000,000 people living away from these seaport centres of population.

The Fruit Dispatch Company was organized to serve this function for the United Fruit Company. During the early days of the business, not long ago, bananas were practically unknown in many parts of the interior of the United States, and it was necessary to create and develop some organization which would be able to handle this fruit product with the intelligence and promptness which its perishable nature demanded.

At its inception as a corporation the United Fruit Company established as a part of its policy the dictum that it would make absolutely no effort to acquire control, directly or indirectly, of either the wholesale jobbing or retail trade. In accord with that policy it has no financial interest in any banana jobbing house or retail store in the United States. Of its own volition the company has consistently refrained from attempting to raise, lower, or control in any

BANANAS
FRUIT DISPATCH COMPANY
IMPORT THE BEST
BOSTON
NEW YORK
PHILADELPHIA
BALTIMORE
CHARLESTON
MOBILE
NEW ORLEANS
GALVESTON
U.R. T.C^o
1500 1500
UNION
REFRIGERATOR
TRANSIT C^o
1500
U.R.T.C
1500

A banana car

way the prices charged by wholesalers or retailers. Students of the affairs and policies of great corporations will find in this novel procedure something well worthy of reflection.

Experience had taught Andrew W. Preston that one of the vital problems of the banana business was to insure prompt and efficient distribution of this perishable fruit to the interior markets of the United States, and as executive head of the Boston Fruit Company he suggested and secured the incorporation of the Fruit Dispatch Company, which has always acted as the marketing and distributing agency of the United Fruit Company. In building up this important department of the United Fruit Company it was deemed advisable to make it stand squarely on its own feet, and, accordingly, to regard and treat it the same as though it were a separate organization selling fruit in the same manner as the ordinary broker doing a general commission business, but with this very important difference — the Fruit Dispatch Company was to perform all of these duties for the wholesalers pratically at cost.

As the business of the United Fruit Company has increased and the efficiency of the Fruit Dispatch Company has been enhanced, the commissions charged by the latter have been reduced. There have been years when this corporation has returned slight profits, and there have been years when it has operated at a slight loss, but its function is not to pay dividends, but to insure that the dealers in bananas in all parts of the United States will receive good fruit promptly and in perfect condition, and the success attained in accomplishing this result has had an advertising and good-will value difficult to express in terms of dollars.

In order to give the requisite assurance to the banana merchants of the interior that their orders could be filled, it was necessary to have local representatives who could advise them of probable importations and receive orders to be forwarded to the seaboard. It was also necessary that these orders should be received at the seaboard by some official whose particular business should be to see that they were promptly and properly filled.

Its most beneficent function is to render the interior dealer absolutely independent of any intermediary interest at the port of banana entry. In the place of a clique of competing or confederated middlemen in all of these ports we see the Fruit Dispatch Company performing an indispensable service practically at cost, and doing this on an enormous scale and with a system perfected after years of study and experience.

Some idea of the magnitude of this duty may be obtained when it is stated that in 1913 the Fruit Dispatch Company handled for the United Fruit Company alone a total considerably exceeding 50,000 cars of bananas, which would make a solid train more than 400 miles long!

The orders from the interior dealers are in before the ship arrives. Let us take a fruit vessel arriving at New Orleans for instance. A considerable part of her cargo of 40,000 bunches of bananas have been purchased by dealers in Chicago, Indianapolis, Cincinnati, St. Louis, Kansas City, Omaha, and other points. The specially constructed refrigerator cars are in waiting at the New Orleans docks of the United Fruit Company.

As soon as the fruit ship is warped to her dock the banana-unloading machines are lowered into position and a small army of men assists in bringing her cargo from her chambered hold. A keen-eyed corps of inspectors is on watch, trained men who represent the New Orleans Board of Trade.

There is no law or port regulation requiring an inspection by these representatives of the New Orleans Board of Trade. Why, then, are they there, and armed with power to reject any bunch of bananas? Because of the request of the Fruit Dispatch Company. A number of years ago the executives of this company earnestly requested and finally arranged for the official inspection and weighing of all of its bananas by such organizations as the New Orleans Board of Trade, the Boston Chamber of Commerce, the Mobile Chamber of Commerce & Business League, and the Galveston Cotton Exchange & Board of Trade. It was the purpose of the Fruit Dispatch Company to give its customers just what they had ordered and had a right to expect. So far as

I can learn, this solicitation of an official stamp of approval by a disinterested outside organization on the weight and quality of a competitive product is not only unique and worthy of praise, but marks a new attitude on the part of corporations in their dealings with the public.

Here is fruit for which the company has paid an independent grower in Costa Rica or Panama 30 or 35 cents a bunch. This particular bunch has been carried by rail by the company from the field to the dock, has been inspected and passed three or four times, has been insured against shipwreck, has been loaded and unloaded at considerable expense, has been carried over a thousand miles of water— and now an inspector makes a dash at the man who is about to put it in the car. So far as you or I can see there is not a blemish on it, but away it goes to join other "rejects" which make a mounting pile to one side of the unloading machines.

Some of these bunches are rejected for interior shipment because they are sufficiently ripe for immediate use, and are sold to local merchants. Others with slight defects are sold to manufacturers who convert them into banana flour, banana vinegar, dried bananas, coffee substitutes, and other valuable edible products which have been discovered.

Each bunch of bananas, in passing from the ships to the cars, is under the careful observation of at least six inspectors who make sure that no guilty bunch escapes. As soon as a sufficient number of cars to constitute a train are loaded they are at once started on their journey to the interior. Accompanying each train are at least two trained experts in charge of the bananas. These employees are known as "banana messengers," and they go with the train to its destination. These banana trains are run on very fast schedules. At each junction or division point it is the duty of the messengers to inspect each car of fruit, ascertain accurately the temperature inside and outside of the car, and to keep informed regarding the probable conditions of weather later to be met on the journey, and to regulate the temperature of the cars accordingly. They are also required to keep a careful record of the time of arrival and

A TOUR OF INSPECTION

The banana railroads are equipped with motor cars of high speed by which a plantation manager can cover 200 or more miles a day

departure from each division point, and to enter this and other data on printed forms.

At the larger division points are stationed other experts known as "resident messengers." These men are required to meet all trains on arrival at their agencies, to make careful inspection of the contents of the cars, to receive and verify the reports of the messengers in charge of them and to give instructions regarding their care until they arrive at the zone of the next resident messenger.

In addition to these officials located along the lines of the principal railroads, each large city has its local manager whose duty it is to take charge of the cars destined for local consignees and care for the same until the purchasers of the bananas are ready to take possession. By this system the fruit is under the observation and care of experts from the time it is cut from the stalk in the tropics until it is delivered to the dealer. At several places along the principal routes large sheds are maintained into which the banana trains may be run, where certain cars may be cut off and diverted to branches leading from the trunk railroad line. These banana depots are equipped with apparatus for cooling in summer and heating in winter. In extreme weather conditions, or where the condition of the fruit may require it, the trains are held in these cooling and heating stations until the bananas are brought to the proper temperature.

The result of the adoption of this system is the delivery of perfect bananas to all of the centres of large population of the United States. With the old methods in vogue it was practically impossible to induce dealers to handle bananas during the periods of extreme heat and cold, but with this service the sellers of bananas pay little attention to the weather.

The Fruit Dispatch Company has also taught the dealer how to take care of his fruit, how properly to ripen it, make it attractive to the consumer, and how best to distribute it. All sales of bananas are made f. o. b. seaboard, and the purchaser takes the risks of interior transportation, but the system maintained by the Fruit Dispatch Company reduces the percentage of damaged fruit almost to the zero point.

Corporations engaged extensively in interstate trade, though administered by executives who are sincerely desirous of conforming not only to the letter but also the spirit of the laws governing such corporations, are sometimes involved in legal troubles because of the overzealousness of employees anxious to make favorable personal showings. The various minor officials of the Fruit Dispatch Company certainly have no excuse for acting counter to the policy clearly and emphatically expressed in a circular letter issued a number of years ago by Andrew W. Preston, President of the company, under the title, "Policy of the Company," from which I quote the following:

"The high principles which govern the business of the Fruit Dispatch Company are entirely inconsistent with unfair competition. It is the policy of the company to obtain and hold its trade by offering extensive variety, constant supply, careful selection, fair prices, uniform treatment, prompt attention, and absolute reliability. Accordingly, you should rely upon these points in soliciting business, and be careful to refrain from criticising or making derogatory remarks respecting any of our competitors, even though it should be called to your attention that some of them are engaged in unfair tactics. Such an attitude on your part, maintained constantly even in trying circumstances, is sure to win the respect of the trade and react strongly to the advantage of the company. It is the object of the company to merit and have the confidence and respect of its trade, and in your business relations with your customers you should have this in mind at all times."

This was not a new theory of business with Mr. Preston, neither was it promulgated to meet some crisis or emergency. It was the reaffirmation of the policy which for years had been urged and enforced in the affairs of the Boston Fruit Company and later with the United Fruit Company, and much of the success attained by these enterprises may be ascribed to the humane, broad, and charitable spirit expressed by President Preston in the above quoted injunction to his official subordinates. It sounds the keynote to the "New Competition" which is rearing itself on the ruins of that ruthless and destructive type which wrecked itself by its own barbarity.

What the Fruit Dispatch Company had done to widen the markets for the sale of bananas is best evidenced by the fact that in 1899 it had only sixteen agencies, while to-day it has sixty and more distributed among all of the large cities of the United States and Canada. The sale of bananas in the United States has increased from about 16,000,000 bunches in 1900 to more than 46,000,000 in 1913.

It is safe to predict that the shipload of bananas cut from the plantations of Panama, Costa Rica, Honduras, or Guatemala will all have been eaten within three weeks from the hour they were removed from the native stalk, and that the cargo will have been distributed over a section of the United States inhabited by from 5,000,000 to 15,000,000 people. And the banana, which was practically unknown a generation ago, now is the source of an industry which demands that from 1,500 to 2,000 shiploads of this tropical fruit shall be landed in our ports each year! Truly, the banana and the automobile, born at about the same time in a commercial sense, are astoundingly lusty youths!

I have attempted to make clear to the reader how the United Fruit Company brings the banana from the tropical plantation to Chicago, Omaha, Denver, Salt Lake, San Francisco, Seattle, and other cities. It is all very simple, but it is also very stupendous. There are the great plantations scattered 2,000 miles along the coasts and islands of the Caribbean; there are the railroads and tramways with their thousands of cars and hundreds or more of powerful locomotives; there is the great fleet with ships plying back and forth from the coasts of the United States and Europe; there is the wonderful wireless flashing instantaneous instructions and warnings to this banana squadron; there is the swift unloading of these tens of millions of bunches of

AN EXPERIMENT IN BANANAS

These are banana plants which are believed to be immune to the disease which has killed those which formerly grew on this plantation

bananas all along the Gulf and Atlantic seaboard of the United States, and there is the perfected system of distribution by which this fruit goes out all over the interior sections of the nation.

The leading competitors of the United Fruit Company operate on a somewhat similar general system, but none of them on this scale. The fact that they are not as large as the United Fruit Company does not prevent them from making fair profits under favorable conditions, but the banana producer and importer must measure up to a certain standard of size and of assets if he expects to meet the prices which are fixed by a keen and unceasing competition. The sole reason why the banana is the cheapest fruit and food product now offered in the United States is because it is produced and handled on a big scale, with an enormous product distributed and sold under keen competition with a minimum of profit per unit.

All of the ordinary commodities which are sold at a reasonable price are produced on a large scale and offered at a minimum of profit, and all of the commodities which enter into the high cost of living are produced on small and unscientific scales and sold in a haphazard way at any extortionate profit which can be forced from the public. This is the alpha and omega of the cost of living, and those who pray for the return of the day of little things have an instinctive longing for an environment suited to their intellect.

The United Fruit Company has invested and disbursed for wages in the American tropics a sum not less than $200,000,000, and two monumental results of world-wide benefit have accrued from this crusade for the peaceful Conquest of the Tropics. This vast expenditure founded an industry and stimulated a competition which have given to the peoples of the temperate zone of the Northern Hemisphere a fruit-food product which has had an immeasurable effect in sustaining human life. Next in importance to this great contribution is that of quickening to industrial and commercial life the neglected republics along the shores of the Caribbean. These are achievements mighty in compar-

Hospital Grounds in Puerto Limon

ison with the question of whether or not the founders of the United Fruit Company have sufficiently profited by this enterprise.

The vast constructive work of the United Fruit Company, coupled with its broad and creative policy, is largely responsible for the measure of success which has attended the building of a comprehensive railway system for Central America. The more progressive statesmen of all of the Central American republics are planning and looking forward to a day when it will be possible to confederate into one nation the present republics of Guatemala, Salvador, Honduras, Nicaragua, Costa Rica, and Panama. The educated peoples of these republics speak the classical language of Spain, they cherish the same traditions, and are naturally linked by the strong ties of mutual self-interests. They have been held apart by the lack of the greatest of all commercial ties, viz: the spanning of their boundary lines by railways which should connect the United States and Mexico through them with the Panama Canal.

This is the great work to which Minor C. Keith has devoted a large share of his active life. Under his direction the International Railways of Central America are now constructing the gaps which will weld these countries into a commercial whole, and possibly pave the way for the statesmanship which will rear a great republic reaching from Mexico to South America.

The International Railway system is now operating 431 miles of railroad in Guatemala, and 62½ miles in Salvador, and has to construct 76 miles in Guatemala and 214 miles in Salvador, which will give these two republics a total mileage of 783.50. This includes the connecting link with the National Railway Lines of Mexico.

Work is in progress on a line through Salvador to the frontier of Honduras, and the company has an agreement with the Government of Honduras for a line through its territory which will connect with the Nicaragua system of railroads, owned by that government. From Nicaragua a line will be constructed to connect with the Costa Rican system, most of which is the property of the United Fruit

Company. The latter is now building a spur to establish communication with Bocas del Toro, Panama, and a railroad is planned to span the remaining 210 miles between Bocas del Toro and Panama City. The total mileage of these missing links is 438, and under normal conditions the work will be completed in a few years. It is difficult to overestimate the commercial and other benefits which will accrue from the completion of this steel highway linking the United States with the Panama Canal, and eventually with South America.

The annual report made by President Andrew W. Preston for 1913 placed the assets of the United Fruit Company at $82,545,384.33, as compared with $16,949,753.58 in 1900 at the end of the first year of the existence of the company. The capital stock of the company in 1900 was $11,230,000, or $5,719,753 less than its assets. The capital stock in 1913 was $36,594,300, with assets exceeding this amount by $45,951,084, an exhibit certainly not approached by any of the so-called "industrials" of financial importance. The protest against "watered stock" so often urged against corporations engaged in interstate or international trade has no point against the United Fruit Company, which, from its inception, has had tangible assets much in excess of its stock and all security liabilities.

The creative character of this tropical enterprise is indicated in the tabulation of its assets, the more important features of which are these:

PLANTATIONS AND EQUIPMENT:		
Lands	$17,964,543.11	
Houses and buildings	3,299,644.98	
Cultivations	9,325,405.22	
Live stock	1,078,133.57	
Tools and machinery	380,736.31	
Railroads	10,004,496.96	
Tramways	1,540,795.42	
Telephones	144,530.24	
Wharves, lighters, etc.	600,709.24	
Merchandise (stores)	1,100,979.97	
Material on hand	1,413,565.37	
Sugar mill	1,455,107.45	
		$48,308,638.84

DOMESTIC AND FOREIGN DIVISIONS		384,155.78
INVESTMENTS:		
Agricultural (bananas)	$ 899,740.06	
Agricultural and manufacturing (sugar)	3,443,447.84	
Tropical railways	1,627,717.03	
Miscellaneous	93,831.44	
		$ 6,064,736.37
STEAMSHIPS		14,136,973.88
NOTES RECEIVABLE		59,653.16
CURRENT ASSETS:		
Cash	$8,627,574.69	
Accounts collectable	3,565,075.93	
		$12,192,650.62
COUPON, DIVIDEND, AND TRUSTEE ACCOUNT		$ 708,341.37
ADVANCE PAYMENTS:		
Charters, wharfage and steamship supplies.		690,234.15
Total assets		$82,545,384.33

In 1913 the United Fruit Company took the important step of purchasing all of the remaining stock of the Saetia Sugar Company. It had formerly acquired all of the holdings of the Tropical Fruit and Steamship Company, Limited, the British steamship company of Elders & Fyffes, Limited, and also of the Northern Railway Company, in Costa Rica. President Preston prefaced his annual report for 1913 with this statement:

"Attention is called to the fact that, in order to make a more complete presentation of the company's financial affairs, there have been consolidated with the figures for the United Fruit Company proper those of several companies in which, with one unimportant exception, the United Fruit Company owns the entire capital stock. In any case where the investment had been carried, at a premium, adjustment has been made on the basis of book value, and the difference charged to income account."

To meet the outlay demanded by the enlargement of its fleet, and to provide for important extensions to the tropical plantations, an issue of $12,000,000 of four-year 6 per cent notes was authorized and the bonds subscribed. New lands were planted to bananas to the extent of 17,141 acres during the year, and additional tracts of 7,787 acres of banana cultivations were purchased, thus increasing the banana acreage of the company by more than 25,000 in 1913. These new plantations should produce more fruit than all of the tracts owned by the United Fruit Company at the end of its first year of operation, 1900.

The great Cuban sugar mills ground out 261,000,000

On the way to market

pounds of sugar and 5,600,000 gallons of molasses, but the low market prices for these commodities greatly reduced the profits from the preceding year. This factor, combined with the policy of making extensive permanent improvements, precluded the payment of any extra dividends in this fiscal year — an extra dividend of 2 per cent being declared just after its close, making a total of 10 per cent for 1913 — but an analysis of the annual income account of the company for 1913 indicates a degree of prosperity rare in a period marked by depression in all parts of the world:

INCOME ACCOUNT OF THE UNITED FRUIT COMPANY FOR 1913

Total Net Earnings of the year were:		
From bananas and miscellaneous tropical fruits, including profits from transportation and merchandise business		$ 5,696,065.49
From the sugar business		452,410.84
Miscellaneous income		49,399.75
Total income		$ 6,197,876.08
Deduct interest charges		882,245.03
Balance, net income for year .		$ 5,315,631.05
Regular dividend of 8 per cent . . .		2,927,544.00
Balance surplus for fiscal year .		$ 2,388,087.05
Brought forward from the close of the previous year a surplus of. . .		16,645,853.16
Making the total amount at credit of income account		$19,033,940.21
Direct charges have been made to income as follows:		
Premiums on investments in subsidiary companies and depreciation on tropical properties .	$ 2,050,349.54	
Investment in wireless telegraph; discount in full on $12,000,000 four-year 6 per cent notes issued during the year, and miscellaneous . .	699,378.90	
		2,749,728.44
Surplus, September 30, 1913		$16,284,211.77

I have compiled from the fourteen annual reports of the United Fruit Company what may be termed an epitome of its financial history. These reports are not only models of accuracy and completeness but also models of frankness. From its inception the company has withheld no essential financial detail from its stockholders or the public. This is in refreshing contrast to many large corporations.

The table now submitted gives for the years inclusive of 1900–1913 the assets, capital stock, amounts of dividends, disbursements, percentage of dividends to capital stock, and, finally, the percentage of dividends to the capital actually invested in these enterprises. The latter is what really counts. The question of whether or not a corporation is deriving unjust profits cannot be determined by its dividend rate. There are corporations in the United States which pay from 50 to 500 per cent annually on their capital stock, and these rates are fair when measured by the capital invested. There are other corporations which pay from 4 to 6 per cent on their capital stock, and this apparently low rate is actually extortionate, it being based on inflated securities.

A banana carrier

It is for the purpose of getting down to bedrock facts that the United States Government is now undertaking, at enormous expense, the task of ascertaining the actual physical cost of the railroads of the United States. The amounts of the capital stocks of these public service corporations mean little or nothing, but the public has a right to know what legitimately has been invested in these common carriers.

As has been pointed out in an early chapter of this book, the individual or the corporation making an investment in the American tropics assumes risks which, in the event of success, justify much higher profit rates than those fixed by competition in the United States. No just complaint can be made against the tropical producer of agricultural or other wealth who fixes prices which yield profits of from 10 to 20 per cent on capital actually invested. I had always supposed that the United Fruit Company made at least 25 per cent on the capital actually invested in its tropical operations, and, being posted through costly personal experience in tropical investments, considered this no more than their due.

Let us see what money rewards have accrued to the men who dared invest their capital in districts which others feared and ignored:

COMPARATIVE STATEMENT SHOWING ASSETS, CAPITAL STOCK, AMOUNTS OF DIVIDENDS PAID, DIVIDEND RATES, AND DIVIDEND EARNINGS IN PERCENTAGE TO CAPITAL ACTUALLY INVESTED BY THE UNITED FRUIT COMPANY IN THE FOURTEEN YEARS OF ITS CORPORATE EXISTENCE

YEAR	ASSETS	CAPITAL STOCK	DIVIDENDS	STOCK PER CENT	INVESTMENT PER CENT
1900	$16,949,753.58	$11,230,000.00	$ 1,119,257.50	10	6.5
1901	18,469,490.48	12,369,500.00	1,084,767.50	9	5.9
1902	19,251,189.21	12,369,500.00	1,051,407.50	8.5	5.4
1903	21,314,675.24	12,575,500.00	877,150.00	7	4.1
1904	22,824,251.99	15,782,000.00	967,675.00	7	4.06
1905	24,413,114.63	17,485,000.00	1,167,792.50	7	4.8
1906	26,599,683.31	17,961,000.00	1,235,745.00	7	4.6
1907	32,721,183.14	18,525,000.00	1,419,350.00	7.75	4.3
1908	35,215,178.27	21,328,300.00	3,524,484.00	18	9.9
1909	40,756,493.72	21,340,000.00	1,707,042.00	8	4.2
1910	45,033,752.97	23,474,000.00	4,011,472.00	18	8.9
1911	52,232,833.51	27,058,900.00	4,624,612.00	18	8.8
1912	67,500,393.34	36,594,300.00	5,101,678.00	18	7.8
1913	82,545,384.33	36,619,300.00	2,927,544.00	10	3.5
			$30,819,973.00	10.8	5.91

Thus it is seen that the stockholders of the United Fruit Company have received average annual dividends of 10.8 per cent, and that the actual money return on capital really invested has been less than 6 per cent. For the average tropical investment this would be an absolutely inadequate percentage of profit, but those who study this question from the investment viewpoint will not ignore the fact that during all of these years the United Fruit Company has been reinvesting a large share of its earnings in new plantations, new railroads, new ships, and other productive assets, and that each share of stock represents a substantial equity in the huge excess of tangible assets over the security liabilities.

When the time arrives that the production of bananas catches up with the increasing world demand for this fruit it will not be necessary for the United Fruit Company to appropriate huge annual sums for betterments. Good business management and average good fortune under such circumstances would warrant an expectation of not less than 10 per cent annual profit on the capital actually invested in these tropical properties. This would mean that the annual dividends of the United Fruit Company would average about 25 per cent, and neither the recipients nor the public would have any justifiable protest.

CHAPTER XVI

Lessons Taught by the Banana

OT until an attempt was made to impose an import tariff tax on bananas did that humble tropical fruit arrive at the dignity of a recognized factor in our national life. From relative obscurity it became in a few brief weeks one of our cherished American institutions. Under attack it forgot that it was a meek and lowly immigrant with a "yellow streak," and when it donned its fighting garb millions of housewives, toilers, and consumers of all classes rallied to its defense and demanded of our lawmakers that it be left free to enter the United States from the tropics without paying for the privilege.

It was a peculiar and most interesting episode, and is a striking illustration of the power of public opinion when wielded in a just cause. A clause taxing bananas 5 cents a bunch was inserted by the United States Senate when the Underwood-Simmons tariff bill came to it from the House of Representatives, which had left bananas on the free list, as they always had been, and probably always will be. The Senatorial sponsors for this banana tax undoubtedly acted in good faith. The reduced tariff rates on other articles of import threatened a deficit. Careless writers and speakers had given circulation to statements calculated to create the impression that there was a "banana trust," and that it made enormous profits. The United Fruit Company, known to be the leading producer and shipper of bananas, was presumed to be the beneficiary of this rumored monopoly, and certain of the Senators saw no reason why $2,000,000 a year should not be collected on the 40,000,000 bunches of bananas imported annually, it being assumed that the prosperous United Fruit Company would pay practically all of this tidy amount.

What ensued was rather amusing. The fruit trade was well aware that there was most spirited competition in bananas, and that the United Fruit Company had powerful and alert rivals and absolutely no control over wholesale or retail prices. Congress was soon made aware that there was no subterfuge about this competition, that it was real and vital, also that the rivals of the United Fruit Company were in deadly earnest. They pointed out that the prices of bananas were not fixed so much by the supply on the market at a given time as they were by the relative scarcity of native fruits, and that no importing company, or all of them combined, could artificially raise the price of this tropical fruit.

They also submitted undisputable evidence which indicated that the average importer receives less than 5 cents net profit on a bunch of bananas, and warned Congress that the proposed tax would annihilate all save the more powerful companies, which would be able to stand losses until a possible time when banana prices should adjust themselves on a higher level.

The Public — that mysterious entity which is respected and reviled, feared and defied, but which always wins when it gets mad — aroused itself and sounded a deepening thunder of protest. The public knew nothing and cared nothing about the mysteries and statistics of the banana trade. It did not care if there was one importer, or ten or a hundred. The irate public was content to know that the banana was the cheapest fruit and food product on the market, and had a dead sure premonition that it would pay all of the tax and a lot more. The public was entirely satisfied with the banana situation as it was. If there was competition, well and good; if there was a banana trust it was a most excellent and righteous monopoly and should not be disturbed in its well-doing by a tax imposed by a political party which had charged high food prices to an iniquitous tariff system.

And the Press fell in line with the Public, as it generally does and should, and the Banana never knew until then how many friends he had and how welcome he was to the millions who had come to appreciate his gastronomic charms. And that was the end of the proposed tax.

An interesting feature of this episode was the fact that cer-

Type of Central American architecture

tain of the competitors of the United Fruit Company found it good tactics to point out and prove that that concern did not exercise, and never had exercised, a monopoly or any control over bananas. The public is inclined to be skeptical when a successful and admitted leader in an industrial enterprise defends itself against such charges, but it is entirely another matter when competitors, presumed to be at its mercy, indignantly declare and prove that they are enjoying a steadily increasing prosperity, and that they have no complaint whatever against the concern which happens to be selected for attack because of its size, and, possibly, because those making the attack had been deluded into accepting as true, certain sensational and false statements.

The facts were obvious and were at the command of any one who cared to verify them. Bananas are not smuggled into the United States. They pay no duty, but the port officials keep accurate count of every bunch unloaded at the various ports, and the records show the number of bunches brought in annually by the various shippers. If the United Fruit Company had operated during its thirteen years of existence in a manner calculated to overwhelm all competition the statistics of banana imports would tell the tale of its merciless rapacity.

What did these trade statistics show? They showed that in 1900 the United Fruit Company shipped to the United States 11,153,881 bunches of bananas, and that in that year its competitors imported 4,862,449 bunches. This indicated that the United Fruit Company then held a very decided trade advantage over its competitors, but far from a monopoly.

In 1913, the year in which the banana became a tariff issue and a subject of acute public interest, the United Fruit Company shipped to the United States 24,975,640 bunches of bananas as against 17,529,801 bunches shipped by its competitors. In these twelve years the United Fruit Company had increased its shipments by 13,821,759 bunches, or less than 124 per cent, and in the same period its competitors had climbed from 4,862,449 to 17,529,801 bunches, an increased importation exceeding 260 per cent, or more than twice the rate of increase enjoyed by the United Fruit Company.

Such officially verified figures are enough to dishearten the most aggressive and persistent of trust hunters.

One of the most interesting and remarkable features of this whole subject is the astounding retail price charged for bananas. Bananas at 10 cents a dozen, 15, 20, and even 25 cents a dozen, are a positive phenomenon in this era of high food prices.

Here is one of the most perishable of tropical fruits, one

requiring a fortune to attempt its large production and importation, one which must be sold within a day or two after it ripens, one which was justly esteemed a luxury a few years ago, and yet it is offered for sale all over the United States at all times of the year for less than the average prices charged for hardy native fruits grown in superabundance within a few miles of the market-places.

If this outcome could justly be charged to the operations of a "banana trust" it would glorify that alleged iniquity. If the prices charged for native grown apples, pears, oranges, and other year-around fruits be the outcome of competition, the sooner we substitute monopoly the better. In an

Palm garden of the SS. *Pastores*

editorial entitled "Consider the Banana," published in the Houston *Post* under date of January 27, 1913, this pointed comment was made:

"How does it happen that the home-grown apple is placed beyond the reach of the average consumer and that the foreign-grown banana has increased in quality and decreased in price? The banana is a perishable fruit. It must be marketed immediately on its importation, and the business is one which requires millions in investment and the risks incident to fleets sailing in waters menaced by hurricanes and northers. It is a farce when apples grown within ten miles of St. Louis or New York sell by weight for ten times the price charged for bananas shipped from Costa Rica or Colombia, South America.

"There is no secret about the low cost of bananas. They are produced and handled on an enormous scale by companies which put them on the market without the intervention of middlemen who extort large commissions. These companies have learned that there is more money for them in selling a huge total of product at a low net profit than there is in extracting a high profit from small sales at prices prohibitive to the average consumer. When those in the apple industry learn this lesson there will be more orchards, less apples rotting on the ground, and more prosperity and happiness for all concerned. Consider the banana."

The New York *Times* later sarcastically remarked that "There is much need of an apple trust, as 'bad' as the fruit trust," and that "people are eating bananas, oranges, and grapefruit because domestic fruits are dear and inaccessible."

It is a common thing to see apples and bananas displayed for sale on stands or in stores, with 10 cents asked for the apple and three fine bananas offered for 5 cents. The apple grew a few miles away and the bananas came from Panama.

The United Fruit Company is primarily responsible for the low banana prices, and the remaining credit belongs to its competitors, who have had the sagacity to imitate its systems of production and distribution.

What would happen if some corporation imitated the United Fruit Company in the production and distribution of apples? Would its officials be hailed as benefactors or would they be sent to jail? This is an interesting conjecture and worth analyzing.

The last ten or twelve years has witnessed an advance in food prices which has dazed the statesmanship of the world and inflicted untold hardships on all classes save those of independent means. This astounding climb in food prices has been most marked in the United States, and it is mere chicanery to ascribe any considerable portion of it to the tariff or any other political or partisan policies. Scores of causes are alleged by intelligent students of this phenomenon, and it is fair to assume that it is the composite result of a number of conditions deeply embedded in our social and economic structure.

It logically follows that in this general rise in the cost of raw materials, labor, service of various kinds both needful and useless, and finally in the cost of the article offered for sale — it logically follows, I say, that any commodity which has maintained a practically uniform scale in all of these years has actually fallen in price. This decided inflation of retail prices for food and other necessities really means a depreciated dollar; a debased dollar which will not purchase as much food as it did ten or twelve years ago. There can be no intelligent dissent from this proposition. It is elementary and painfully obvious.

Now, are there any food products which are exceptions to this decreased ability of a dollar to acquire them? Yes, there are two such products, and only two of consequence — bananas and sugar — and it happens that these are the two food necessities on which are based the extensive operations of the United Fruit Company. If there be any other corporation catering to the food hunger of the public which can claim and prove this distinction, its identity has escaped my observation.

Why are bananas and sugar conspicuous exceptions to the rule of high and advancing prices? It is impossible to escape the conclusion that the reason is to be found in the fact that bananas and raw sugar are produced and marketed under comprehensive and scientific systems which avoid the wastes and losses inevitable to petty and badly organized production. Every known fact points to this conclusion.

The United States Department of Labor issued early in 1913 a comprehensive bulletin containing startling statistics relative to the mounting prices of food. The table which I now submit was compiled from this official report. In this table "100" stands for the average retail price of the food stated in the decade 1890–99. For instance, surloin steak in 1902 cost at retail the equivalent of "115," which means that it had advanced in price 15 per cent. over the average established in the ten years inclusive of 1890–99.

The prices stated for bananas are compiled from the trade statistics which show the prices paid by the dealers to the importing companies in these years. There has been so little fluctuation in the actual retail prices that one quotation would practically serve for the entire period considered. The rates given indicate fairly the part played by the banana producers and importers in determining what the consumer should pay.

Here is a table which is well worth studying by those who wish to understand why millions of people rallied to the defense of the banana when the proposal was made to impose an import tax on it. It also throws an interesting light on the low and steady range of the sugar used to sweeten sliced bananas:

RELATIVE RETAIL PRICES OF THE PRINCIPAL ARTICLES OF FOOD CONSUMED IN ALL SECTIONS OF THE UNITED STATES AS CONTRASTED WITH THE SELLING PRICES OF BANANAS IN THE YEARS SINCE THE INCORPORATION OF THE UNITED FRUIT COMPANY

	1900	1901	1902	1903	1904	1905	1906	1907	1908	1909	1910	1911	1912
Sirloin steak	107	109	115	110	111	111	114	116	119	126	134	135	153
Round steak	109	114	122	116	121	120	124	128	135	141	149	153	174
Rib roast	109	113	118	117	117	116	120	123	128	132	138	139	156
Pork chops	109	109	127	126	123	125	136	141	144	159	178	170	188
Bacon (smoked)	110	121	135	140	138	139	150	158	163	176	214	197	199
Ham (smoked)	106	111	121	122	119	116	127	131	134	142	159	156	160
Lard (pure)	105	120	136	126	116	116	127	133	134	150	173	145	154
Hens	100	105	114	119	121	124	128	132	135	146	155	152	158
Flour	95	95	96	102	118	119	108	118	127	139	136	128	133
Corn meal	96	108	124	122	123	123	124	133	143	146	148	147	160
Eggs (fresh)	99	108	119	125	131	131	134	138	143	155	158	150	162
Butter	101	103	110	110	108	111	118	127	128	134	140	131	147
Potatoes	93	114	117	115	119	109	115	122	130	133	119	157	168
Milk	100	101	104	107	107	108	110	119	123	126	132	133	136
Sugar	104	102	93	94	100	102	97	99	101	100	102	111	109
BANANAS	86	81	94	91	93	83	97	103	95	91	104	95	93

NOTE. — In this table 100 is the average retail price in the ten years preceding 1900, and all above or below is a percentage of increase or decrease in price compared with that preceding decade.

It will be noted that bananas sold in 1912 at a figure below that of ten years previously, during which period sirloin steak advanced 38 per cent in price, round steak 52, pork chops 61, bacon 64, flour 37, eggs 43, butter 37, potatoes 51, and sugar 16 per cent. In the period between 1910 and 1913, when all of these food products made their most astounding advances, the price of bananas actually dropped more than 11 per cent. If this tropical fruit had advanced only slightly in sympathy with this gigantic elevation in other food prices it would have been a result for which the harassed consumers would have been thankful, but bananas actually dropped 11.6 points or per cent — and, unless the people had protested, this kindly feat would have been rewarded with a tax!

The newspaper poets probably were not familiar with all of the statistical virtues of the banana as now set forth, but they knew how the masses felt on the subject, and the theme was chosen by many able versifiers. Here are two selected from an impressive collection, Poet Nelson proving that it is not difficult to find words to rhyme with "bananas":

THE TAX IS OFF!

Bananas will be restored to the free list. — *Joy Message from Washington*

Come all ye good citizens, raise
Your loudest hosannas,
With pæans of popular praise
For taxless bananas.

Food fit for the gods of Olympus,
For doughty Dianas
And heroes of legend: who'd skimp us
Of blessed bananas?

Meat fit for an Orient sultan,
For dusky sultanas —
The infant one or the adult un,
Soul-filling bananas!

Giuseppis and Abrahams eat 'em,
And Gretchens and Hannas,
Vox populi says you can't beat 'em,
World-building bananas.

And whether it's clay you'll be smoking
Or fragrant Habanas,
None thinks you are lying or joking
If you praise bananas.

They're slender and tender, nutritious,
  Most mighty of mannas;
They're yellow and mellow, delicious —
  Praise be for bananas!

You tax us for air and for water,
  For faith and bandannas;
We go like a lamb to the slaughter —
  But halt! on bananas.

What sound from the northernmost mountain,
  From southern savannahs?
The East and the West are thanks shoutin'
  For untaxed bananas.

—E. T. Nelson in New York *Sun.*

Poet John O'Keefe tuned his harp and sang:

THE FREE BANANA

You may tax the silk stockings from Paris
  Or the hat from the street of peace,
Or the jewels the womenfolk carry
  From the land of the aureate fleece,
Or the smoky old Scotch from Glengarry,
  Or the braid that was made in Milan;
    But the President's sure
    You will injure the poor
  If you tax the nutritious banan'!

If a damsel who dances ta-ra-ra,
  Till it seems that her foot is a wing,
Should arrive with a lovely tiara
  That she got with the heart of a king,
You may call it an avis that's rara
  And assess it by Congress' plan;
    But our people are such
    You'll be getting in Dutch
  If you venture to tax the banan'!

We are anxious that beef should be cheaper,
  So we'll lower the tariff on cow;
Though it come from the Platte or the Dnieper,
  We will lessen its price to the frau;
And the wheat of the Muscovite reaper
  May sustain the American man;
    But far greater than these
    Is the joy that he sees
  As he lives on the handy banan'!

Oh, a poet of stature Miltonic
Should be happy to write on this theme!
To the ghost of Beethoven symphonic
It should furnish an orchestra scheme!
Let the tariff protectionists chronic
Raise objections from Maine to Japan;
But we'll cry, "It's a hit!"
(If our mouths will permit)
While we gulp the untariffed banan'!

— John O'Keefe in New York *World.*

Pleasing bit of steamship architecture

There is no mystery concerning the cheapness of bananas. Three factors combine to make them the minimum cost article of fruit-food ever offered to the American public, viz:

(1) Bananas are produced on an enormous scale and are transported and distributed on a scientific plan which has been developed to approximate perfection.

(2) The producing importers receive only a nominal percentage of profit over the actual cost of cultivating and delivering bananas to the great centres of distribution.

(3) The wholesalers or jobbers obtain only a nominal profit for services which are indispensable, and the retailer receives profits insignificant when compared with those extorted from most food products.

For a standard bunch of bananas containing nine hands and, we will say, 144 individual bananas, the producer and shipper will receive on the average less than a dollar for such a bunch of fruit.

Enormous quantities of bananas are sold at retail for 10 cents a dozen, and I doubt if the average price exceeds 15 cents a dozen. On this latter basis the retailer would receive $1.80 for the 144 bananas in the bunch which the importer sold to the jobber for $1. At 20 cents a dozen the retailer would receive $2.40 for this bunch. When we add to the original dollar charged by the importer the various items of freight, a few cents to the Fruit Dispatch or some similar company, and also a fair profit for the wholesaler, we have the entire bill with the exception of what the retailer receives as his share. We do not begrudge him that. It is not a profit in the true sense of that word. It is a wage for manual services performed.

Thus the banana bunch which was sold by the producer and importer for $1 reaches the consumer with not more than another dollar added to it for freight, delivery, and all of the charges imposed by middlemen. Does the American consumer obtain any native farm product at any such proportionate charge? Hardly!

According to one of the railroad authorities of the country the potatoes for which the farmers received $8,437,000 in 1910 were sold to consumers in New York City for more than $60,000,000. Onions, for which the farmers got $821,000, consumers paid $8,212,000. Consumers paid $9,125,000 for cabbages the farmers had sold for $1,825,000.

This means that when a housewife spends $1 for cabbage that only 20 cents of her money goes to the farmer who raised these cabbages, and that the remaining 80 cents has been absorbed by transportation charges, commissions, profits to various classes of middlemen, and to the retailer. This means that when the housewife spends $1 for potatoes that 14 cents of this represents the farmer's share, and that 86 cents of her money is absorbed in the process of bringing them from the farm to her. In the case of onions the farmer gets almost exactly 10 cents out of every dollar expended by the consumer.

But when this housewife spends $1 for bananas she can rest assured that about 50 cents of this goes to the producer and importer for honest value delivered, and that the remaining 50 cents stands for legitimate and indispensable services rendered by railroads, truckmen, and the retailer. In its banana business the United Fruit Company is a farming enterprise, its ships serving in place of wagons to bring its produce from the fields to the markets. Counting all of the services of distribution and selling under the head of "Transportation and Middlemen," let us see what sort of an exhibit these four food products make displayed in a cold-blooded table:

Food Article	Percentage of retail price received by the farmer	Percentage of retail price received by transportation and middlemen
Onions . . .	10	90
Potatoes . .	14	86
Cabbages . .	20	80
Bananas . .	50	50

Plain enough, isn't it? Bananas are produced scientifically, and distributed and sold with a minimum of service by the middlemen. Onions, potatoes, cabbages, and scores of the other necessities of life are produced unscientifically, and handled by a lack of system which invites and assures all forms of extortion.

Farmers living within five miles of my residence in Hastings-on-Hudson, New York, in the autumn sell such apples as are not left to rot under the trees from 40 to 60 cents a bushel, and my neighbors and I buy them a few months later at from $2 to $3 a bushel. We pay 5 cents for a decent eating apple raised a few miles away, but we can buy for this 5 cents three delicious bananas which were raised in the valleys of Central or South America.

Busy scene on arrival of banana cargo at New Orleans

FOOD VALUE OF THE BANANA

The banana will never enjoy the popularity it deserves until the people of the temperate zones learn to know when it is ripe, and learn not to eat it in its raw state. There is popular delusion that the banana has ripened when it turns from its original green to a golden yellow, and those thus deluded decline to touch this fruit when dark spots appear in the yellow skin of the banana.

The banana is not fully ripe when it is yellow. This change from green to yellow is the first outward appearance of a chemical process incidental to the ripening process. Not until a considerable portion of the skin has turned to a deep brown has this ripening process sufficiently developed to give the fruit its greatest value as a delicious and healthful food. A writer in a recent number of the *Journal of the American Medical Association* brought this fact out clearly when he said:

"The dictum that fruits should be eaten 'in their season' finds its limitations as regards variety in the temperate zones at certain periods of the year. There is, however, one fruit which is readily available fresh in the American markets at practically all seasons. It is unfortunate that an article of diet which meets nutritive requirements so well and so easily obtainable at reasonable cost as the banana should be the subject of so much misunderstanding among both physicians and laymen. For, despite the fact that over 40,000,000 bunches are reported to have been brought to the United States last year, it is popularly stated in many quarters that the banana is difficult of digestion and may give rise to alimentary distress.

"The fruit is brought to our northern markets green, and is ripened by artificial heat. The color of the peel gives evidence of the degree of ripeness. The green banana contains, in the part exclusive of the skin, about 1.5 per cent of protein and 20 to 25 per cent of carbohydrate, almost entirely starch. In the ripe banana with the yellow-brown peel the edible part contains somewhat less of carbohydrate; but that which remains is now almost entirely in the form of soluble sugars. Broadly speaking, then, the ripe banana is about one-fifth sugar; the green, one-fifth starch.

"Inasmuch as bananas are commonly eaten uncooked, it is obvious that more or less raw starch will be ingested if the fruit is not ripe, i. e., if the skin has not begun to shrivel and darken. No one would advise the use of uncooked potatoes; yet many people eschew a thoroughly ripe banana in the belief that this wholesome fruit is 'rotten' when the skin becomes darkened, whereas they eagerly eat the yellow-green starch-bearing fruit at its stage of incomplete ripeness."

It is an entirely different matter when the green or semi-ripe banana is cooked. The application of heat renders the pulp nutritious and readily digestible, and the tropical natives prepare many delicious dishes by baking green bananas in ashes.

The *Magazine of the Housewives' League* discusses the food value of bananas entertainingly in a recent article, from which the following extracts are selected:

"The food value of the banana, long known in tropical countries, has within the past twenty years begun to be more highly appreciated by the masses of the northern countries, and the following facts, collated from authoritative sources, will indicate the progress made by science and commerce in familiarizing the people living outside of tropical countries with its value as a foodstuff.

"From a sanitary point of view, the banana is superior to many other fruits. Exposed on stands on the street, in fruit stores and otherwise, by reason of the fact that it is always first peeled to get at the edible portion, it escapes all forms of germ life communications either by the air or contact with polluted substances. The skin of the fresh apple is generally eaten, with the risk of dirt and disease, by the ordinary people. Cooked, the baked apple is open to the same objection — and the same facts apply to many other forms of fruit in a greater or less degree.

"For further comparison, the following table has been prepared by the Government:

	BANANAS	PORTERHOUSE STEAK
Price per pound	.07 cents	25.00 cents
Cost of 100 calories	23.30 cents	22.50 cents
Energy —		
Total weight food material . .	1.43 lbs.	.40 lbs.
Fuel value, calories	429.00 lbs.	444.00 lbs.

INDIAN AND MARIMBA

The marimba is a musical instrument similar to the xylophone

"This table indicates that the most strenuous form of labor can be supported by a banana diet equally as well as by the highest class meat diet. It is a well-established fact that in the States of Parana and Santa Catarina, Brazil, the entire population subsists exclusively on bananas as a food, and coffee as a drink; and these sections are famous for the strength and endurance of their laboring classes.

"The familiar form of the banana in the tropics, other than the fresh fruit, is the flour or meal made from the dried fruit. The tabulated statistics show, among other data, that banana flour contains an average of 85 per cent of carbohydrates, as compared with 75 per cent from wheat flour, but it is lower in protein or flesh-forming values. This flour is used in combination with milk, sugar, etc., in the preparation of cakes, custards, and similar articles. It is very palatable and never cloys. It is particularly adapted for persons of weak or inferior digestive organs, and is now marketed by a New York company. Seven hundred weight of fruit are used to make a hundred weight of flour.

"The banana is further used to make breakfast foods — like the ordinary cereal; one preparation taking the place of coffee as a nutriment instead of a stimulant; banana biscuits are now on the menu of many households; banana vinegar is said to have many excellent qualities to recommend it; banana marmalade, banana prepared as a substitute for figs, raisins, grapes, and currants are some of the other commercial articles which are rapidly making their way into everyday use in households, and are advertised by supply houses.

"In view of the importation of upwards of 44,000,000 bunches of bananas per annum, under the auspices of several powerful American corporations, subsidiary companies, equipped with scientific laboratories, have been established in New York City and elsewhere, supplementing the efforts of the United States Government for the definite purpose of continuing the study of how to increase the value of the banana in new forms of foodstuffs."

While the banana can be prepared in various ways, it is surprising to find the number of persons who are amazed to learn that it can be served baked, fried, or in many other ways. The American and European people are just beginning to appreciate the advantages and desirability of the banana as a most appetizing vegetable cooked for the daily consumption of the rich and poor alike.

The test of the food value of any article of diet is found

in the relative proportion of flesh-forming principle it contains, viz: proteid; after this the amount of carbohydrate and fat is taken into consideration. The following analysis showing the composition of the apple, orange, and banana is by Atwater:

	Water	Proteid	Fat	Carbo-hydrate	Ash
Apple	84.6	.4	.5	14.2	.3
Orange	86.9	.8	.2	11.6	.5
Banana	75.3	1.3	.6	22.0	.8

The exceptional qualities of the banana as a wholesome and nutritious food are recognized and extolled by the leading medical authorities. Albert Harris Hoy, M. D., in his famous book on "Eating and Drinking," says:

"It is a remarkable fact that the albuminates are present in the banana in almost the same proportion that they are found in milk, this substance, according to three investigators, containing them to the extent of 4.03 per cent. Dry wheat flour contains 12 per cent of albuminates, and hence one pound of it would be equalled in nourishment by three pounds of bananas. Were these dried and reduced to flour, one pound of this flour would probably equal two pounds of wheat flour in nourishment. The analysis of the banana then but confirms that which experience has proved to be true, that it is a fruit of high nutritive value. In fact, it stands alone in this respect, as well as being the only sweet fruit which can be obtained fresh and in a suitable condition in all parts of the country and at all seasons of the year."

This very important fact is also generally recognized and commented on by the leading medical authorities abroad. No less an authority than Dr. Arnold Lorand of Carlsbad, in his recent book on "Health and Longevity through Rational Diet," says:

"There is probably no more nourishing food, or one whose cultivation is of more value to mankind, than the banana. . . . In view of the very great influence of fruit upon the health of the population in general it would be very desirable that the duties collected on fruits be abolished."

In the course of a speech delivered recently on his return to London from Jamaica, Sir James Crichton-Browne, M. D., F. R. S., a leading medical authority of England, said:

"I wish all of our school-children could have bananas from time to time. The banana is not a flavored fruit, that is to say, a little sugar and water with some essence thrown in, but a fruit-food containing, in an agreeable form, all of the essential elements of nutrition. As an adjunct to our other foods it is of great value, being at once acceptable to all — for it is not an acquired taste — giving variety to the domestic diet and mingling well with other comestibles. I am quite sure that the Jamaica banana, than which there is none finer or better flavored when it is of the proper degree of ripeness, is, in the guise of a cheap luxury, a substantial addition to our food supply, and one which is certain more and more to commend itself to the working classes of our large towns. Its portability, palatability, and digestibility are immense advantages, and I am glad to see that it is largely taking the place of the stale sandwich on railway journeys."

HOW TO COOK BANANAS

As has been explained, the banana should not be eaten raw until its yellow peel is mottled with brown. It is then not only readily digestible but delicious. On account of its natural protection from contamination, it has well been said that "The banana was put up and sealed by nature in a germ-proof package," and so long as that package is intact the banana itself furnishes absolute guarantee that it is pure food.

Professional chefs and amateur cooks are constantly finding new ways to cook bananas. Here are a few recipes which have attained wide popularity:

BANANA FRITTERS

One-half cup of flour, one-quarter cup of cold water, one egg beaten, one-fourth teaspoon of melted butter, one pinch of baking powder.

Beat the yolk of the egg; add the water, and stir into the flour; add the salt, baking powder, and melted butter, then the white of egg whipped to a stiff froth.

Put sliced bananas into this batter and fry About three or four slices should be incorporated in each fritter. When done, dredge with powdered sugar and serve hot.

FRIED BANANAS

Select firm and rather slender fruit; peel and cut into sections about three inches long. Fry in hot butter, and, as the bananas cook, sprinkle with a little sugar, and roll about carefully in the frying pan until a light brown all over. Dish, pouring over any butter and sugar remaining in the pan. Serve very hot.

BANANA CROQUETTES

Peel the bananas, cut into short lengths, round the cut edges, dip in beaten egg, roll in sifted crumbs, and fry until tender and brown. Serve hot with any kind of roast meat.

BANANAS WITH BACON OR HAM

Prepare fruit as above. Cook in the same manner, using bacon or ham fat in place of butter, and serve on the platter with broiled bacon or ham. This dish, with a salad, makes an exceedingly good luncheon.

GELATINE OF BANANAS

Make a lemon, an orange or a wine jelly, according to the rule for the kind of gelatine used. Mould this with sliced bananas only, or with oranges, white grapes, a few figs cut up, nuts, or any mixture liked.

Turn out and serve with whipped cream.

BANANA SHORTCAKE

When berries or fresh peaches are out of season, use sliced bananas between and on top of layers of shortcake.

Add the fruit the moment before serving, as the heat will discolor the fruit if allowed to stand after slicing when uncooked.

SPICED BANANAS

Stir gently thick slices of bananas in a syrup flavored with cinnamon, cloves, and a very little mace.

BANANA LOAF

Take a small loaf of sponge cake or angel food, and cut a well in the centre. Fill with sliced bananas and heap with whipped cream sweetened to taste.

BANANA CAKE

Bake a sponge cake or a plain cup cake in two layers.

Just before serving, put freshly sliced bananas between and on top of the layers of cake. Cover the top thickly with whipped cream and serve at the table in wedge-shaped pieces.

BANANA ICE CREAM

One quart of cream. One cup of sugar, pulp of five or six bananas, juice of one lemon, a pinch of salt.

Heat the cream with three-fourths of the sugar. Let it cool. Peel the bananas, split and remove the seeds and dark spots; rub through a sieve; add salt, lemon juice, and the fourth of a cup of sugar. Mix with the chilled cream and freeze at once.

BANANA BAVARIAN CREAM

One pint of cooked banana pulp sweetened, one-half box of granulated gelatine, one-half pint of cold water, one pint of cream.

Stew ripe bananas in a little water until there is a pint of pulp. Sweeten to taste. Soak the gelatine in the cold water. When thoroughly dissolved, beat through the pulp and stand in cracked ice, and stir until it begins to thicken.

Add the cream whipped very stiff, and a cup of chopped nuts. Put in a mould to harden. To serve, turn on a platter, surrounded with whipped cream, dotted with maraschino cherries.

At the meeting of the British Medical Association in July, 1910, Dr. Eric Pritchard recommended the use of banana flour in infant feeding. Dr. Pritchard asserted that it was cheap and wholesome, rendered the milk more digestible, and possessed high nutritive value. He stated that for many years he has recommended the addition of mashed banana to the milk mixtures with which babies are fed when the natural source is unavailable. As the results of careful experiments he recommended the substitution of banana flour, made into a gruel or decoction, for the more expensive proprietary infant foods. It is of great importance that infants should be trained early to digest cow's milk, and this cannot be done by giving them artificial substitutes which are predigested, and Dr. Pritchard finds that a decoction of banana gruel has much to recommend it.

Thus we see that the banana is a fruit, a food, a drink, a breakfast dish, a dessert, a confection, and a medicine. It shares with bread the distinction of a staff of life, and is a welcome addition to the menu of the affluent.

Created into an industry by the men who founded and who have made of the United Fruit Company a mighty enterprise, the banana has bequeathed to the United States a vast extension of its commerce, and has pointed the sure and honorable way for the further peaceful conquest of the American tropics. It already has taken a place as a fixture in our social economy, but it is destined to a much higher rank in the future as a factor in promoting the health, happiness, and prosperity of hundreds of millions of people who were strangers to this tropical fruit-food only a short generation ago.

The United Fruit Company is more than a corporation. It is an institution, an American institution founded by certain of its citizens and conducted with a broadness of policy and an industrial statesmanship which lift it out of the class of mere money making and profit hunting corporations.

Myrtle Bank Hotel, Kingston, Jamaica

It is doing for the American tropics and the American people what the Hudson Bay Company did for the British Empire in the frozen north of Canada. It has awakened the slumbering nations bordering on the Caribbean with the quickening tonic of Yankee enterprise. It has proved to the world that these tropics can be converted from a harassing liability into an asset of stupendous value, and it has solved for the world the problem of transforming deadly swamps and jungles to gardens on which can be raised the food products demanded to keep pace with the ever-increasing hunger of the city-housed multitudes.

Andrew W. Preston is, and always has been, President of the United Fruit Company, and is the active executive head and directing spirit of it and all of its subsidiary interests. His rise from a fruit merchant in Boston to the front of vast enterprises, national and international in their scope, is a striking illustration of what opportunity offers in America to the one who hears the call, and is swift and earnest to take honest advantage of possibilities in new fields reached by untrodden paths.

I called on Mr. Preston in his Boston office and asked him to explain the general policy which has been followed by the United Fruit Company in relation to its competitors and to the consuming public which purchases its products. In his frank answers to my rather pointed questions Mr. Preston takes a position which may be studied with interest by all who have intelligent concern in the vital problems which have arisen with the growth of wide-reaching industrial corporations. My first question was:

"What is the competitive policy of the United Fruit Company?"

MR. PRESTON: "Competition, in its ordinary trade sense, is not a vitally important factor in the banana industry. The total of marketable bananas produced in the American tropics is not sufficient to meet the demands of existing markets and those which are yet practically untouched, and there is every indication that the demand in the established market centres will continue greatly to increase. There are periods, of course, when there is an over-supply of this fruit, and at such times prices automatically fall below the cost of production and handling, but the slight fluctuations in the wholesale prices are seldom reflected in the rates paid by the consumers. The United Fruit Company and its competitors are planning in confident expectation that the banana is destined to have a decidedly enhanced use as a fruit and a food in the coming years. Since the known field is large enough for all of us there is no incentive to waste money and energy in a struggle for something which would be of no advantage if won."

"Is there any understanding or agreement, written or

implied, between the United Fruit Company and any of its competitors?"

MR. PRESTON: "There is absolutely none, and there has never been a time when our company has attempted to direct or influence the policies or acts of its competitors. We have been busy with other and vastly more important matters. Whatever of success we have attained has been because of creative and not of destructive endeavor. No combination or agreement would have any appreciable influence in determining banana prices. If an artificial increase in banana prices were possible, and if we were so foolish and criminal as to participate in such a conspiracy, the very success of it would precipitate business disaster. There are legitimate profits in the banana industry only because the natural laws of trade and of free competition have made this tropical fruit a staple article with a recognized food value, and because the consumers know that it can always be obtained at an unvarying low price.

"We have keen competition with the steamship companies which bid for the passenger and freight traffic to and from the ports in the American tropics. We have keen competition in the production and sale of our Cuban sugar output. The leading railroads of the United States carry for us not less than 50,000 carloads of freight annually. In these and in all of the other ramifications of our business we have rigidly adhered to the policy of making no alliances, combinations, or agreements with competitors, and we have neither solicited or received any discriminating favors from railroad lines. Our company has not been a party to any pooling agreement, to any agreement having as its object a division of territory, division of traffic, or any other stipulation which would interfere in the free exercise of competition."

"Would not the weaker rivals of the United Fruit Company be at its mercy in the event of a cut-rate war?"

MR. PRESTON: "Possibly, but what pretext could justify a cut-rate war in bananas? It is not only illegal but immoral for a strong competitor to use such a weapon on a weaker one. It is true that this was not a part of the general business code years ago. Selling below cost was frequently resorted to, and there was no law and little public sentiment against this feature of competition in a period not far remote. But the records will show that no such tactics ever have been employed in the banana trade.

"With our widely scattered plantations and highly developed systems of transportation we have legitimately acquired advantages over all of our competitors, but we exercise these advantages fairly and, I believe, generously. It sometimes happens that a competitor loses a ship or has one disabled. If it is possible for us to do so, we do not hesitate to place one of our ships at his disposal. Again, it happens that a flood or a wind or some other disaster may ruin the plantations from which he draws his supplies. Instead of taking advantage of this calamity to invade and absorb his market we make it a practice to furnish him with bananas from our own plantations until such time as he can arrange for a permanent source of supply. We claim no special merit for this, and we should expect an honorable competitor to do what he could for us under similar circumstances. It is in accord with the spirit of the new competition. When a newspaper building is destroyed by fire its most bitter rival is likely to offer the use of its plant. The United States has evoluted from the savagery of old-time competition, and I am glad to say that our company never has been afflicted with it."

"What is the general policy, the aim, and the ultimate ambition of the United Fruit Company?"

Mr. Preston: "A corporation has the double duty of conserving the interests of its stockholders and of rendering a service to the public which has authorized its corporate existence. These duties do not conflict. The stockholders are entitled to fair profits on their stock investments, and the public is entitled to the benefits of prices and services based on just dividend rates. That has been our general policy, and the present management will continue it. We deal mainly in bananas and sugar, the two cheaper food products now at the command of the American consumer.

"The aim of the United Fruit Company is to continue its

work of linking the United States commercially and industrially with the American tropics, and to share in the rewards of the mutually enhanced prosperity of both sections. We are proud of what we have already accomplished. We are jealous of a prestige earnestly fought for, and we shall do our best to preserve and increase it."

I have presented in these chapters the operations of the United Fruit Company as I have seen and studied them. If I am prejudiced in its favor it is because of an admiration for great enterprises which perform great services in a comprehensive and scientific way and which, consequently, de-

The United Fruit Company SS. *Tenadores*

servedly are crowned with success. The fair-minded traveller or student who analyzes the record and achievements of this far-reaching tropical and international enterprise may, in his verdict, recall President Woodrow Wilson's eloquent summing-up of his attitude toward big business:

"I am not jealous of any progress or growth no matter how huge the result, provided the result was indeed obtained by the processes of wholesome development, which are the processes of efficiency, of economy, of intelligence, and of invention."

THE END

INDEX

INDEX

THE COUNTRY LIFE PRESS
GARDEN CITY, N. Y.